'YOU DON'T KNOW'

EASA Series
Published in Association with the European Association of Social Anthropologists (EASA)
Series Editors:
Jelena Tošić, University of St. Gallen
Sabine Strasser, University of Bern
Annika Lems, Max Planck Institute for Social Anthropology, Halle

Social anthropology in Europe is growing, and the variety of work being done is expanding. This series is intended to present the best of the work produced by members of the EASA, both in monographs and in edited collections. The studies in this series describe societies, processes, and institutions around the world and are intended for both scholarly and student readership.

Recent volumes:

53. 'YOU DON'T KNOW'
Precarious Methods and Life in a Workers' Hostel
Jacob A. E. Nielsen

52. THE HIDDEN MINORITY
Perceptions of Belonging and Otherness in the Finnish–Russian Borderland
Helena Jerman

51. PERFORMING STATE BOUNDARIES
Food Networks, Democratic Bureaucracy and China
Christof Lammer

50. RE-TURNS, ENTANGLEMENTS AND COLLABORATIONS
Anthropological Experimentations
Edited by Jelena Tošić, Sabine Strasser and Annika Lems

49. THE POLITICS OF RELATIONS
How Self-Government, Infrastructures and Care Transform the State in Serbia
André Thiemann

48. DIFFERENCE AND SAMENESS IN SCHOOLS
Perspectives from the European Anthropology of Education
Edited by Laura Gilliam and Christa Markom

47. THE FAMILIAL OCCULT
Explorations at the Margins of Critical Autoethnography
Edited by Alexandra Coţofană

46. AN ANTHROPOLOGY OF DISAPPEARANCE
Politics, Intimacies and Alternative Ways of Knowing
Edited by Laura Huttunen and Gerhild Perl

45. ETHNOGRAPHIES OF DESERVINGNESS
Unpacking Ideologies of Distribution and Inequality
Edited by Jelena Tošić and Andreas Streinzer

44. ETHNOGRAPHERS BEFORE MALINOWSKI
Pioneers of Anthropological Fieldwork, 1870–1922
Edited by Frederico Delgado Rosa and Han F. Vermeulen

43. TRACING SLAVERY
The Politics of Atlantic Memory in The Netherlands
Markus Balkenhol

For a full volume listing, please see the series page on our website: https://www.berghahnbooks.com/series/easa

'You Don't Know'

Precarious Methods and Life in a Workers' Hostel

Jacob A.E. Nielsen

berghahn
NEW YORK • OXFORD
www.berghahnbooks.com

First published in 2025 by
Berghahn Books
www.berghahnbooks.com

Library of Congress Cataloging-in-Publication Data

A C.I.P. cataloging record is available from the Library of Congress
Library of Congress Cataloging in Publication Control Number: 2024046822

British Library Cataloguing in Publication Data

A catalogue record for this book is available from the British Library

ISBN 978-1-80539-897-4 hardback
ISBN 978-1-80539-898-1 epub
ISBN 978-1-80539-899-8 web pdf

https://doi.org/10.3167/9781805398974

Contents

Illustrations

Figures

Table

Acknowledgements

Thank you to all the people who throughout the research process carved out some valuable time in an overburdened academic life to read and give me feedback. Their deep insights, open-mindedness to difference, and endless patience with my confusing explorations helped develop this research into its final form. Their approach to research and life in academia also served as a constant positive inspiration throughout the research process and without their continued support, the research would without a doubt never have been finished.

My early career colleagues and perhaps particularly my fellow Graduate Teaching Assistants have been an inspiration both in terms of their extensive knowledge and creative research explorations, and in terms of how they have sought to deal with and shape the process of study and work at the University of Liverpool. More than anything, the chats, conversations, emails, texts, shared coffees, and timezone-distanced phone calls have all supported me more than they can imagine.

I would also like to extend my deepest appreciation to Elin, Peter, Juan, Ana, Elana, Matt, Rafael, Ranvid, Catina, Thomas, Maja, Mahmud, Malik, Zofia, Natalia, Mathias, Celeste, Ibrahim, Lucio, Lise, Karl, Gloria, Abbas, Nikola, Saaf, Viktoria, Sadia, Emma, Ahmed, Shahu, Tarun, Eduardo, Sorina, Tejas, Adam, Charlotte, Kobi, Julianna, Endri, Aurora, Charles, Primin, James, Josephine, Tahiro, Luz, Lilou, Fabian, Antonio, Max, Emilia, Traian, Chia, Mai, Fleur, Cristofor, Dinu, Dorin, Faye, Joyce, Mutya, Patricia, Benilda, Benjamín, Andrés, Rosario, Attila, Fransico, Jorge, Miguel, Aisha, Nashwa, Ejaz, Fateh, Oliver, Alfie, Matthew, Lewis, Amita, and many others I was fortunate enough to meet during the research process. Your names are all made up for anonymity, but without your kindness and warmth, I could never have finished this agglomeration of words that despite my best efforts still has all too few of the traces you left behind.

Finally, a thank you to all the unmentioned people who have supported me and been part of my life through parts of this research project. Some of you are still here, others are not, but the weighted presence of you all is still palpable.

Prelude

Another Place

The sun shines brightly as you get out of the London tube station. You go down the stairs, out through the ticket gate and take a right. You walk past a small council estate with a few people leaning up against a fence whilst they are enjoying the sun and watching people go by. You take another turn and walk up the street where the hostel is located. The hostel is not a single building, but a collection of houses across the area. There are no signs to indicate it's a hostel – there is no reception and there are no permanent staff present at all times. Instead, when you first come to check in, you have to call a number and someone will come and meet you. You call the number and after 10 minutes a person from the hostel arrives. His name is Fabio and he is perhaps in his late twenties. He tells you that you are staying in another house up the road. You make your way there and Fabio lets you in. First, you have to sort out the formalities, so you go down to the common area where you are asked to pay the money for the first week. You pay, in cash, but you don't have the exact amount so you overpay and Fabio promises that you will get the change at another time. You get the Wi-Fi password and a set of keys to the front door and the bedroom you are staying in. Fabio then gets some bedsheets and takes you to your room. You are told that you can choose between any of the free beds. Then Fabio leaves.

You are alone. It is the middle of the day, but the room is dark because the curtains are closed and the small window doesn't let in much light. There are seven double bunk beds and three fridges in the room, and not much space in between it all. You choose the bottom bed in the corner and start to put the sheets on. There are small pieces of rotten food under the bed, the floor is pretty grim, and the bed you choose is squeaky. When you finish, you go down to the common room, where there are tables lined up and a sofa with a TV in front of it. There is also an unattended but big garden at the back. Coming back to the room, you meet one person. You say hello and engage in some small talk, but then he has to go to bed because work is waiting in the morning. More people have arrived in the hostel. At first, you might get a small nod or nothing much at all. It is a new place that you are not yet part of. You are alone, a separate thing thrown into a world bound together through mutual chatter, smiles, heated discussions, shared cigarettes, and people moving like they somehow belong. You are reeling, and you can't see anything but walls, materials, and floating figures with nothing to hold on to.

Questions for Precarious Lives

Do you ever feel vulnerable? Do you ever feel like your, our, world is coming apart? That your life as you imagined it would be turned out to be messier and more complicated than it was supposed to? Do you have a sense that things always fall out of reach and out of your control? Is it perhaps your job that makes you feel like this? Was it supposed to be more secure? Give you more wealth? Did it promise to soothe your daily worries about how to survive? No more stress about bills, food and a roof over your head, and no more worries about whether your heart and head can survive the pressured intensities to make it through another day? Is it worth all of the living life that you sacrifice to it day after day? Or is it perhaps something else? Do you feel at home? Do you have a place where you belong? Where the quiet rhythms of life gently bring you together with new and old people you hold dear? Or has belonging become a chase? Is it never more than a horizon of possibilities that never seems to arrive no matter how hard you run, crawl, and drag yourself towards it? Is your home nothing but frail dreams in restless nights? Does the world seem to always be incomplete, fragile, and incomprehensible? If so, how do you survive and belong in such a precarious world? How do you make your way through a world characterised by multiplicity, messiness, fragility, distortions, incoherence, and instability? How do you make sense of it all? How do you even start to apprehend a world characterised by fractured truths, a shattered sense of belonging, and unrelenting pressures to work and survive it all?

This book does not try to provide definite answers to any or all of these questions, but it does try to navigate this precarious world by experimenting with precarious methods in the hope that it will allow us to ask these questions in ways that are more in tune with the vulnerable and wrecked positions that they emerge from and seek to address.

To do this, the book experiments with precarious methods. This also means that the format of the book might look a little different from other academic books. There will, for example, not be an overall introduction and conclusion to hold on to. The book consists of three different parts that enact different methods to try to apprehend and write about life in precarious worlds. The three parts do not have to be read in consecutive order from beginning to end. The first part seeks to use traditional academic methods to provide a coherent analysis of precarious work and life in a London hostel. The second part provides a variety of scribbles to give a sense of an always messy, precarious and vulnerable research process. The third part experiments with more fragmented ways to apprehend something about life in unfolding precarious worlds. Where you prefer to start and how you relate the different parts to each other is something I prefer not to preconfigure and predetermine.

If you want to read about some of the background, motives, theories, and potential interpretations of this experiment with precarious methods, there is a Postscript and Q&A section at the end of the book. There I try to provide some of my perspectives on different aspects of precarious methods and the content of this book. However, these answers should not be seen as defining an imagined singular meaning of this book; instead, they are just my own, always changing attempts to make sense of precarious methods and the worlds filled with uncertainties, contradictions, and multiplicities that they seek to apprehend.

Part I

Settlement

Surviving Work

An Ethnography of Precarious Workers in London

Drawing on long-term ethnographic research with people living and working in precarious circumstances in London, this volume will examine what role work played in their lives and what practices, tactics, and imaginaries they had in relation to work. The aim is to show that, when examining precarious work from the perspective of precarious workers, many political and academic assumptions about work and its relationship to precariousness turn out to be problematic. This will illustrate how work in itself emerged as an inherently problematic part of people's lives. This also meant that in order to address the exploitative aspects of work, people were less focused on particular working conditions; instead, most of their creative efforts were guided towards finding ways to minimise the impact that work in general had on their lives.

The relationship between precariousness and work is an odd one. On the one hand, the emergence of precarity as both a political and an academic concept is heavily tied in with changing economic and political transformations that are perceived to create increasingly precarious and exploitative working conditions (Standing, 2011). On the other hand, the 'right' kind of work is often conceptualised as a transformative solution to the issues that precarious workers are faced with.

These perceptions about work's simultaneously problematic and transformative qualities underpin most political initiatives and agendas related to precarious work. However, to what extent these political and academic perceptions of work reflect the everyday experiences of precarious workers themselves are rarely explored in any depth. To achieve a more grounded understanding of the relationship between precariousness and work, it is therefore necessary to move beyond established political and academic assumptions about the nature of work in order to explore how work is perceived and experienced in the everyday lives of precarious workers themselves.

Unpacking Assumptions about Work

Work is fundamental to global capitalist production and it plays a key role in shaping most people's lived experiences, determining their income, their access to social rights, and spheres of sociality (Weeks, 2011). In work-centred societies like the United Kingdom, paid work is still a central and ubiquitous part of people's lives, and the vast majority of people have to work to afford the bare necessities of life. Large amounts of people's time are spent on work or doing activities related to work, whether that is 'upskilling' their qualifications to become more employable, applying for new jobs, or spending most of their time off work trying to recover from the physical and mental stress that work causes (Mumby et al., 2017). Politically the benefits of creating new jobs in the pursuit of ever more economic growth are rarely publicly questioned for long. Work is held up as a channel for personal development and achievement, and when new jobs are created and new efforts are put into cultivating an employable and hardworking workforce, this is celebrated as being beneficial both to society and to the individual (Frayne, 2015).

For instance, when the UK government claims that it has 'helped millions of people into work, halving the unemployment rate' (Conservative Party, 2019: 7), it is therefore not surprising that this is portrayed as a political success that will help to 'unleash Britain's potential' (Conservative Party, 2019: 7). Furthermore, despite ample evidence that expanding employment is not a way out of poverty or a way to address inequalities, work continues to be espoused as the main solution to address the consequences of poverty and inequality (Human Rights Council, 2019; Xu et al., 2019). A somewhat similar picture emerges when looking at the main political opposition in the form of the Labour Party. In its political manifesto, the Labour Party has a long list of potential improvements to the quality of work and emphasises the importance of a life outside work; nonetheless, it still considers work as having the potential to 'provide a decent life' and serving as 'a gateway to learning new skills, the creation of opportunities and the opening up of horizons' (Labour Party, 2019: 5).

The Problem and Continuum of Work

Although pro-work positions remain the default, there is widespread recognition that something is not quite right with all types of work. However, the criticism tends to focus on the conditions of work rather than questioning the value of work itself. There are two dominant perspectives in the United Kingdom when it comes to examining the problem of work. One perspective centres around the issue of precarious working conditions and tends to interconnect with progressive and left-leaning policies. The other perspective that has received increasing attention politically is the issue of labour exploitation, which ties in with wider discourses on modern slavery and human trafficking, and has been championed by right-leaning politicians as well as those on the left. Both of these perspectives are part of particular assemblages of academic research, organisational activities, policies, and activism.

The current UK government, with the support of most parties in Parliament, has for several years been a part of wider political and academic assemblages that work on tackling the issue of labour exploitation and modern slavery. Within these assemblages, there has been a range of different narratives about what exactly constitutes labour exploitation and how to delineate it from good work practices (Weitzer, 2014). Some approaches have taken a sharp binary view that makes a clear-cut separation between work conditions that are considered to constitute an abhorrent crime that needs to be eradicated (Bales et al., 2009; Home Office, 2014) and work conditions that are generally good, but might have some minor issues of compliance (Department for Business Innovation & Skills, 2016; Gangmasters and Labour Abuse Authority, 2017). The understanding that all work conditions and practices fall into one of two binary categories has been nuanced by research that views work as taking place on a continuum of different patterns of working conditions from forced labour to decent work (Potter and Hamilton, 2014; Skrivankova, 2010).

Although there are different shades to these approaches concerning what constitutes labour exploitation and how it should be defined, they are similar in terms of the way that they focus on conditions of work such as pay, hours worked, and the security of the job, among other things, and the protection of labour rights as a practical way to delineate exploitative labour from decent work. In a similar vein, political and academic concerns have been raised for some time about the rise of precarious work. The links between work and precariousness can be traced back to the 1960s when precariousness started to be used as a concept by both social movements and some academics to differentiate between what was seen as secure standard employment and the growth of insecure work with fewer rights and benefits (Armano et al., 2017).

Although the emphasis of perspectives on precarious work is somewhat different in policy and research engagements with labour exploitation, they share a similar focus on the conditions of work. Just as with approaches to labour exploitation, research into precarity has sought to conceptualise work conditions in ways that either seek to make binary distinctions between standard employment models and precarious forms of work (Castel, 2003; Kalleberg, 2009) or conceptualise work as a continuum organised around degrees of precariousness (Lambert and Herod, 2016). The degree of precarity is then conceptualised and rendered measurable based on several dimensions such as earnings, social security, regulatory protection, and influence on work arrangements (Millar, 2017).

This focus on the importance of working conditions has consequences for how policy solutions are imagined, shaped, and designed to be implemented. It also presupposes that it is possible to have decent and unproblematic work. Work therefore often ends up being imagined as being both part of the problem and the solution to the issues that workers are facing. For example, when the government seeks to tackle the issue of labour exploitation, the business sector is not only considered to be generally unproblematic – with the vast majority cast as 'honest, upstanding employers' (Department for Business Innovation & Skills, 2016: 3) – but is also seen as a key stakeholder and a victim of labour exploitation practices, as their growth and job-creating potential is perceived to be undercut by 'unfair, illegal competition' (Department for Business Innovation & Skills, 2016: 3). When workers are 'rescued' from their exploitative conditions, it is therefore not surprising that regular employment is brought up as a crucial aspect in their rehabilitation (Home Office, 2019; Idris, 2017) and that programmes have been set up with the business sector in order to create 'a pathway to permanent employment for survivors' (Balch et al., 2017: 2).

Similarly, the imagined solutions to the problematic rise of precarious work are often tied in with the prospect of decent or good work as a panacea for the issues that workers are facing. For instance, in the much-lauded, government-supported but 'independent' Taylor review on good work and modern work practices, the focus is on precarious work and the imagined solutions to the issues are 'explicitly directed toward the goal of good work for all, recognising that good work and plentiful work can and should go together' (Taylor, 2017: 9). In other words, more but better work is conceived as the way to address the issue of precarious work.

The approach from traditional unions follows along much the same lines, in that they argue there is a decent job deficit and that new policies should be introduced 'to encourage the creation of decent jobs, with decent hours and pay' (TUC and Hudson, 2015: 4). From a wider academic perspective, the expansion and development of the 'standard employment relationship' (Bosch, 2004), conceptualised as measures provided by employers and the state to provide 'substantive protections against a pure market relationship' (Rubery et al., 2018: 510), is still widely considered to be the best way to address issues of precarity, even though it is recognised that this might risk creating new patterns of division and exclusion of the margins (Alberti et al., 2018).

The Problem of the Worker and Its Solutions

This focus on decent work as a transformative solution to the precarious and exploitative conditions of workers is often faced with the conundrum as to why the workers are not actively and consistently pursuing what is considered decent work themselves. This conundrum takes a slightly different form depending on whether it is approached from the perspective of labour exploitation or precarious work, but both examine issues relating to the lack of agency amongst workers and what factors might structure this lack of agency.

Within labour exploitation assemblages, there is still limited research on why workers in some situations seem to put up with their exploitative circumstances. Although there are some extreme cases where leaving is impossible due to threats and forced confinement, in many cases the type of exploitation does not in itself prevent workers from leaving their work (Davies, 2019; Weitzer, 2015). To explain why workers sometimes choose to put up with their exploitation, several factors, most of them related to the characteristics of the workers, are used to explain why they behave the way they do. Issues around their ignorance of their rights, limited language skills, cultural differences, and mental health issues, have all been identified as personal characteristics that make workers vulnerable to exploitation, with more structural factors such as the lack of unions and the hidden nature of their work raised as side issues (Beels, 2017; Harris et al., 2014). Whilst highlighting how these different factors tie in with patterns of exploitation can be useful, they also often end up portraying the workers as being without much real agency or influence on their situation. By linking labour exploitation with characteristics of difference and marginalisation, it also implies that the blame for labour exploitation is at least partly on workers who 'lack' knowledge, skills, health, or some other characteristics. This focus on perceived causational factors amongst the workers also risks shifting the focus away from the underpinning political and economic factors that shape exploitation and work.

Within political and academic assemblages that perceive the issue to be about precarious work, the focus tends to shift to concerns about why people are not more actively organising in unions in order to promote decent work. In most Western European countries, trade union density has been falling for decades (Tailby and Pollert, 2011) and a similar pattern is found in the United Kingdom, where despite a small increase during the period from 2017 to 2020, union membership density in 2022 fell to the lowest recorded levels at 22.3% (ONS, 2023), far below the levels seen in the late 1970s, when membership peaked at 53% (Machin, 2000).

There has been extensive research into union membership decline, and this has tended to cluster around demand and supply-focused explanations. The demand-focused research traces how changing values in relation to work and increasing individualisation amongst younger generations has meant that there are more diverse expectations about work, whilst at the same time there is increasing scepticism towards the collectivist aspect of unions (Margalioth, 1998; Ng et al., 2010; Oliver, 2006). By contrast, the supply-focused perspective highlights how changing political and economic conditions have resulted in a shift in the labour market so that more precarious work, which tends to have lower union membership rates, now makes up a larger proportion of the total workforce (Bryson and Gomez, 2005). Some argue that this has resulted in workers becoming like 'boiled frogs' as they slowly and uncritically become accustomed to increasingly precarious working conditions, coming to rely on their individual abilities to navigate insecurities rather than seeking to resist and create better conditions through collective action (Berry and McDaniel, 2020; Furlong et al., 2017).

Although there are differences between supply and demand-aligned approaches, they share similar assumptions about the centrality of working conditions and the role of traditional union membership as a way of dealing with these 'real' concerns of workers. This is problematic both in terms of assuming that the real concern of all workers is job security and slightly better wages, and in terms of assuming that traditional union membership plays a crucial role in dealing with the concerns of all workers. Unions tend to focus on issues around job security, wages, and pensions (Berry and McDaniel, 2020), and for some this might be important. However, it is problematic to assume that these issues reflect the concerns of all workers.

The notion that the best way to address these issues is through union membership is also problematic as it ignores other ways of seeking change, whether through direct action-focused rank-and-file unions or other individual forms of resistance (Woodcock, 2017). This is not to say that issues of working conditions are not important in some contexts or that traditional unions have no role to play. However, the view that it is only some kinds of wage labour that are problematic and that membership of a union is the solution to all work-related problems should not be assumed, at least not without first taking into account the multiple and varied lived ways in which work is experienced in the everyday by precarious workers.

Patterns of Resistance and Control

In order to examine some of the underlying assumptions about decent and precarious work, it is therefore necessary to examine the everyday lived experiences of workers more closely. Previous research has examined how workers in their everyday life themselves are critical of work and the impact it has on their lives, even if the work is what would be considered 'decent'. Some research directions have pointed out that how work is experienced is more complex than just the external conditions of work.

It is argued that there are different layers of meaning attached to work and whether a job is experienced as meaningful or not is linked to contextual and processual factors relating to the social constitution of power, control, isolation, self-estrangement, and occupational timescapes within particular jobs and work practices (Bailey and Madden, 2017; Costas and Fleming, 2009; Seeman, 1959; Volti, 2012). For others, it is not just that work can occasionally be meaningless, but that an increasingly large part of work is made up of so-called 'bullshit jobs' without any meaning for the workers whatsoever and with work practices that mainly serve to create more work for the sake of work rather than having any meaningful impact on the world (Graeber, 2018). In Mills' study of white-collar workers, the view expressed by the workers is more critical, with white-collar workers accepting that 'work *per se* is unpleasant' (Mills, 1953: 229) and that one type of job is only considered more satisfactory in comparison with other types of work or jobs, but not necessarily in comparison with not working at all. This kind of research indicates that the issue is not just about improving the external conditions of work and liberating all workers by ensuring decent work for all; instead, what becomes more important is to start to notice how workers tackle the issue of work in their daily lives. To explore these issues, the notion of resistance and control as an analytical concept can be particularly useful.

Resistance at work has often been conceptualised in terms of formal acts of resistance such as union membership and official strikes. However, resistance can be seen to incorporate a range of different activities, including more everyday acts of resistance (Woodcock, 2017). Scott explored this issue by drawing out how peasants and other marginalised groups rarely resort to open refusal against 'those who seek to extract labor, food, taxes, rents, and interest from them' (Scott, 1985: 29), but instead use more invisible methods such as 'foot dragging, dissimulation, false compliance, pilfering, feigned ignorance, slander, arson, sabotage' (Scott, 1985: 29). These patterns of everyday resistance can also be found in other settings, such as in Irish and British call centres, where practices such as taking extra breaks, absenteeism, cheating the system, or leaving the work altogether have been linked to activities of resistance in workplaces characterised by highly regulated and technologically enabled regimes of labour control (Mulholland, 2004; Woodcock, 2017).

However, there are some issues with how control and resistance are often examined as a binary opposition, where control is either considered as being inescapable and total, leaving the workers as dupes for management control, or where resistance is romanticised in terms of pure spaces of total freedom. Instead, resistance and control should be seen as being interconnected and mutually constitutive so that the everyday practices of workers 'are simultaneously enabling and constraining, coherent and contradictory, complex and simple, efficacious and ineffectual' (Mumby, 2005: 38).

Mapping Precarious Resistance

There are other studies that explore contemporary patterns of precarious resistance and control in particular workplaces. These include studies of call centres where resistance evolved around the flight from work (Woodcock, 2017), Sheffield steel factories where kinship relations were incorporated into processes of capital accumulation (Mollona, 2009), and studies of Deliveroo drivers where new technological developments enabled new patterns of control and resistance (Cant, 2019). These research findings have already highlighted some of the contemporary dynamics and changing nature of precarious work and patterns of resistance, control and capital accumulation, and this research will seek to build on these views of precarious work.

Where the research I am presenting here is different is that rather than focusing on one particular type of workplace, it draws on the experience of people with diverse and constantly shifting work patterns. If the precariousness of work cannot be delineated as a characteristic that only applies to some work experiences and 'if precarity is instead theorized as inherent to all labour-capital relationships, to varying degrees' (Alberti et al., 2018: 449), then we also need to notice 'commonalities across the diverse situations in which labour is at work and on the move in the world today' (Neilson and Rossiter, 2008: 58). By noticing the partial connections and points of commonality of diverse and changing work experiences, we can tease out how patterns of resistance and control transcend particular industries and workplaces.

Furthermore, it is also important to take into account how patterns of resistance and control are shaped outside the workplace. The move towards more flexible production patterns to maximise wealth accumulation results in new dynamics where workers are expected to be flexible and always ready to work at a moment's notice. Always having to be ready to start work at short notice and always having to seek out new work opportunities means that 'free time' becomes further occupied by the demands of work. Not only do the workers have to actively look and wait for work to emerge, but they also still have to recuperate and brace for the impact of another stretch of work (Anderson, 2007). In this way, processes of wealth accumulation seep into the everyday life of workers by trapping them in a continuous present where they are always anticipating, waiting, or seeking work without being able to plan for the future (Tsianos and Papadopoulos, 2006). Therefore, to understand the impact of changing patterns of work, it is also important to move away from a confined focus on the workplace in order to pay attention to patterns of resistance and control in people's 'free time'.

Perspectives from the Field

To both get a sense of how diverse patterns of precariousness play out across different work sectors and to take account of the impact that work has on people's everyday lives, this research draws on ethnographic fieldwork where I lived and worked with people in precarious circumstances. By living for months at a time in a hostel together with precarious workers, it was possible to gain a sense of how different forms of precarious work impacted people's lives. Furthermore, by working in call centres and warehouses, I could experience firsthand what practices people used to address the issue of work.

For the people I lived and worked with, there was no one defining characteristic that encompassed all of their different working experiences. There were people working on full-time contracts and people working as day labourers. Some people earned much less than the minimum wage and some people earned somewhat more. The types of work people were doing in the hostel were also very diverse. Some people worked in jobs that are often associated with low pay and insecure working conditions, such as builders, kitchen porters, hairdressers, waiters, cleaners, security staff, and warehouse staff. However, there were also people whose jobs might normally be associated with more secure and prestigious types of work. For example, some people worked in information technology (IT), office administration, finance, high-end restaurant chefs, entrepreneurs, app developers, and estate agents.

During fieldwork, I would meet hundreds of people at work and in the hostel who all had different sets of backgrounds and experiences. Some I might only encounter for a few minutes and others I would get to know better than most of my friends. Any attempts to align and divide these different work experiences along continuums of standard employment and precarious work, or decent work and exploitative work would quickly run into trouble as there were too many partial connections and contradictions to fit any such framework.

The patterns of precarity were different and people's individual circumstances would change more often than not, but the issue of how to deal with work and the precariousness and vulnerability it brought with it was one aspect that in some way unified these diverse experiences. Examining these diverse experiences partially connected through shared patterns of precariousness can help give a sense of how patterns of work, precariousness control, and resistance are evolving and adapting.

By examining some of the commonalities in terms of how the issue of work was dealt with by this wide range of people in precarity, we can also start to get a sense of how the issues and concerns might be conceptualised differently from how they are viewed in political and academic assemblages concerning precarious and exploitative work. Importantly, however, the view given here should not be seen as a definitive exploration of how people living in precarious circumstances experience work, as the ever-changing diversity of precarious work practices and patterns of resistance and control precludes that possibility.

The Everyday Issue of Work

For all of the people I encountered during my fieldwork, there was rarely any doubt that 'work' was the most important single aspect that shaped their everyday practices. Large parts of their day would be taken up by working, going to and from work, recovering from work, or looking for work. As such, work also often came up during the conversations people had. When starting a new job, I and the other newcomers would normally try to get a better sense of what it was like to work there, but initially our inquiries would be met with short nondescript replies such as 'it is OK', 'pff, it's alright' or 'it's good'. It would be the same kind of short reply people at the hostel would get when they initially inquired about work with someone they didn't know.

It was only as people started to get to know each other more at work and in the hostel that this talk about work expanded. Once in a while, the conversations would focus on concrete details about the conditions of work. How often did you get paid? Was there any overtime bonus? Would they cut your pay for 15 minutes if you were 1 minute late? How long were the breaks and how strictly were they enforced? How intense was the work? Was discipline tight or could you do your own thing? What was it like working there before and was it getting worse? Had there always been these rules or was that just a new thing? Were the other colleagues stressed, relaxed, nice, scheming, or fun? And how about management – were they wannabe dictators or soft and distant?

Conversations like that did come up, but they were relatively rare. Much more common were stories about events that happened at work. Most of these stories would be about bosses treating the workers unfairly, disciplining them for no reason, taking away their bonuses, asking them to do impossible things, moving them to work tasks they hated, being abusive, yelling, throwing things, or humiliating them in front of others. At other times it was people's colleagues or the customers who got on their nerves, giving them even more stress and hassle to deal with. These ways of talking about work might give some outer indications of some of the differences and particularities of whatever job people were doing at the time, but they didn't address the underlying practices of having to work and, more importantly, they didn't say much about how to make it through another day of work.

Only after settling into a job and being part of different practices at work did it start to become clear that the conditions of work, the pay, the hours, the intensity, etc. were important, but the main thing that the workers were concerned with on a daily basis was how to get through work as quickly, and with as little harm, as possible. Most conversations did not seek out the details of work conditions, but were searching for hints, guidance, and tools to help make it through to the end of work and to minimise the impact of work outside of the workplace. However, the issue of how to deal with work was not just an everyday issue that could be dealt with one day at a time. People also imagined, planned, and sought to achieve futures where the impact of work was absent or at least minimised.

To explore how people dealt with these aspects of work, I will link up my own embodied experiences of working in the field with how people in the hostel experienced and dealt with the issue of work. When I examine how work was dealt with at the workplace, a large part of my discussion will therefore be based on my own work experiences, as the details of how to deal with work were mostly something that became clear through participating in it. Similarly, how work impacted people's lives outside of work and how people planned for work-free futures will mainly be based on the ethnographic research I did in the hostel, although I will supplement it with the conversations about how to overcome work altogether that came up in the places where I worked.

Getting through Work

'Think only of the next break, finishing time, and the weekend. Break, finish, weekend. That is it. All you need.' I am being trained together with a group of other new recruits to work in a warehouse that belongs to Iroha, a global retail company. Saaf is our trainer who is going to show us how to do the work, but the thing he repeats continuously throughout the training sessions is that sentence. Think about 'break, finish, weekend'. Think about nothing else than the next upcoming point where work finishes for a little while. Saaf has been working there for years on a regular contract with better pay than us temps, but he knows that the daily concern of all the workers is to get through the day as swiftly and as unscathed as possible. His advice is well heeded, but alone it is not enough. To get through a day at Iroha, you need an arsenal of different tactics to avoid work and pull time along so that you can get out of there as quickly as possible.

Iroha was not unique. In the other warehouses, the call centres, the market research odd jobs, and when hearing people in the hostel's stories about their work, the problem of getting through work seemed central to people's experiences of work. To deal with this problem, people sought to manipulate the particular work assemblages they were part of at any particular time in order to minimise the impact of work. Every work situation, no matter how simple it might look from the outside, was always complex, changing, and fluid. The dynamics between workers seeking to minimise the impact of work and managers seeking to increase control in order to facilitate productivity were central in shaping how work was experienced.

However, these patterns of resistance and control did not happen in a vacuum. They were always shaped within constantly evolving assemblages where temporal, spatial, embodied, and material aspects came together to create new sets of opportunities to escape work and new ways for management to enforce control. This is not a new finding. Research has been done on the wider links between capitalist and technological developments and the temporal, spatial, and embodied dynamics of the world (Berardi, 2009; Brenner, 1999; Wajcman and Dodd, 2017). It is also crucial to notice that time, space, embodiment, and materials are not static entities, and that they are shaped in evolving assemblages that are interdependent on social processes, including wider capitalist processes.

However, my focus here is less on evaluating the extent to which capitalist processes have led to particular spatial, temporal, material, and embodied changes. Instead, it will be on how the workers themselves, in order to deal with the issue of work, made sense of, utilised, navigated, and sought to manipulate these assemblages' temporal, spatial, embodied, social, and material features.

Furthermore, the examples I include here should not be seen as an exhaustive examination of the different patterns of resistance that took place in the places where I worked. Even in what from the outside would seem like simple and predictable patterns of work, there were complex dynamics at play that always created new situational flows in which different patterns of resistance and control could emerge. The examples I have chosen here are designed to highlight some of these issues rather than to give a full sense of all the different ways these patterns could play out.

Body and Mind Separation

Saaf's advice that all we needed to do was to think about the break, finish and weekend was good advice, but how to make it to the break unscathed still presented plenty of hurdles for people to overcome. There would be long stretches were getting through the next minute seemed like an impossible task beyond any of the powers workers had available to them at that time and place.

One of the methods that people could use was to seek relief in the potential of a body and mind separation. The goal here was to take themselves away from the material reality they were faced with so that they could be consumed by free-flowing daydreams, friendly hidden chats, or achieve a state of complete absentmindedness. Different tactics could be used to try to achieve that. At call centres, although all distracting material was usually banned from the workstations, people could always find a way to have a sneaky look at their phone, smuggle in a hidden book or magazine under the interview scripts, or have hour-long whispering conversations in between calls with the person next to them.

At Iroha, the immense number of different items that were stocked in the warehouse could be used to set off a flow of thoughts that would allow the minutes fly by. Whether it was the strange Halloween hat, a tabletop game to play with, a new trainer with an enticing design, hair colour products that could give a new look, or books that could bring new narratives to play with, these could all be useful instigators to let the mind wander away from the world they were part of at that moment.

It was not only physical items that could be used to instigate a mind stroll. Daydreams of childhood, about the latest superhero film, sexual fantasies, anticipating going to the pub, what they were going to eat for dinner, and the plans for their days off were just some of the things that people mentioned in passing had occupied their minds whilst working, but there were doubtless endless other streams of thoughts that people used to separate themselves from the material imposition of work. Letting your mind wander was not the only way to use your mind to get away from things. Spacing out (Conrad, 1997) was also an important tool that could be used. Spacing out was a kind of applied on-the-hoof meditational skill that, if you could master it, would bring you to a state of nothingness where you would be untouched by the nagging trivialities of the world of work.

The biggest hindrance to this kind of manipulation of the mind was the work itself. If the job involved any mental effort, such as having to count all the items in 'a bin' or shelf space, it made it significantly more difficult to let the mind wander or space out. The same was the case for call centre work, where any interaction with people on the other end of the line would end up occupying and binding down the mind in the present.

In contrast, work that required minimal mental effort was conducive to separating and setting your mind free to do its own thing. So, at Iroha, if your job for the day was to scan all the items in a bin, it was easier to almost entirely let go of this world for extended moments and go wherever your mind might take you. As Molstad (1986) points out in his study of brewery workers, if workers were inclined to pursue these tactics of getting through work by letting their mind wander or seek out pleasurable daydreams, it would be beneficial to do more boring and simple work tasks to keep the mind free from work. For management, this presenteeism, where a worker is there in body only (Cederström and Fleming, 2012), might be seen as problematic for some tasks, but it was almost impossible to guard against, unless the whole work process was changed to involve more mental work tasks that could prevent workers from spacing out to get relief from work.

Chasing the Rush

If manipulating the mind to minimise the impact of the work was not possible either because of the type of work people were told to do or because they were not in the right frame of mind to do so, another tactic was to try and chase the rush. This tactic fed off pressure and expectations for how quickly management expected things to be done. The aim was to make time pass more quickly by making themselves feel like they were starved of time (Perlow, 1999). Putting themselves in a situation where time was in short supply reversed the problem of time, from being one where time needed to be dragged along to a problem of how to slow time down so that they could do what they needed to do. In a sense, they were playing a reverse psychology game with themselves. They wanted to feel the pressure of being short on time so that they could ride time's ability to suddenly disappear without a trace.

There is an important distinction to be made here between the types of work they were doing. There was the task type where they were in an actual rush, where their work didn't end until they finished certain tasks. Here time was in actual short supply and not finishing on time just meant that work was extended and their free time was consequently shortened. Being in a state of rush in this type of work did indeed make time go faster, but it was a vicious and cruel type of speed that relentlessly devoured their time. On the other hand, when work was to finish at a set clock time no matter how much work they had done, achieving a state of being in a rush had far fewer trade-offs, but it was consequently harder to achieve.

There were almost always targets set by management that the workers were supposed to aim to achieve, but these targets were rarely enough to create a rush (and being in a rush did not necessarily mean being more productive and achieving higher targets). At Iroha, for example, all job functions had targets that the workers were supposed to try to achieve and the targets were set so high that it was impossible to achieve them all. From Iroha's management perspective, setting impossible targets might have been part of a ploy that would induce constant stress and thereby higher productivity. However, people quickly realised that it was impossible to meet the targets and they also realised that if they did, management would just come up with new targets. So, as time went on, people stopped caring and feeling stressed about meeting the targets.

Instead, it was the specific job function and their embodied particularities that had a greater impact on whether people could achieve a rush. At Iroha, I was attached to the Quality Assurance unit together with roughly sixty other people. Within this unit, there were three 'work processes': Single Bin Counts (SBCs), which involved counting all the items in a bin; Simple Record Counts (SRCs), which involved counting a specific type of item; and Circle Counts (CCs), which involved scanning all the items in a bin. Doing SBCs and CCs involved moving very little at a time. They might count one bin and then be told by the scanner to count the bin above it or very close to it. To feel rushed in these job functions was almost impossible. The slow methodical almost standstill nature of the work made it difficult to get the blood rushing and time passing by.

SRCs, by contrast, were different. In SRCs they first had to search through a bin for the item they were looking for, then count it (and often there would only be a few of those items in the bin) and then they were told to go to another bin that would often be hundreds of yards away. This constant movement between places and frantic searching through items to find the item that they needed to scan was inducive to creating a rush. That SRCs were a relatively rare work process to be assigned also helped. The fear of being taken off an SRC and put back on the other processes could further increase the pressure that could bring the workers closer to achieving a state of rush. For those people who favoured being in a state of rush to get through the day, being put on SRCs was therefore like being given a partial pardon from the hardship of work. It was almost like the actual work time had been considerably shortened.

In the morning, when people were told their initial work assignment, they would be exalted if they were put on an SRC and if they were later taken off it, they would be visibly distressed. One of the main grounds for workers' complaints was also the lack of opportunity to do SRCs and some theorised that if a particular manager didn't like a person, they would punish them by taking them off SRCs. Although management could use this desire for SRCs to discipline and entice people to put in extra effort, there were still fractures in the system that allowed the workers to resist. It was possible to change the work task on the scanner that each worker had by themselves. If a worker changed their work task by themselves it would, in theory, be instantly visible to the manager, but even managers work in rhythms and there would be periods where their attention and effort would fall off. If the workers timed it right, it was therefore possible to sneak in some 'free' SRCs without the managers noticing it.

Yet, being in a rush had its drawbacks. Being rushed on SRCs, for example, meant that people would have to half run between the bins (even though running was strictly forbidden) and if a worker were on SRCs the whole 11 hours of the day, their body would pay the price with blisters and aching muscles and joints. The stress of trying to chase the rush was therefore not worth it for many people, who preferred the more relaxed approach of using mind wandering as a method of manipulating time to their advantage.

Spatial Oases

Seeking to separate the mind and body, or using the stress of the rush to get through work could help things a great deal, but they were far from a foolproof way to be protected from the impact of work because at the end of the day they would still be working. To seek out and create spatial oases where they would not have to work at all was therefore by far the most reliable way of getting away from work. The particular material and virtual form those spatial oases would take would again depend on the particular assemblages of the work.

Going to the toilet was one of the favourite ways to create a spatial oasis. In call centres there would often be the physical presence of managers at the end of the workers' table and going to the toilet would involve having to physically go under the prying eyes of managers who threatened to keep a tab on their every move. However, at Iroha going to the toilet meant logging out of the scanner to indicate to the algorithm that now they were going to the toilet and at the moment they had logged out of the system, it would be registered as a toilet break. This systematic virtual registration of toilet breaks also meant that the workers didn't physically have to move to the toilet. I would often find people wandering around 'being on the toilet'; drinking tea or coffee in the cafeteria 'being on the toilet', or just taking a rest on a box whilst 'being on the toilet'. Sometimes people were reprimanded for spending too much time on the toilet, but because the toilets could easily take 10 minutes to get to and since going to the toilet involved somewhat taboo activities that the managers didn't want to hear about in too much graphic detail, the managers would normally let it go with an inconsequential warning of not using the toilet for too long.

A more advanced technique involved using the surveillance system to create a mirage of work activity that could hide the spatial oases. Here the goal was to not work whilst making it look like they were working from the point of view of the surveillance system. Doing market research at call centres where the managers' eyes would constantly be scanning the room, people could still present themselves to the manager as if they were working, even though they weren't. One way to do this was to set up appointments with a string of numbers that they had called before and where they knew that long-winded answering machines would be the only response they would get. They would still have to call the numbers, but since they knew that no one would pick up, they could carve out a few moments of work-free time whilst they let the answering machine go through the motions of notifying them of a respondent's absence. These small moments of freedom could then be used on better things like reading, clandestinely whispering with the person next to them, or just spacing out.

At Iroha, the surveillance technology was different as it was done via the scanner, which could check how the workers progressed in work through the scans that they made. The workers were supposed to scan a specific numbered item every few minutes and failing to do so would raise the alarm to management, who would send a text telling them to go back to work. If, however, the wrong item was scanned, it would still look like work was being done and that the only problem was that the worker was struggling to find the right thing to scan. People would elegantly take advantage of this loophole and purposely scan a wrong item over and over again whilst chatting with someone, sitting down for a rest, laying down for a little nap (for the brave ones), or just wandering around the warehouse. All these activities would, from the point of view of the surveillance system, come across as people working hard, albeit in a somewhat lost and incompetent way.

There were of course risks to seeking and using these spatial oases. At Iroha, managers would sometimes make the rounds and try to catch people out, though most of the time the rumour that the managers were on the floor would quickly spread and people would make sure they looked busy should one of them suddenly turn up. Also, if someone were deemed to be too unproductive or having too much time on the toilet, they could risk disciplinary punishments, such as being given less work or being let go altogether. In the call centres people were sometimes caught out by managers checking their call records or listening in on their calls, but the rewards for seeking out spaces where they didn't have to work were too tempting for people to give up on them altogether, despite the risks involved in doing so.

Break Time, Leaving Early, Finishing Early, Bonus Time off

The management-approved and controlled work-free periods, whether that was in the form of paid and unpaid breaks or the time you would get off work, were also the target of different practices, considerations, and impulses about how to approach them. When it came to paid breaks, there was not much debate about what the goal was – the longer the break was, the better, and there were always a few things, such as being deliberately but acceptably late, that could be done to try to extend these breaks. However, whilst paid breaks were ultimately seen as being an unproblematic good and any extension as a positive thing, the issue of how to approach unpaid breaks, the option of leaving early without pay, and calling in sick was more complicated. The main reason people worked was for money and giving up on some of that money voluntarily in exchange for freedom did raise various sets of deliberations.

At Iroha, we would sometimes be asked to volunteer to leave early via a message on our scanner. Before that, there would often have been rumours spreading about that possibility and everyone would start discussing what to do. Multiple things spoke against taking voluntary time off. For one thing, Iroha was located outside of London and to get there Iroha provided a special bus service from a range of stations around London costing a couple of pounds. If people had arrived on the bus, leaving early meant that they had to make their own way back, which could involve a 20-minute walk to the nearest bus stop. There they would have to wait for the hourly bus to arrive to take them to the train station, where another train would eventually take them towards their home. It could easily expand the travel time by an hour or two and it would cost close to almost two hours' salary. Another issue to consider was that in Iroha the overtime system meant that if they worked more than 40 hours, the pay for those hours increased by 50% and if they worked more than 50 hours a week, the hourly pay would double. Leaving early would then mean giving up on potentially lucrative overtime bonuses. Despite this, the excitement was palpable when the rumours spread that we might be able to leave early. Eventually, some people would stay behind because 'well I'm already here', but for most people, the promise of an early release was too great a temptation to resist and they would jubilantly, sometimes with half-joking sounds of 'freeedoom', choose to leave work despite the economic cost.

These kinds of considerations also came into play when deciding when to call in sick. Calling in sick was not an uncommon feature and within the first four weeks of starting work, the group of eight people I had started with had all called in sick at least a few times. What constituted sickness from management's point of view and the workers' points of view tended to differ. Management had clear expectations that sick days should be used to deal with medically accepted definitions of being sick. For the workers, when they needed a sick day, it was to gain some more time off work, which, from their perspective, was the best cure for the stress and hardship that work caused, even if that was not yet fully accepted as a medical reason to call in sick.

Calling in sick became even more prevalent during the so-called peak period, where the standard hours went from 40 hours a week to 55 hours a week. Although the overtime bonus provided a strong economic incentive to work all 55 hours, for most people the price they paid for losing more of their freedom from work was not worth it and to seek respite, they resorted to calling in sick. At the end of the two-month peak period, most of the people I knew had only managed to work the full weekly shifts for around half of the time, thereby losing hundreds of pounds.

Another example illustrating that time off work would trump economic incentives became visible with the so-called power-hour bonus. During the peak period, one hour would be designated 'the power hour'. Here everyone would be forced to work on the boring, simple processes (SBCs) and the goal was to have 'fun' by seeing how much the unit as a whole could count in one hour. To increase the 'fun', the worker who counted the most bins would win a prize that would either be an extra half-hour break or the pay for half an hour's work. When people were given this direct choice between extra money or extra free time, almost everyone without hesitation opted for the extra half an hour of freedom from work. When the other workers after a too short break started to go back to work, they would sometimes see the relaxed and tranquil figure of the power-hour winner staying behind for another 30 minutes of freedom and at that moment most people were in no doubt that they had made the right choice.

When working on market research projects in call centres on zero-hours contracts, the tension between wanting to earn money and yearning for freedom from work took on a dynamic that both enabled workers to seek out freedom from work and enabled zero-hours contracts to become more profitable. When working on a market research project, there would be a project target for how many interviews needed to be done and when that target was reached, the work would finish. Unless there happened to be another project coming up, most people would then be let go and would have to start searching for some other job.

Most places didn't have any bonus system in place and amongst the ones that did, the targets were so high that it was well known that they were impossible to achieve. Without this financial incentive to achieve a high number of interviews, there was a financial incentive to not get any interviews because that would mean that the project would be extended and people would get more hours of work. If people prioritised the possibility of extra work and income against the prospect of finishing and being released from work, they could then have slowed down, deliberately trying to avoid completing the project to squeeze out as many working hours as they possibly could.

Avoiding interviews was easy. Calling up busy businesses and asking another overworked person to dedicate 10–30 minutes of their time for nothing so that they could help another company that preferred to stay anonymous was a difficult sell. To get an interview required a light-touch approach to the true length and purpose of the survey, and putting emotional energy into circumventing the truth demanded extra effort. More importantly, the only way to get an interview was to create a momentary emotional connection with the respondent by invoking respect, sympathy, awe, pity, fear, laughter, or some other emotion that could tie the respondent down to spend

10–30 minutes of their time and investing that kind of affective labour was something that demanded considerable effort. Just by talking in a normal and disinterested tone and being truthful about the full extent and length of the survey would result in an instant rejection. Therefore, if workers had wanted to, it would have been easy to keep extending the project until the client who had ordered the project ran out of money and patience.

However, not once did I experience a project that lasted for the full period it was initially projected to last. The interview targets were always reached early and therefore people were let go earlier than they had expected. When first beginning a project, which would normally be set to last around a couple of months, people wouldn't think too much about how long the work would last. But once a few weeks had passed, the dreariness of the work started to be felt more heavily and people would start to dream of a future where they would no longer have to do the same boring interview with the same type of businesspeople over and over again. When, after a few weeks into the project, managers would start to say how many more interviews they needed before the project could finish, the work intensity started to pick up. The end felt like it was in sight and rather than trying to extend the financial rewards by slowing down work, most people put all their emotional efforts into finishing the project so they could be finally liberated from this work. In this quest for freedom, any concern about money barely mattered when put up against the prospect of freedom from work.

In these instances, the dislike of the work was beneficial for the market research company and their clients as it would mean that the project could be finished quicker and cheaper. However, as always, there were patterns of resistance that emerged. To achieve the targets quicker and avoid some of the affective labour interviews involved, people would start to fill in half of the survey by themselves, ignore the mistakes of their colleagues when they did 'quality assurance checks', and create entirely fake interviews by themselves. The clients and the company might think that they had found the perfect model to exploit workers, but there were always unexpected ways to sabotage and disrupt the imposition of work to be found.

After Work

All of these different tools were deployed by workers to survive until they were liberated to stop working. However, making it to the end of another workday did not mean that the problem of work had been solved. Everyone knew that another day of work would surely come and that any short interval of work-free time would evaporate before it had really started. Also, getting off work did not mean that the impact of work disappeared as if nothing had happened.

Work festered, lingered on, sticking to every aspect of their being in the world. The ceaseless, repetitive rhythms could mould their body with blisters, cuts, worn-down joints, and surges of pain rushing through them for no apparent reason. Work could colonise their entire behaviour. It could mangle their dreams into repetitive nightmares – 'I had another dream of work again, why do I work in my dreams!'; discipline them to inadvertently continue their work processes – 'I can't stop counting, I counted rows of cars going back home yesterday'; rationalise and benumb their affective relationships – 'When talking with friends, I just want to finish the talk as quickly as possible. It is like I'm doing an interview'; petrify them into silence with the prospect of another day at work; or coerce their thoughts to gather around the endless stream of stress and mistreatment that work would bring.

Work had different intensities with periods of greater calm and periods where it could overflow people entirely. When living with people in the hostel, these intensities of work intruded into the rhythms of everyday life in the hostel. In the periods around the seasonal peaks of work, where most people worked long hours, the hostel became more polarised. The use of cannabis went up drastically and I would often find people unmovable in slightly awkward positions staring into an unknown void. In normal times when people came back from work, they would usually be met with warm greetings, and if there was energy left in them, and soon they would settle into the social rhythms of the hostel.

When it was peak period, coming back to the hostel would at best receive a little nod of tired and spaced-out recognition, and most people could only muster up a few struggling attempts at being social before having to shut down mentally and physically in order to prepare for the followings day's onslaught of work. People had been fighting with the imposition of work their whole life, so they knew a thing or two about how to handle it and they were normally adept at some separation between work and their own lives. However, when the pressures intensified, everyone had their limits and work could for extended periods occupy most of the people's mental and physical energy.

In the peak periods, the number of conflicts also increased, with more people almost coming to blows, only being separated by the quick interventions of other residents. There would also be more instances of people taking out their anger on whatever material things that happened to be near them. The marks and traces after angry and frustrated punches, kicks, thrown chairs, lifted-over tables, smashed windows and broken bottles would steadily grow and leave yet more evidence to posterity about the real impact of work. The spontaneous social events that would normally fill the days would also suddenly come to a standstill and the lively conversations that would echo around the common areas would die out. People would quickly prepare their food, eat it and hurry to their bed to sleep or they would focus on creating that perfect joint to bring distance to it all. This was also the period where ambulances were called when people fell over due to being too exhausted and it was the period where residents who had stayed there for years would suddenly disappear, leaving only vague rumours about their whereabouts behind.

The intensity of work and people's response to it could also take on particular individual characteristics. It could be that people were starting a new job where they both had to learn new work processes and all the different defence tactics that made work survivable. It could be that a new manager had arrived with new ideas about how to enforce control and compliance, which would mean that new defence tactics would have to be invented yet again. Or it could be that it was the sheer accumulation of constant work that relentlessly stole away their lives, a fact which, even for the strongest, at some point would be too much to deal with without breaking just a little bit. When people entered these particularly hard stretches, their energy would become drained and their whole embodied presence in the hostel would diminish into vague shadows that could do nothing but seek to barely survive until the onrush of work-related suffering died down.

The Future of (Freedom from) Work

The ripple effects of work on people's everyday lives meant that work as a problem was something they had to deal with regardless of whether they were at work or not. People knew that using different tools to make it through the day was only a short-term solution and did little to solve the problem of work in itself. If they wanted to find a permanent solution to the issue of work, they had to eliminate or at least reduce the impact of work on their lives. People knew that this was difficult, but it did not prevent them from trying to constantly grapple with how to eliminate the impact of work from their lives.

The three main paths people imagined could lead to a life free from the impact of work were: seeking to do what they loved; acquiring capital; and achieving a better type of alienation.

Enjoying Work to Kill Work

The idea that work can be pleasurable and a means to personal fulfilment if only people 'do what they love' might still be a favoured political and management-promoted discourse to entice worker compliance (Sandoval, 2018), but for most people at work and in the hostel, there was rarely any doubt that work was always bad for them.

There were still a few who had hopes that if only they found the right job where they could do what they enjoyed doing, it wouldn't feel like working at all. Some people had long-time dreams of wanting to pursue careers as designers, marketing professionals, chefs, photographers, police officers, or IT programmers. Some people were already doing their 'dream job' or had done them in the past, but in every single instance they had found that the promise that work would be better if only they loved it enough never held true and that ultimately work was work, no matter what they did.

This is not to say that there could not be some benefits to working with something in which they had an interest, but that was just one of the factors that shaped the experience of work and often it would be drowned out by all the other factors that made work feel like work. A chef might sometimes show with pride the piece of art they had created as a dish, the builders might justifiably brag about the enduring quality of the door frame they had made, and IT programmers could dive into hour-long conversations about the metaphysical philosophy of virus protection, but these moments were the exception. For the vast majority of the time, regardless of whether people's work aligned with their interests, the devastating impact of work on their lives did not stop just because they were doing what they liked.

The people I worked and lived with in the hostel had mostly experienced a whole range of different jobs. Some of these jobs would have been closer to their dream jobs and the external conditions in terms of pay, pension, rights and hours worked had sometimes been better than the jobs they were doing now. However, no matter how 'good' the working conditions had been and regardless of whether the job had involved activities that they had enjoyed doing outside of work, in the end, they had left and in most cases, they had done so on their own initiative. The growing range of experiences of work seemed to make it increasingly clear to them that no matter what work they would have to do, it would still be work and therefore inherently problematic.

Capitalist Utopias

Abstract discussions about the nature of capitalism very rarely formed part of any conversation, but most people knew that any talk about hard work paying off was false. It was as if they had studied the inner workings of the relationship between the rate of capital and the rate of economic growth (Piketty, 2014) to come to the conclusion that the acquisition of capital was the only way to set themselves free from the constraints of capitalist work.

The specifics of their aspirations would take different forms and how much capital they estimated they would need to be truly free from work would depend on the person. Some had dreams of becoming landlords and living off the rent, like John, a semi-mythical figure who would come to the hostel once a year after travelling the world using the money he got from renting out his London flat. Some had hopes of one day doing something similar and they had dreams of saving up to buy a couple of properties in London that they could then renovate, living off the rent for the rest of their lives. People knew that these kinds of ambitions were close to being unachievable and they would often be spoken about in the same daydreaming way as fantasising about what they would do if they won the lottery. They knew that in a world where they could barely afford to pay the transport to work, the idea of saving up the hundreds of thousands (if not millions) of pounds they would need to buy some London properties could be nothing more than a dream of a better life.

For others, the focus they hoped to enable wealth accumulation by setting up their own successful company. For a few, this was tied in with the expectation that owning their own business would make them free from the constraints of having a boss, so even if they had to work, it would not feel like real work. However, most had bigger ambitions and wanted to create a company that was so successful that it could run itself without them having to worry too much about money and work again.

A few people did try to set up their own business and they could often be found in the common area making phone and sales calls with potential investors, coming back from failed business meetings, and talking with the other residents about how their business ideas would change their lives. For most people, the dreams of setting up their own business were more fleeting and would rarely go beyond daydreams of better lives. Sometimes, though, the entrepreneurial spirit would overcome people who, in a small burst of wild optimism, would put in some intense hours of work to plan out how they could set up a new sofa business empire, a wellbeing garden company catering to the billionaire class, a tutorial app company to take over the London education market, a new YouTube channel to break the internet or something else that could finally emancipate them from work. These spurts of optimism and entrepreneurial dreams would rarely last too long as soon as new waves of work would overwhelm their lives and dreams yet again.

Finally, some people believed that capital investments would enable them to become free of the constraints of capitalism. Here the ambition was to not only get enough to live on without working but also to become rich. This was not so that they could buy all kinds of things or spend a lot of money, but rather so they would be completely free from any capitalist constraints society might put on them. As Amita, a tutor in her forties, told me once in the hostel:

> I want to be a billionaire. Not a millionaire. My family earned hundreds of thousands and they were still consumed by worrying. They would always be counting their money and pushing it around. It is not much different from being in a council estate. As a woman, I can't be happy with being a housewife. I know my worth and after 20 years of being Joe Bloggs I am done with that and I'm not going to settle for a few million cause you can lose that easily. Every billionaire has to have hit rock bottom like me that is how it is.

The most popular way of imagining a path to liberating wealth was to invest in blockchain currencies such as bitcoin, which in that period had seen a surge in price and publicity. There was a range of digital platforms where it was possible to exchange different cryptocurrencies and there was a whole host of auxiliary services that for a 'small' fee would handle the practicalities of investments with the promises of unlimited growth towards wealth.

Although the investors in the hostel were often different from the people in the hostel who gambled, it could be hard to distinguish them. The daily emotional rollercoaster of seeing their investment double or completely disappear in a matter of minutes was not much different from the people who lost half their weekly salary to gambling in an instant bet on red. The end result of steadily accumulating debt rather than wealth was also strikingly similar. Yet people would often continue to try to invest, as achieving the capitalist dream of almost unlimited wealth was seen as the only realistic way to overcome a life determined by the forces of capitalism and work.

Contained Alienation

For the people who did not believe that capitalism could liberate them from the destructive aspects of work, whether that was through the promise of the perfect job or freedom creating wealth, their focus tended to cluster around how best to prevent work from colonising more of their life than necessary. Whilst Marx might have said that workers only feel at 'home when he is not working, and when he is working he is not at home' (Marx, 1844: 74) as a critique of capitalist work, for some this type of alienation would have sounded like an improvement compared to the life they were currently living.

Being able to live a life where there were at least some places that remained detached and protected from work was the best thing people taking this stance could ever hope for. For them, work as a problem would always be part of their life, and the only way to get away from it was to build up mechanisms that would ensure perfect separation between the destructive powers of the world of work and their own life. This approach was linked to the way in which people tried to deal with the impact of work on an everyday basis, but its ambitions were grander. It sought to make a more complete separation between the spatial, temporal, and material assemblages where work happened and the life that was lived outside of work. If the impact of work could at least be contained, then they would still be able to live part of their lives free from the imposition of work.

One way to seek to establish this kind of separation was by trying to achieve a state of mind where no matter what trouble they were put through in their working life, it would not impact their mental state. These approaches were often tied in with different meditative practices, such as Yoga and Tai Chi, and sometimes it was partially connected to underlying religious beliefs as some people aligned these practices with their Buddhist, Hinduist, Christian, or Muslim faith. Whilst there might have been different underlying beliefs and emotions tied into these practices, when they came up in the discussion at the hostel, it was mostly in connection with practical discussions about how best to deal with the daily frustrations of a life dominated by work.

When the benefits of meditative practices were shared and tried out in the common rooms or the parks, it was in the hope that they could help build up a better defence against the neverending reality of having to deal with the impact of work. For this approach, accepting that work would always be part of life was one of the first steps. Once that was accepted, they could use these different meditative practices to let go of the negative aspects of work so that they didn't linger in their lives outside of work. As Ranvid, one of the Buddhist-inspired people, said in a late-night philosophical discussion: 'I just let it flow. I listen to my breath and just let it all flow out. I can't change it, I can't do anything about it, so I just let it flow.'

Trying out these practices was not enough for everyone and to help things along, some would enlist the help of drugs to maintain a proper separation. They knew that drugs might be damaging, but the relief they could give was often found to outweigh the downsides of using them. As Daniel, one of the believers in the use of cannabis, explained on a relaxing Sunday afternoon just before his first spliff of the day:

> I stopped smoking [weed] one time and started to eat all healthy and exercise, but then all I ever did was work, sleep, and try to stay healthy. There was nothing left to enjoy. I thought weed was the cause of all my problems but after I stopped, I found that all my problems were still the same. At least when I smoke I can feel something different.

Despite the potential of drug use to help deal with the issue of work, some acknowledged that relying on drugs ultimately did not change anything. As Gabriel would regularly shout out in a singing voice that would echo through the common rooms:

> We smoke weed every day, every day we smoke weed hahaha, but everything stays the same. Nothing ever changes. Every day the same work, the same drugs, the same music.

Making Sense of Precarious Work and Life

This part has drawn out how people living and working in precarious circumstances engaged with the issue of work. When the issue of precarious and exploitative work is examined from the perspective of the workers themselves, many of the assumptions that underpin dominant academic and policy perspectives on these issues become problematic. In contrast to how precarious and exploitative work in dominant political and academic assemblages is conceptualised as being related to specific conditions of work, for most people, work per se was perceived to be the main problem. Furthermore, whilst decent work is often conceived to have the potential to transform society and people's lives, most workers did not think that work in any form had the potential to change their lives for the better.

Looking at the economic aspects of work, the earning potential of work was rarely perceived to be transformative and the importance of earning a bit of extra money was most of the time a concern that faded in comparison to the quest for freedom from work. Given the choice, people would readily give up on easy opportunities to earn some extra in exchange for some freedom from work, even if just for a little stretch of time. Money did of course matter, but it was only when it reached the levels where, as capital, it could support life without work that it was perceived to have truly transformative potential. People knew that no matter how hard they worked, it would never be enough to acquire that amount of money. The wages earned by work were therefore a minor concern in the overall picture of dealing with the imposition of work.

When it came to issues concerning the regularity and the predictability of the job, it was not perceived to have transformative potential either and it did little to change their daily concerns of getting through work. Most places would have a mix of regular and temporary staff, but for the most part, the formal employment status did not change the makeup of the challenges they faced in their everyday struggle to get through another working day. There were some instances where working on a short-term or zero-hours contract would be beneficial. With short-term and infrequent work, freedom from work was never felt to be too far away, and even though the breaks between different jobs would always be temporary and filled with uncertainty, they still provided some form of respite. In terms of the academic and policy assemblages' much-prized decent and stable jobs with defined hours of work, which some of the people in the hostel did have, they seemed to offer little added advantage when it came to the issue of how to deal with the everyday hardship of work.

Some people might still have harboured some hope that the right kind of job could transform their lives: some people were still seeking their dream job, one that could change the underlying life-draining experiences of work and make it pleasurable and enjoyable. However, most people at the hostel and work had already been let down by their experiences of past or present dream jobs that had turned out to be just other types of work. Even if they had never found their dream job, the range of work experiences they had accumulated had highlighted to them that work was mostly similar and they had lost any hope that there would be any dramatic differences between any type of work. The transformative potential of work was therefore nothing but a naïve and hopeful narrative that had been quashed by their lived experiences a long time ago.

To say that work was not considered transformative in itself did not mean that the particular conditions people worked under were completely unimportant in terms of how work was experienced. Getting a higher wage might make it more economically feasible to take more days off work. Lowering the workload could make it easier to get through the day (although in some situations it could also make it more difficult). Receiving longer breaks meant that there was less work to overcome. Having the right to sick pay could mean yet more opportunities to avoid the impact of work. Differences in work conditions could therefore relate somewhat to how work was experienced and it could interlink with some of the tactics and methods people used to avoid work, but these varied conditions of work were never considered to be truly transformative of people's lives.

In policy assemblages, working conditions are often delineated on a continuum from exploitative and precarious work to decent work, but for most workers, all work was considered to be exploitative and precarious. No matter what work they would do, their lives would still be subordinated to the devastating forces of work. Having to work meant that their everyday lives would always be precarious and vulnerable to the ebbs and flows of work pressures. This shared precariousness and vulnerability to the imposition of work was also what connected people. Their particular work practices and experiences might be different in terms of salary, working hours and patterns of control, but all people shared the same concerns about how best to deal with the havoc that work wreaked on their lives.

Facing this stark reality of work, the main concern of the workers was how to minimise or escape the inherent exploitation that work entailed. To do so, they utilised an array of different tactics and practices in the specific workplace, outside of work, and in the way they imagined better futures. It was this daily resistance against the imposition of work and management patterns of control that was central to how they engaged with work. These patterns of resistance were never static, but were interlinked with, and constituted in relation to, constantly changing patterns of control.

In order to resist the imposition of work in the workplace, people sought to manipulate the embodied, spatial, and temporal assemblages of the particular workplace. These patterns of resistance were in a fluid and interactive relationship with management's attempts to enforce control and increase productivity. This meant that sometimes people's initiatives to minimise the impact of work would go against management's desires, but in other instances, it could be co-opted and used to promote the goals of management. This constant dialectic between control and resistance was visible in the types of tactics that workers used.

For example, when workers used certain work tasks to 'chase the rush' to make work feel shorter, management could use that dynamic to increase productivity and enforce discipline. However, workers in turn quickly developed new ways to resist these patterns of control by learning, as at Iroha, to manipulate the scanners in relation to the work patterns of the managers. Using scanners that could monitor the work activities of workers in real time might also seem like the perfect tool to ensure compliance, but once the technicalities and algorithmic particularities of the scanner were figured out, it could be used to create an algorithmic mirage of work activity that the workers could employ to create a spatial oasis where they could hide for hours in freedom from work. In the name of productivity, management might also have designed intensely boring and repetitive tasks, but the sheer repetitiveness allowed people to take their minds off work to daydream, chat, read, or just space out.

The destructive impact of work was not something that people only had to deal with whilst at work. The processes of exploitation that work entailed would creep into and start to disrupt their 'free time'. The logic of work would colonise people's thoughts and dreams, the intense stress and exhaustion that work caused would cut through social relations, and the sheer weight of dealing with a life defined by work would leave marks of violent frustration.

To seek out futures that could emancipate them from work, people would seek out practices and foster aspirations that could transform their lives. Most people had given up on the social and political narratives that imbued work with transformative possibilities. Instead, their practices and aspirations focused on transforming their lives either through acquiring capital or by seeking out better kinds of alienation.

The quest for capital drew on common capitalist narratives and patterns of wealth accumulation. People would plan out how to become landlords, pursue entrepreneurial dreams, and some would seek to figure out how to profit from the wild financial flows of the markets. These attempts at acquiring capital without having any capital to start with faced multiple difficulties, but the potential of capital to save them from the constant exploitation of work was a dream that for many was too great to ever give up on completely, however unlikely its realisation might be. For the people who did not rely on dreams of capital to bring relief, there seemed to be little option but to accept that work would always form some part of their lives. Yet, this did not mean that nothing could be done, and people tried to use a number of different methods to move towards futures where work was an alienating but separate and contained part of their life. That said, whether people subscribed to religious, meditative, pharmaceutical, or psychological practices, the intrusive patterns of work exploitation proved hard to fully contain.

It could be tempting to interpret these future aspirations as the complete victory of capitalist patterns of control and exploitation. Precarious workers whose dreams of better lives centre around the acquisition of capital so that they can become the beneficiaries of the exploitative patterns of capitalist wealth accumulation do not seem to bear many promises of a world free from the exploitation of precarious work. Precarious workers whose aspirations are limited to a strategy of containing the alienation caused by work by building up religious and pharmaceutical protective walls around the few work-free patches of life they have left might also not seem like a clear path towards a life free from the alienating consequences of work. However, these interpretations rest on assumptions that the relationship between patterns of resistance and control around capitalist wealth accumulation is always binary and oppositional. If the relationship between resistance against work and capitalist patterns of control is seen as being interlinked and constituted in relation to each other, then the picture might become less clear, but also in a sense more hopeful.

It is in this light that people's patterns of resistance and imagined futures should be interpreted. The way in which people living and working in precarious circumstances seek to deal with the imposition of work might not result in neat and pure anti-capitalist patterns of resistance, but neither are they ever close to becoming mindless drones ready to be controlled and used for state-capitalist purposes. Every day, people are creatively seeking to navigate and manipulate the work assemblages and patterns of control they are exposed to, and every day there are small stories of success and failures. The dreams of work-free futures that the people in the hostel had might not seem to offer much resistance towards capitalist narratives, yet they were acutely aware that the imposition of work was inherently problematic, and no amount of political and management promotion of the benefits and transformative potential of work could change that.

Drawing on the experiences of some people who are part of precarious work and living assemblages can never give the full picture of the multiple ways in which precarious work exploitation is experienced and dealt with by all people. However, it continues to be essential to pay attention to how patterns of resistance and control emerge in particular assemblages, as this can provide a better sense as to where the faultlines, points of conflict, and fractures are erupting in the ever-evolving patterns of resistance and control that define capitalist wealth accumulation.

Failing to do so and seeking to put all hope on singular solutions to the problem of work would miss out on the constantly changing nature and pervasiveness of the issue. Whether the solution to precarious and exploitative work is imagined to be a strengthening of traditional unions and the expansion of decent work or the eradication of organised crime groups that seek to exploit vulnerable workers or something else entirely, it is doubtful whether they will be able to address the multitude of ways work impacts, disrupts, and interlinks with people's lives. Instead, paying attention to the shared precariousness and vulnerability that people have in their daily struggle to deal with the exploitation of work, and taking inspiration from the multiple creative ways in which people, despite the overwhelming odds, seek to resist the imposition of work, is perhaps where hope and possible paths towards better work free futures can be found.

Part II
Rifts

Research Management

The work of trying to contain, control, and secure the sprawling mess of lived fieldwork realities and interlinked academic wildernesses of text, whilst somehow producing coherent and linear textual outputs, was not something that happened by itself. It required continuous attempts at enforcing and maintaining embodied self-discipline. As an early career researcher, the patterns of control and resistance can only be constituted through oneself. This results in an interesting situation where an embodied self is twisted and pulled by an ongoing dialectical dynamic between self-imposed processes of control and self-management, and a self that constantly engages in creative acts of resistance against the imposition of work.[1]

In contrast with being in the field, for most of the research process I found myself deliberately trying to do my utmost to collaborate and comply with the desires of (self-)management. Like perhaps other managers will tend to do, I found myself focusing more on all the potential riches that were lost through inefficiencies and lack of productivity rather than on what my 'slacking' working self did end up producing. From my management-self's point of view, any time period that did not result in productive work was seen as problematic. Was there ever a good justification for taking any form of inconvenient and wasteful breaks? Was sleep really necessary? And perhaps all those pro-sleep and pro-rest studies were nothing but exaggerated discourses made up to sabotage the creation of ever more analytical wealth.

Despite my best efforts to control my work, I always had a sense that valuable productive time was being lost. Although I had strong intentions to implement my management-self's authoritarian demands, I found that seeking to control the ever-changing creative patterns of resistance from my working-self so that every last ounce of productivity could be squeezed out was no easy task. Being a manager, even of oneself, was a lonely task, so I sought out allies in the form of different enforcement tools and techniques that I hoped had the potential to swiftly quell the pesky rebellious act of resistance that kept on sabotaging my quest for maximal productivity.

I tried to use my powers as a manager to control and define clock time. As if I had taken on the role of a call centre manager, I attempted to make a strict and compact schedule where any break was timed to the minute and strictly enforced. The so-called Pomodoro Technique where work is delineated into clearly defined intervals with short breaks in between seemed like a perfect fit. Implementing this method was made easier by the abundance of choices I had when it came to finding a Pomodoro app that as a good management assistant could keep time and shout out commands when the break was supposed to start and finish.

However, ensuring that I sat in front of my workstation did not mean that I would do any work. Similarly to working in the call centre, there were plenty of possible distractions on my phone or the internet that could distract my working-self to the point of halting all production. To ensure that productivity was not harmed by wasteful periods of dawdling, I again borrowed a page out of the call centre management book and tried to implement an enforcement software tool that in perfect dystopian fashion was called 'Freedom'. Once the software was installed on the workstation (my laptop) and my phone, it gave me the possibility to impose a curfew-like shutdown of any possible 'distractions' that might tempt my impressionable mind to stray away from what really mattered: work.

When 'Freedom' was activated, dangerous freedom-undermining activities like watching YouTube kittens sleeping on dogs; texting WhatsApp gifs with friends; scrolling through Twitter and Reddit (for 30% dog and cat-related videos); reading circular news stories; streaming the 144th episode of a random comedy series; traversing the whole Asian continent one Google Streetview step at a time, and similar undermining activities were quickly shut down and eliminated by 'Freedom' before they had a chance to encroach on my freedom to work. The introduction of 'Freedom' brought a short-lived hope of more complete control, but my working-self quickly worked out other ways to waste impressive amounts of time, despite the heavy-handed regime I tried to maintain.

Undeterred, I tried other management techniques. I tried setting more or less random targets that would make any Iroha manager proud. Yet despite strict management demands of having to write or read x amounts of words within x amount of time, like at Iroha and the call centre, just living up to measured targets didn't mean that work was being done as intended. Calling up clients and hanging up the phone before they could answer would give an excellent calling rate and writing a string of words in the form of 'affdf ggrgrg' so that the target of 1,000 words could be reached did technically meet the target, but alas, 95,000 words of 'affdf ggrgrg' do not a research book make.

I also tried to use a reward system and made motivational promises to my working-self that I would be awarded an extra-long break if only I just finished a few more pages or if I just finished this part. Like Iroha's 'fun' attempts at encouraging increased productivity work through the 'power hour' reward system, it rarely worked as most of the time I was already too drained by work to be able to muster any extra effort, especially considering the minuscule awards.

Trying to ensure work compliance, productivity, and motivation was hard enough by itself, but there was also the issue of other types of work encroaching and taking over time that could be better used on writing up the research. Teaching and administrative-related tasks would mostly take precedence due to their perceived urgency, and it was not uncommon for research activities to be put on hold for long periods. I wasn't the only academic facing these issues and in both universities where I worked during this project, there were different forms of writing retreats that were designed to carve out and protect a chunk of time so that we could focus on (research) work without being disturbed by (admin and teaching) work. Unfortunately carving out space so that it was possible to concentrate on one type of work did not mean that the other work magically disappeared. Whilst the protected space of the writing retreat could be effective in ensuring targeted productivity, once I left those spaces, the pent-up pressure of other work tasks would immediately swallow me up with vengeful glee.

At times, my management-self would find worrying signs that work motivation was faltering. I would come across troubling traces that clearly indicated that my working-self did not fully appreciate the transformative benefits of the work it was doing. One time, I came across this trace of disturbing dreams.

Clearly, my working-self's mind wasn't in the right frame of mind. To convince them of their folly and to refocus my mind(s) on work, I drew up charts about the minuscule probability of winning (1 in 139,838,160), which my management-self presented with glee and conviction. Unfortunately, my working-self was in a snarky mood and replied: 'Well then, tell me what are the chances of saving up £43,838,281.89[2] as a part-time employed academic?'

Rational arguments clearly did not work, so to boost morale I started to look for examples of how other academics had succeeded

Figure 2.1. Even academics dream of capitalist utopias. © Jacob A.E. Nielsen

through hard work and dedication. I found David Frayne – a key theorist on anti-work. He had published in abundance, his work had been translated into unknown amounts of languages, and he was now the recipient of a prestigious fellowship. He was a perfect example of all the things that hard work could achieve. Success stories like this would surely lift the spirits, my management-self thought. Unfortunately, my working-self was getting more erratic and the working days would be continuously disrupted by uncalled-for emotional outbursts like in the leftover note below:

> 7:12 pm, flat, Yorkshire
> It is the first day of a long weekend, but I'm tired after an intense burst of conducting online summative student presentations. It might be a long weekend, but the flow of students' essays and portfolios has already started, and the long weekend is long only in name. In my 'free time' from the part-time lecture job I'm working, I have to work, to finish my research. When I say part-time, it is part-time in salary, but rarely part-time in terms of the hours I work. When I first moved to this city to work, no landlord would accept me as my salary was too low, so soon I yet again found myself living in a hostel, sharing a room with eight other people, this time not by research design, but by sheer necessity.
>
> Part of me enjoyed being back at a hostel, but at the same time, I felt uneasy about living there as in the hints dropped in conversations with colleagues, it didn't fit with how life as an academic was supposed to be lived. After a while, I finally found a place. The place where I live now and where this is written has more mould and vermin seeping through it

than even the cheapest London accommodations would expose me to. Yet its walled-in space that in its short-term rented form 'belongs' solely to me comes across as a type of place that aligns better, from the outside, with the expectations of how an academic ought to be living after returning 'home' from their excursion to the 'field'.

My situation doesn't seem to be unique here. Academics rarely divulge financial or other insecurities but in small chattery fragments you can trace stories of struggling to withstand the work pressures without financial rewards; of having to rely on others to survive; of not being able to afford to pay the transport to go to work; of earning less than the minimum wage; of being haunted by stressful bursts through sleepless nights.

On this bank holiday, the first of a long weekend, I want to go back to writing some research. In the morning I start by reading Butler's *Frames of War* (2009) in PDF form. I have read parts of it before, but I need another perspective on it. I skim-read and make use of the search function to quickly find relevant parts. She refers to Chetan Bhatt's work, which I think could be relevant so I end up skimming through a couple of articles of his work, I copy some parts I could use and then, for whatever reason, I google him to find his extensive resumé in leading academic and management roles, involvement in government committees and how he even made it to a Ted Talk.

Searching out other people's success doesn't set me at ease and time is running out, so I seek to get back to 'work'. I find an article by Garfinkel (1996) where he mentions Durkheim. In one of my drafts, I had tried to draw on Durkheim, Weber, and Marx to illustrate different perspectives on ideology and order and I didn't realise the connection to Garfinkel. Time is slipping away so I end up using a dirty academic trick that in my imagination surely would be scorned by my academic patrons – I use Wikipedia[3] to get a summary of how Garfinkel and Durkheim are connected. I get a sense of what the connection is, but it feels shallow and insignificant, so I look up the source, which is Garfinkel's (2002) *Ethnomethodology's Program: Working out Durkheim's Aphorism.*

Before the proper introduction by the editor (Anne W. Rawls), there is a short prologue by Charles Lemert and it is in one of the paragraphs that he writes that the idea for this possible shallow path of interpretation emerged. In the paragraph, he paints a picture of sociology as a discipline that has progressed immensely since the 1960s and he attributes part of the success to Garfinkel. He goes on to say:

> But just pause for an instant to consider what it must be like to have done what these great thinkers, Garfinkel included, have done. To have, that is, invented an original idea, then explained it so that it could be used by others younger or less original than its inventor, then to have guided (if that is the word) new workers along the paths of their proper intellectual, artistic, and professional development. (Lemert, 2002: xii)

> At the time I read it I had just looked at the clock, it was soon 5 pm and not a word on the screen about the analytical perspective I wanted to explore. All I had 'achieved' so far in the day was to trace out what seemed like neverending potential theoretical links that called for a deeper understanding, a more thorough engagement, and most of all, more time. Time for understanding and creative engagement with these 'great thinkers' (Lemert, 2002: xii) we as academics are supposed to stand on the shoulders of and time that would allow me to move along the paths of 'proper intellectual, artistic, and professional development' (Lemert, 2002: xii).
>
> Yet, time was already running out and another precious rare 'free' day to do some work had almost gone by with nothing tangible to show. I started to feel flows of stress pushing my heart rate up whilst my thoughts started to fluster and scatter. At that time, in that particular moment when reading that paragraph, my first reaction was not a rational analytic appreciation of the aspirational achievements of 'great thinkers'. Instead, my first reaction was something along the lines of the emotion evoked by saying:
>
> Ok boomer.

Despite these hostile utterances I tried to be magnanimous and continued to make motivational speeches about how lucky I was to be able to work on this research. However, when the work pressure intensified, I felt like these narratives sounded as convincing as the managers at Iroha's daily attempts at trying to convince us all that we were just a group of friends having fun whilst playfully counting boxes for 50+ hours a week.

Despite my management-self's abundance of kind-hearted efforts to protect my own interest and guide me towards ever-greater productivity filled with promises of future work rewards, my working-s elf was getting increasingly frustrated and despondent, as the trace below might indicate:

> I sometimes doubt the sanity of what I am doing. For four days in a row I have worked from around 8 in the morning to 1 at night on my research and tomorrow my real work begins again. I am writing on anti-work and resistance, and part of the argument I make is that workers are not dupes. That they actively resist their exploitation and that their activities should be taken seriously as such, but when it comes to my own actions I have doubts about whether that is the case. There is a certain underlying expectation that the sociologist is more critical towards taken-for-granted assumptions in society and it would therefore be natural to consider that a sociologist like me would act in a way that resisted exploitative patterns. Yet here I find myself working harder than I ever did during my field-

> work and on top of that this work is unpaid. And for what? A better job with more money and prestige? In other words, the only possible reward for my free work on anti-work is the frail promise of more work. If there are gods, they must be having a laugh.

To make matters worse, together with other Graduate Teaching Assistants, my working-self was planning to organise open acts of resistance against our workload and working conditions. The horror! Meetings were called, complaints filed, and evidence of work conditions was collected and presented to management. The supposed purpose of all these activities was that a rigidly crafted reality that in solid numbers would display the real precarious conditions of working as a Graduate Teaching Assistant would instigate something. Luckily, for my management-self, these plans were quickly eliminated and hardly made a dent in the ongoing quest for ever greater productivity, individual excellence, and organisational efficiency. These mostly hidden activities did, however, leave some worrying traces behind. I have included one such example of an abandoned and burnt trace from this troublesome period that supposedly shows the excessive workloads of Graduate Teaching Assistants. It is a poignant reminder of the many struggles, unruly movements and discourteous facts that management continues to face whilst trying to make a better world.

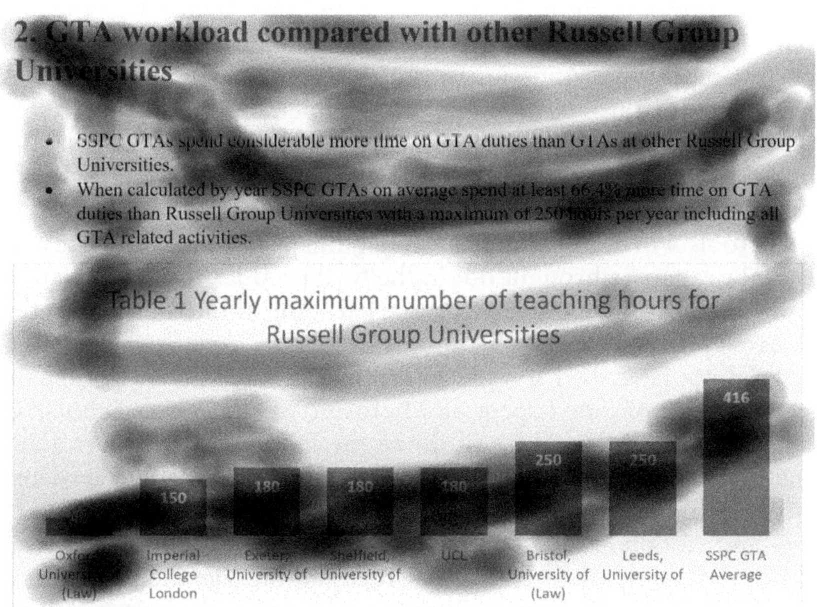

Figure 2.2. Management's struggle. © Jacob A.E. Nielsen

My management-self's attempts to manage and impose work on my working-self were never static, easy, or straightforward. Similar to the realities that were portrayed in the first part, it was a complicated co-constituted process involving different interlinking patterns of control and resistance. Regardless of whether one would take the perspective of me as the manager seeking control or as the worker resisting the imposition of work, the success and failures of the different tools and techniques of control and the patterns of resistance were always unsettled, incomplete, and unpredictable.

Tools and Gifts of the Trade

What matters more: Google Scholar or the field? Microsoft Word or the cacophony of voices and movements I encountered during fieldwork? As an ethnographer who continuously claims authority by referring to the extended period of fieldwork, this might seem like an odd question. Surely, the sheer weight of the fine-grained and lived ethnography would outweigh a blank digital page or a search box on an almost bare background.

On the front cover of *Writing Culture* (Clifford and Marcus, 1986), there is a picture of an ethnographer who is sitting in the field deeply engrossed in writing in his notebook, and this picture becomes the starting point of the argument that ethnographies should start to notice the aspect of writing in the research process. If a similar picture was taken for this research project, then perhaps we would see me, the researcher, sitting in a room bent over his laptop, with his word processor, browsers, sites of academic index engines and journals, and citation software open in a row of digital windows. Are all of these tools worth noticing? Do they perhaps impinge on what kind of realities can be brought out in the final product? Do they matter? What happens if we start to notice what some of the tools did in this research process?

I did not have the foresight to measure in standard clock time the 'real' amount of time I spent on Microsoft Word, Google Scholar, or other tools over the course of the research. How many hours, days, and months did I spend on searching, finding, and reading academic work? How much time was swallowed by drafting editing, redrafting, and responding to comments on Microsoft Word? And what about the tools I used to analyse order and manage the data? I have not got clear measurements. But the undefined sense I get is that the combined weight of all of these tools by far outweighs the ever more vague and distant memories I have of life in the 'field'.

Trying to notice what these tools do in solitary research and work processes will be very different from research done by ethnographers who parachute into the field to observe how other people use particular tools.[4] I will not claim to make a fully rounded and conclusive analysis in a traditional academic way, but I hope these scribbles can give some sense that these tools did something.

The Hidden State of Word

For a long time, I hardly noticed my quiet word processor as a tool at all. I thought about search engines, library websites, citation software, and coding software, but the one tool that played the greatest part somehow managed to escape my attention and hide in the background. Why was that?

At first glance, it might seem that a word processor like Microsoft Word is nothing but a glorified typewriter as all it does is to produce texts. Although this might seem obvious and unproblematic, it is perhaps this ability to produce texts as if they had been written on a typewriter and then printed that is both its greatest power and why it remains mostly unnoticed and unquestioned.

Social research is a complicated process involving countless hours of editing, receiving feedback, reading and applying theory, and redrafting and redrafting and redrafting. From the first vague note taken in the field to the final product, an almost endless range of influences shapes the text. Take a look at the screenshot below in Figure 2.3. It is from the later stage of the research process where the text has already been through several rounds of feedback and analytical settlements, yet it is still being thoroughly torn apart and reconstituted.

The relationship between precariousness and work is an odd one. On the one hand, the emergence of precarity as both a political and academic concept is heavily tied in with changing economic and political transformations that are perceived to create increasingly precarious and exploitative working conditions (Standing, 2011). ~~Yet the relationship between precariousness and work is an odd one. On the one hand, the emergence of precarity as both a political and academic concept is heavily tied in with work and with the economic and political transformations that are perceived to create increasingly precarious and exploitative working conditions.~~ On the other hand, the 'right' kind of work is often conceptualised as a transformative solution to the issues that precarious workers are faced with.

Figure 2.3. Red gore. © Jacob A.E. Nielsen

However, with a click of a few buttons, Word and similar processors allow the author to hide this complex history and erase the hands of others. This ability is perhaps not trivial, as it enables the framing of a reality where the document and the words it contains seem like they are unmediated and unproblematic reflections of pure realities from the field. With a click of a button, as if by magic, gone are all the messy entanglements that for years have pulled, pushed, and remoulded this document so that it can now be presented as a pristine miracle of knowledge that has descended upon this world fully formed and without a scream.

Word's ability to cleanse past entanglements also allows for a particular vision of authorship to be maintained. There is a strange relationship between the author and the researched world in academia. On the one hand, there are all the scientifically inclined narratives where the author should minimise their presence in the text so as not to pollute a singular reality, but at the same time all the credit, blame, authority, and sense of inferiority in relation to this reality is put squarely on the author(s).[5] Whenever this reality is then discussed, analysed, and cited by other academic authors and measured and calculated by algorithms, it is done in a way as if the author singlehandedly managed to capture, transport, and keep alive a wild but now disentangled and entrapped specimen of reality for us to admire, critique, and devour. The word processor's ability to quickly and cleanly cut away all the bloody and messy fragility and how the research has been shaped by others in order to present an immaculate, clean, strong, and measurable product that can be tied to a single author is perhaps ones of its greatest strengths.

When the word processor has cleansed and locked down the text in its final impenetrable form, the fixity and rigidity of the text also imbue it with strict linearity. Any signs that the text might have taken other directions, that it might have arrived at different conclusions, that it might have shown other realities have now all been purged. Left behind is a text, walled in and guarded against any attempts to escape its conclusive reality. Caught in this situation, the reader has little choice but to proceed towards the predetermined conclusion. There can be notes to break up the steady march towards the finishing line, the readers are still free to leave and to jump in and out at various points in the text, and it might be possible to find experiments with concurrent parallel paths of (still walled in) narratives on each page.[6] Yet the text remains solid, unchangeable, and with linear fortified paths that connect the clearly defined start and finish line.

The reader might be unimpressed or highly critical of the reality they have been firmly but gently pressed towards seeing, and they might ignore and leave the presented reality altogether. However, what the fixed, solid, and linear nature of the word processor text makes it more difficult to do is for anyone or anything to become entangled and interconnected with it so that it will change and reveal other possible realities.

While these techniques of fortifying single meanings into a text are always doomed to fail as creative interpretations can take a text in multiple conflicting interpretive directions, this does not eliminate the role that the form of a text can have. With the right tools and determination, it is always possible to climb any wall, but that still makes the wall materially different from an open field of grass. Similarly, it is perhaps more difficult to move towards other possible realities with texts that seek to anchor and tie down rigid analytical meanings.

The characteristics I have mentioned so far might not be unique to the word processor and they would be similar to how texts were shaped and printed with other techniques such as the pen, typewriter, or printing press. However, that might not be the whole story. A word processor does not only replicate the typewriter, but also intensifies the speed of writing and enables easier control of all phases of the editing process, resulting in an extension of possible work tasks.

Before the text is finalised and locked down, in almost an instant, anyone can edit, cut, paste, and change the size and order of the texts and paragraphs. In a few efficient clicks, a whole section can be transformed, moved, or deleted, thereby changing the whole analytical flow of the text. Errors can quickly be adjusted and contradictions can be located and cut out in a ruthless and timely manner. Compared to the typewriter, the word processor can seem to be more efficient and allow for greater productivity so that in theory, more text can be produced in a shorter amount of time. If the printing press changed the speed and intensity with which books could be copied and spread across the world, the word processor perhaps equally helps facilitate the ever-increasing amount of publishable texts and research findings.

However, I wonder if these improvements that in theory make the work process more efficient benefit working academics. Have these new possibilities of efficiency resulted in flocks of academics lying around admiring the slow growth of a world with oceans of time to ponder new possible realities? Or has the amount of research that needs to be produced by academics increased exponentially? Has the ability to easily and quickly shape all parts of the editing process meant that there is ever more freedom to shape the text as one likes? Or has it meant that the editing workload has been shifted from the publishers onto the academics who are now expected to follow complex guidelines for how to edit the text before it can even be read and judged?[7]

I have a sense of what the answers look like from the academic worlds of which I have been part, but I will not claim to have more than a sense. I have a slightly stronger inclination to believe that without the vast and growing array of tools and techniques[8] that the word processor provides that can speed up and enable the writing and editing process, any changes in responsibility, expectation, and workload might not have happened in quite the same way.[9]

Now, there might be some who say that at least some of the aspects I have brought up here are inherent characteristics of what written text just happens to be. They might also point out that only by experimenting with other verbal, visual, audio, and sensual ways of expression can these textual limitations be overcome. Nonetheless, even with just a textual output, many of the characteristics that are embedded in the text as it is created and finalised within a word processor do not have to be that way.

Does the messy research and editing process where the vulnerability of the text becomes apparent have to be hidden? Does a text's precarious interconnectedness with others have to be concealed behind the steely textual visage of an authoritarian author? As sites such as Wikipedia illustrate, it is technically possible to keep at least a few visible links to the traces of an editing and reshaping process that continuously transforms and impacts a text that never settles.[10] There is also the possibility of removing the immutability of the text and its attachment to a single author. By detaching the ownership of the text from the author, the authority, but also the heavy responsibility, is taken off their shoulders and now there is space for others to impinge on and become part of an unfolding knowledge-making process. This might present a range of limitations and problems of its own, but it still shows that other textual realities are possible.

Does the text have to be linear so that the meaning and intention are set in stone? Take a look on Twitter or Reddit and you will find that although there is a textual starting point, the threads of comments have the potential to spread out in multiple directions along sometimes wild and diffuse paths of meaning that can be confusing, enlightening, absurd, laughable, enraging, and consoling.

For example, when I started this research, I set up a Twitter account so I could follow stakeholders, often police officers, working on tackling the issue of modern slavery and labour exploitation. To my amazement, almost every tweet they put out was quickly contested by workers or charities, who would swiftly point out that the police raid to save 'victims' had resulted in the arrest, abuse, and deportation of women; that new anti-trafficking policies now meant that women could be arrested for going alone to a bar; or that the safe houses for trafficking victims were more like prisons. None of these tweets is verifiable in an academic sense, but they resulted in more precarious knowledge claims that were more vulnerable to being taken apart and intertwined with the experiences of others. These textual forms differed considerably from the closed-down and static texts of official reports or academic work that never once allowed such precarious moments to emerge.[11]

Imagine an academic text where the people who were the focus of the research could continuously impinge on and leave traces of their influence on a continuously developing text related to the realities they were living. Imagine a text where the analysis, the theoretical links, the interpretations and claims made in it were always unsettled, interlinked, and spreading out in multiple directions full of unfinished possibilities. Would such an imagined text perhaps be able to present and reflect a wider array of precarious and vulnerable realities? Would it make the academic text more open for collaborations that are better attuned to survive in a precarious world? Or are word processors, like Word, with their comforting but cold fixity and familiar linearity a state in which we as academics always prefer to live and to know? Regardless of what we might think of these questions and possible answers, starting to notice the impact and consequences of using this quiet word processor can perhaps spark something else.

Google Scholar: Faith and Suspicion in a Time of Giants

If the word processor provides an integral but quiet shadowy influence on the text, Google Scholar is a blizzard of giants crying out for attention and significance.[12] Whenever a vague glimmer of possible analytical life springs to mind, I have an almost compulsive instinct to run towards and seek out support from the deafening chorus of intellectual greats. I might occasionally use other methods, library websites and references within a single academic work, but Google Scholar remains the main jumping point I use to descend into the storm to try to catch one of the most essential elixirs that can keep a vulnerable analytical point alive – the reviewed, confirmed, and finalised textual realities of academic peers.

There is an eerily deceptive calm to the start page of Google Scholar, which is mostly blank, with an empty simple search box in the middle. One of the few things that indicate what lies ahead is the slogan written in soothing green: 'Stand on the shoulders of giants'. This slogan is not the making of Google Scholar, but one that refers to a general vision about how academic knowledge works.

One of my supervisors mentioned to me how in hermeneutics there is talk about reading a text with suspicion or with faith and that I perhaps tend to read the academic parts of my research with more suspicion than faith. So let me first try to venture into this world of knowledge and giants with some faith in my heart.

In this adventure filled with faith, the giants are friendly creatures that gently lift me to their shoulders so that new, exciting, and previously unknown worlds can be revealed, whilst I, the researching explorer, duly take notes so that these splendours can be retold to the curious readers stuck on the ground. Standing on the collective shoulders of others enables me to see further than I would otherwise be able to see. By recognising and building on the achievements of these intellectual giants, I can uncover more complete perspectives and details that merely standing on the ground would never have allowed. Without having made my way up to the shoulders of Butler, Tsing, Law, Stewart, Breeze, and all the other intellectual greats who so gently have lent their shoulders to me, this research would lack vision and insight, as all I would have been able to see would be the same muddy ground as everyone else.

Read in this spirit of faith, Google Scholar is a tool that allows the researcher to reach and gather knowledge quicker and more extensively than was previously possible. A simple quick search on 'precarious work and living' will in 0.06 seconds present 344,000 possible giants that with happy reassurance are ready to give new vision and life to my barely breathing analytical realities. Before it might have been possible to traverse for hours through barren library shelves and desolate print journals before any useful giants hiding in the shadows were uncovered, but now with a single vague search, a dense throng of useful perspectives storms towards me ready to serve.

In this faithful adventure, Google Scholar emerges as a world of endless possibilities and perspectives that can give ever-greater analytical support and nourishment to newborn and precarious analytical realities. The caring intellectual giants that Google Scholar has introduced me to have gently nurtured this research from a fragile analytical creature into what might turn out to be another full-grown giant ready to gently lend its mighty shoulders to others in the name of the common good.

Suspicion...

When 344,000 giants storm towards me within 0.6 seconds of having been foolish enough to drop a few random words into a scholarly vortex, the feeling I get is not always one filled with faithful hope of new possible horizons. When my reading of the world is filled with more suspicion than faith, this scenario feels more like a badly imagined nightmare where I feel overwhelmingly lost in a swarm of intellectual giants running amok.

It might at times feel like a swarm, but the powerful ordering processes of the algorithm coerce the swarm into a long ever-expanding line of giants begging for me to choose them. How this line is ordered, and what kind of measurements and calculations are involved are not immediately obvious. Factors such as the prestige of the journals in which they are published, the name recognition of the author, and the number of citations they have accumulated might all help in deciding who gets to stand first in the line, but in the end, that reality is not for me to know.

Climbing all the way to the top of the textual shoulders of a single academic work in a way that reveals all of its intrinsic and complicated perspectives takes time and effort. There are various inbuilt techniques in the text that allow the reader to get a sense of the essence of the perspectives that the work presents. The abstract, introductions, and conclusions can serve as shortcuts, but nonetheless even making it onto the shoulders of these parts of the text takes time. Let's imagine that it was possible to get a sense of ten academic pieces of research in a day.[13] Some might only be skimmed and others would be read in depth. With such a pace of reading, it would still take around ninety-four years of nonstop reading to get through the 344,000 giants that were waiting in line to show me their perspectives on 'precarious work and living'.

If this was only a matter of a happy-go-lucky explorer looking for new experiences and perspectives on the world, this line of giants might be seen as a lifetime of opportunities to see even further. However, when the exploring researcher is part of a world where their continued existence and worth partly rely on the perceived ability to comprehensively master all of these giants, then it is a different matter. When there are more or less explicit underlying and internalised expectations that the researcher ought to have a comprehensive understanding of the academic literature on the topic they write about, is it any wonder that the mere thought of having to conduct a comprehensive literature review can make any brave explorer feel dread and trepidation about the impossibilities of their situation?

There might be particularly diligent researching explorers who are determined to truly master all the relevant work, and I can imagine how they to this day are still dragging themselves through the wilderness and the nth piece of relevant academic research. What I, and perhaps most people, do is to try to fake full comprehension so that we can survive and make our way out of this neverending wasteland of academic giants. This is possible to do because what matters, in the end, is not whether the researcher has climbed and conquered them all, but whether the tales they tell afterwards make it seem that way.

However, this also changes the dynamics of how tools like Google Scholar are used. Now the purpose is not just to open up the endless possible adventures and realities that the researcher can retell to adoring audiences. Instead, it also becomes about covering up and protecting the vulnerability of the tales the researcher is telling. The intellectual giants within this dynamic are not so much being used as shoulders to stand on so that we can collectively see further into ever-brighter horizons. Instead, they are enlisted as intimidatingly muscular intellectual bodyguards who can fend off any unwarranted intellectual probing that might reveal that the analytical tales we tell are faking it to cover up the precariousness of their claims.

If a reader doesn't think that work can be inherently problematic in the way I presented it in the first part, well here are the giants of Weeks, Frayne and Karl (expletive) Marx(!) who all stand ready to support *my* analysis. Before any weakness guarded by these giants can be exposed, the reader would first have to try to take on and get past their validated intellectual splendour and strength. In this antagonistic sense, the giants are an intellectual security detail that can be called upon to close down any unruly disagreement that might expose the vulnerabilities of my authoritarian claims to reality.

This fear of being exposed also results in slightly paranoid urges to call upon as many imposing giants as possible to protect and secure every single possible weakness in the analysis. Search algorithms like Google Scholar play into this paranoia by making it deceptively easy to locate a giant to serve almost any cause. In the first part, I at one point used ninety-nine mostly academic sources to support my analysis and within a minute of trying to start to write this part an almost compulsive thought crept up on me. Should I Google Scholar 'google scholar' to find academic proof for my concerns?

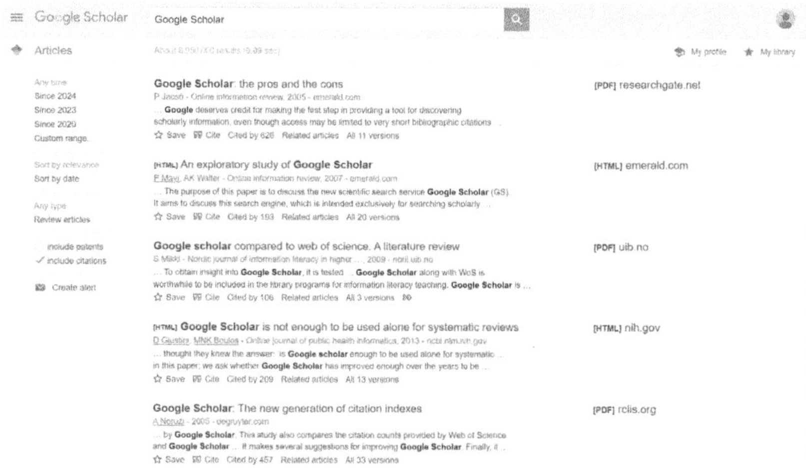

Figure 2.4. Giants upon giants. © Jacob A.E. Nielsen

I of course did and with gleeful delight, Google Scholar in 0.5 seconds presented me with millions of giants ready to show me all their worlds if only I had a mere 2,024 years to spare.[14]

There is another twist to this dynamic. If I managed to fake it in the right way, part of the research might one day become ordained as an accepted peer-reviewed academic textual giant that has a searchable perspective on Google Scholar. In such a future, these very words can then become part of an algorithmic search vortex that researchers exploring the intricacies of Google Scholar for better or worse can be sucked into with hope and trepidation.[15]

I have tried to read and tell Google Scholar and its implications allegorically with faith and suspicion.[16] Do the masses of giants Google Scholar can bring to your feet in an instant lift you up to see new worlds or do you tremble below their feet? Or, in less allegorical terms, do each of our academic publications lift us up to new intellectual heights and possibilities of better worlds? Or is it a tool of our own oppression that stands ready to crush any troubling realities from emerging that might expose our precarious and vulnerable lifeworlds?

I don't know the answers to these questions, but I do know that in the end, I managed to mostly resist searching for any giants to support the words I have written here. Whether that is a sign of lost opportunities, an act of resistance, or something beyond my single-minded imagination, I cannot pretend to know.

The Alluring Gift of Research

> Liverpool, 2019
> I am chatting with three Ph.D. students before going back to work and one of them mentions how they need to read up on their supervisor's work so that they can cite it in their work. I ask what they mean by that, and they reply that they think that it is expected that you cite your supervisors as a show of gratitude for their support. I express a bit of surprise and say that it doesn't seem uncommon for supervisors to try to steer their students in a certain theoretical direction that might result in the students citing the supervisors, but I didn't know it was expected that you cite them. The other Ph.D. students chime in and all say that they had a similar impression.

When teaching undergraduate students about why they need to cite academic references, the reasons that are raised often tend to align with the official arguments that the University of Liverpool tells its students:

- To show where your information came from.
- To allow your reader to identify your sources and verify your data.
- To show the extent of your research.
- To strengthen your academic argument.
- To avoid plagiarism. (University of Liverpool, 2020 top section)

Beneath these technical views of referencing, there might be ideals of seeing further by standing on the shoulders of giants, or there might be insecurities that encourage the researcher to seek support and defence amongst the academic greats, but the ethnographic vignette perhaps speaks to something else.

Maybe what makes references and citations so central to academic research is not only because they can help bring out better 'truths' or because they can help defend an argument, or because they can be measured and calculated. Perhaps it is also their quality as a gift that can be exchanged to build up social relations that makes it difficult to not use them. Maybe one of their purposes is to build up and maintain a community and a sense of belonging.

The exchange of academic references within academia doesn't only happen through the depersonalised use of reference lists and aggregated search tools like Google Scholar. A lot of the exchange happens in more socially entangled ways. In any supervisor and student relationship, the supervisor (and perhaps more rarely the student) will often provide new academic readings as a gift that can help to improve the work. When talking with peers, recommendations of possible useful readings can often come up as part of the conversation. Emailing, mentioning, and texting possible useful readings to peers or students are seen as a friendly gesture, and I have been on the giving and receiving end of this countless times. Why does this exchange happen in this way?

After spending several years in academia, trying to write this without immediately seeking to cite any academic work is a very strange feeling. My first impulse when thinking about writing this is to reread Mauss' (2002) work on the Gift, Malinowski's (1922) work on the Kula exchange, and Graeber's (2004) argument that the role of academics in changing the world should not be as an intellectual vanguard that like Bolshevik revolutionaries prescribe solutions, but as givers of academic research that communities can then use however they like.

At least part of the reason that I have this reaction is that it feels odd not to cite. It is almost like when I had to stop learning to bow after spending years in Japan. Coming to the United Kingdom, having to stop bowing in certain situations felt akin to shouting swear words at people – it just felt out of place (and years later I still occasionally unconsciously do it). Similarly, it feels almost like a social transgression not to cite in a text, like a silent middle finger towards the place you want to call home.

If academia in general and academic disciplines more specifically are communities, then perhaps the circular gift-giving of academic research is one of its core elements that build up, maintain, and stratify this community? When classical research work such as Marx, Durkheim, Weber in sociology and Malinowski, Mauss, and Mead in anthropology is continuously exchanged, is it because like shell-disc necklaces and white shell armbands in the Kula ring,[17] they are now part and parcel of an exchange system that can build up a sense of community as well as create and maintain social status and prestige?

If a young Malinowski had ventured to the island chains of ivory towers instead of the Trobriand Islands, would he have wondered, as he did with the Trobriand people, why academic people would spend so much time, energy, and effort on exchanging something that didn't seem to have much intrinsic value? And would he have arrived at similar conclusions about the socially interlinked nature of value and exchange systems to explain that conundrum? Would he also have noticed that which items ended up being exchanged was less about intrinsic value than about social and cultural norms?

Can this also explain why the exchange and circulation of academic work can feel like it ties in with existing academic hierarchies?

Do most informal gifts and recommendations not tend to happen between academic peers or the people who are considered below them in the hierarchy? And is the trepidation I felt when trying to circulate classical academic work within my own research because the social ceremonial stakes are higher than when 'gifting' my interpretations of disciplinary classics to my students?[18]

Whilst gift exchanges might maintain communities and give a sense of belonging, they can perhaps also become integral to the boundary-making practices and patterns of exclusion on which cultures and communities sometimes rely.[19] Participating in the gift exchange of academic research does perhaps hold the promise of becoming part of an academic community, but is it also imbued with darker dreams of excluding and keeping people out?[20] Perhaps with each exchange of academic research, social ties might be built up and strengthened, but simultaneously with each friendly gift, new borders are erected to separate academic royalty and their tribes from the silenced and forgotten rest.[21]

As I write these scribbles, I am tempted to embark on a journey to make these unfinished ideas part of academic analytical circles of exchange – 'Maybe I could explore this or this academic work so that soon my ideas will belong? Maybe I could quickly read 20 or so gifted references to make the thoughts more acceptable and exchangeable?' – but as I think these thoughts, I know I am running out of time and fuel for thought.

Broken Tools on Broken Orders

Not all tools leave a lasting impact. Many tools will entice with explicit promises of order and efficiency. They will call out to fantasies about having the power to slow down the breakneck passage of time, and their whispers about harmonious and calm analytical worlds will feed into a growing hunger to cut through the analytical mess so that finally something conclusive can be said to end it all.

Breaking NVivo

This coding software was no stranger to me. When working on government-directed research projects I would sometimes utilise it to code and order interview data. After fieldwork, playing the role of a proper social scientist, as I knew it, I duly copied my fieldnotes into the program and started coding. Initially, I had a few master categories that I tried to keep to. However, as I read the notes, they would invoke a surge of memories, emotions, and a tangible sense of past lived entanglements. Reading the notes would bring up unruly traces of people's movements, overflowing rhythms of conversations, and intertwined and inseparable contours of people in the moments of time and space. How can you ever order and master that in ten to twelve categories? As I went through my notes, more and more diverse aspects of life were thrown under the purview of a master category that concurrently became ever more distant from the matter to which it was created to represent. For example, my master category of 'Everyday Life and Work' slowly grew to contain a diversity of topics. One moment, the master category could refer to the importance of getting a good bed in the hostel so that people could better sleep and recover from work; but soon after a note and memory of how technological measurement tools created shifting patterns of control and resistance was thrown into the same category. Below is a list of some of the topics that were contained within the master category 'Everyday Life and Work'. It is not a full list. Exactly 100 categories found their way into this master category, which is perhaps the only bit of neat order it managed to create and contain.

Despite these setbacks, I didn't give up in my quest for clarity, but as I was reminded of moments I had lived and been part of, steadily the number of categories grew. Despite my best efforts to stem the tide, in the end, NVivo buckled and broke down the moment I reached my 323rd different code. In silent shame, with an NVivo that had crashed under the weight of all my codes, I conceded defeat.

Containing Giants on the Run

If we stick with the allegory that an academic piece of research is a giant on whose shoulders you can stand, then deciding on what giants to use was only the start of my problems. Getting to grips with a piece of academic research is as disorderly and tumultuous a process as I imagine it would be to try to climb onto a running giant whilst desperately trying to take notes of the experience. Using giants as an allegory is perhaps limited, as one of the biggest challenges is that a piece of research can easily contain within it a seemingly neverending amount of links to ever-expanding worlds of possible meaning and perspectives.

Take the relatively short 11-page text 'In, against and beyond Precarity: Work in Insecure Times' (Alberti et al., 2018) that I cited a few times in the first part. Eleven pages might not seem too bad for any-

10. Iroha branch differences
11. Iroha feedback
12. Iroha fired
13. Iroha planned fun activities
14. Commuting
15. Control
16. Control and measurement
17. Hierarchy at work
18. Debt
19. Emotional cost of living in a hostel
20. End of work relations
21. Ethnicity
22. Ethnicity at work
23. Everyday malaise
24. Fairness at work
25. Financial cost of working
26. Finishing work
27. Finishing work greatest motivator
28. First day
29. Fitness and preparation for work
30. Fuelling consumption desires
31. Getting a good bed
32. Good and bad about work
33. Health and safety own responsibility.
34. High end work
35. Hipster work'

Table 2.1. Coding the everyday. © Jacob A.E. Nielsen

one who is supposed to be a highly trained academic reader. However, let's imagine I wanted to explore one of the many perspectives it touches upon, such as citizenship precarisation in more detail. So I look up and locate the citation (Lori, 2017). Twenty-nine more pages to read. However, the discussion on the relationship between precarious legal status and precarious employment seems like it could be important so another 19-page article is located (Paret and Gleeson, 2016). I have still only touched the bare surface of condensed information that can be unleashed. Paret and Gleeson can lead to Burawoy's (2015) 30-page discussion of Polanyi's theory and precarity. Burawoy also points to Milkman and Ott's (2014) 340-page work on new ways for labour to organise. Their work, in turn, can drag me towards McCartin's (2014) 58-page research on creative union tactics that, in a mention of the decreasing value of work vis-à-vis capital, points gently in the direction of another 505-page tome of potentially relevant work-related research (Mishel et al., 2012).

This is but a fraction of the possible underlying research that is used to support this 11-page article. I could continue to follow the thread further back or I could choose to go down one of the multiple possible paths and perspectives that each text could lead to. For example, Burawoy's piece could also have led me to Hasegawa's (2014) work on nuclear protests in Japan, which in turn could bring me to Nakane's (1970) classic research on Japanese culture that in theory could open up for discussions and explorations of every single piece of work ever produced in relation to Japanese studies.[22] My hunch is that most, if not all, published academic work will be linked to this 11-page paper if only the dense webs of meaningful citations are followed all the way through.[23]

That these intertwined links exist between most if not all academic work is in itself perhaps a good reflection of the messy interconnectedness of the world. Where the problem emerges is that when I, as an academic researcher, use a piece of research in my analysis, I have to present it in a way that keeps this messiness hidden. There is a self-imposed expectation that if I cite a work, it is because I have fully mastered and comprehended the details of it so that I now with authority can use it to propel my analysis forward. This, in turn, creates extra pressure when reading an academic text with the intention of using it as a possible citation, because how in-depth and comprehensive an understanding do I need to achieve before I can claim to have mastered it?

Besides having to deal with the expectation of mastery, there is also an underlying concern, almost fear, of losing out on an invaluable piece of information that might slip right under my nose if I'm not careful. When each piece of academic research contains countless perspectives that could be linked to possible points of analysis, knowing what to notice and note down so that it could be used for future analytical purposes is almost impossible to know. What analytical points seem important is also constantly changing as the direction and the main argument of an unfinished analysis remains precarious and undetermined right up until its final printed and fortified state.

To address these concerns, there were luckily more tools in the form of reference and knowledge management software that could lure me in with promises of order and clarity. However, despite any notion that academic giants might bring clarity to the world, trying to order, code, and control them proved just as difficult as trying to rein in the messiness of the field into separate NVivo boxes. Again, it didn't take long before my ambitions of simple and comprehensive order and structure were dashed. In a repeat of history, my confined categories quickly overflowed and led to another 326 categories, at which point I yet again had to concede defeat.

Feedback

Feedback is tied in with the academic process that delineates what analytical realities become validated and which ones are left out. The 'peer-reviewed' academic piece of work is often seen as the gold standard for validated academic truth. The feedback and evaluation that is provided by fellow academics are seen to solidify the realities that research brings out and ensure that the final version lives up to acceptable academic standards.[24]

Feedback might play a central part throughout the academic research process, but in the finalised version it is purged from the view of the reader. Gone are the traces of others who have impinged on and drawn the text towards academic validation, and left is the illusion that this piece of research belongs solely to the author(s). There can be many reasons for this. Maybe it is done to avoid exposing any trace of dreaded vulnerabilities and inconsistencies in the text. Perhaps it is done because of the author's desire to keep totalitarian-like control over the message. By removing the traces of any dissenting voices, is it to ensure that nothing can disrupt the analysis's fortified meanings and strictly enforced conclusions? Is it to safeguard the notion that the carefully crafted textual reality remains in the sole possession of the author? Or is it perhaps because anything that would threaten the notion of a clearly delineated author would also threaten the systems that are in place to evaluate, rank, and measure academic success, impact, and financial rewards?

I don't have any definite answers to these questions, but by trying to see what happens when the feedback is not cleansed entirely from the final text, I want to open up the possibility of exploring these questions. I will leave a single trace of the feedback I received out in the open, but I will also use it as a ploy to develop tentative discussions about the aspects they comment on. The feedback is not chosen without ulterior motives, and it should not be seen as a reflection of all the ways in which this research has been shaped by feedback of different kinds.

Feedback Remnant

The following excerpt is from feedback received on the first part:

> There are places in the chapter where I think you could be more consistent in your analysis and that might mean spelling out your position more explicitly early on. I find the discussion of Fordism (though not the discussion of the valorisation of standard employment models) slightly distracting for several reasons and wonder instead if you could just contrast epochal models of capitalism/state-capitalist relations focused on the inter-war and post-war periods (of which the concept of Fordism is just one version), one root of the analytical and policy nostalgia you diagnose around the valorisation of decent work, with the dynamic, dialogical or dialectical account you find in the practices you found/participated in during fieldwork? I'd try to avoid Gambino's 'have it both ways' argument: either nostalgic accounts falsely simplify past worlds of work they don't actually have real insights into at all (because the workers' experiences are missing for example) or the things they present are/were real but were negative. I personally wouldn't take a stand on what the past was really like as you don't have to; the critique of the way the approaches you discuss present and past reality as a way of valorising decent work in the present is enough I'd suggest. Where you do seek to replace their accounts of the past with counter-accounts, you're playing the same analytical game they are only in mirror-image whereas I think your observations about the dynamic/dialogical/dialectical, never settled nature of such things break with the whole frame and allows us to see how much be lost from view when we make the assumptions they make – whole lifeworlds and their histories disappear into what's assumed as you show.

The Art of Creating Single Realities

I think the feedback highlights many of the underlying tensions within this research, which is why I have chosen to include it. The first aspect I want to comment on is the concern with how Fordism was used in prior versions of the text and whether it is necessary to 'take a stand on what the past was really like'. Besides the aspects about whether I had discussed Fordism and the past clearly or comprehensively (which I probably didn't!), it is interesting because it illustrates what is probably a common situation in academia – conflicting analytical advice from different academics.

The link to historical developments, including Fordism, as well as the more theoretical aspects of Part I, was developed in response to feedback from other academics at conferences and within the school.

This feedback steered me towards trying to situate work experiences in a wider social and historical context. Before taking that analytical direction, my analysis did not seek to take a stance on the past.

It might be possible to mould the text so that it addresses the different lines of feedback. However, it also speaks to a situation in which different sets of feedback seek to move the text in what can seem like opposite analytical directions. From talking with other students and academics, from attending various workshops on publishing, and from the experience of publishing myself, this doesn't seem to be an uncommon experience. Maybe it is useful to start noticing why it is a problem that many academics seem to face whenever they try to finalise a text.

If the world is approached as being complex, messy, and never fully comprehensible, and if the methods we use to frame this world are also what shape the reality we end up creating, then it is perhaps not surprising that multiple possible and oppositional analytical perspectives and realities can emerge from the same set of 'data'.[25] When different academics, with their own particular experiences, concerns, and views of the world, then examine and evaluate the validity of an academic piece of research, it would be almost odd if somehow they ended up aligning with the single analytical reality it seeks to present.

This is in itself not problematic, but where the issue emerges is when the text has to be closed down and finalised. Whilst a text can take multiple and contradictory analytical directions throughout the research process, when it becomes finalised, all of these uncertain vulnerabilities are supposed to be hidden under the pristine carpet of analytical coherence. When I finalised Part I, it would have been difficult to make a rigorous analysis that both argues that it is important to situate the workers' experiences in a wider capitalist and historical context whilst also arguing that utilising these fixed social and historical categories is inherently problematic.

If, however, we resist the lure of order, coherence, and finality, then perhaps it is not necessary to settle the analysis into a single consistent reality. Perhaps by keeping and exposing some of the analytical inconsistencies, impurities, and multiplicities, the analysis can remain somewhat unfinished and vulnerable to being reshaped, pulled apart, and cared for by unknown others.

Internal Consistency

Another related aspect of the feedback that I found interesting to comment on is the recommendation that I should seek to avoid a 'have it both ways' kind of argument. On one level, I have a lot of affinity with that recommendation. I tell it to students all the time and even during fieldwork I would use it when having discussions about conspiracy theories. When having discussions with people in the field about conspiracy theories, I would say that I wouldn't mind what their analysis showed or concluded as long as it was analytically coherent. If someone was very critical of evolutionary theory because they were sceptical about the truth of every single letter ever written in support of it, I would not contest that. I would, however, say that if they were critical to that degree about scientific claims concerning evolution theory, then maybe they should be equally critical about what user:nandeyanen68xy wrote on a ch4 forum about a deep-state conspiracy to cover up the existence of alien gods. My point was that if they maintained analytical consistency, then evolution theory might still be problematic, but perhaps less so than many other claims that are out there. So I have an affinity with arguments that seek consistency in the analysis, but I also have a sense that academic knowledge, perhaps all or most knowledge, at some point is always inconsistent and is always trying to have it both ways, at least momentarily.

The potential problem with the analysis I had offered, as was pointed out, is that I sought to replace accounts of the past because they don't take account of the complexities and lifeworlds of the workers. However, I then replaced them with other accounts of the past that ended up erasing the complexities and lifeworlds of the workers. In a sense, I was doing what the conspiracy-happy people in the hostel were doing – I was applying different standards to different parts of the analysis.

What then happened when I took out the claims related to the past and just related them to the ideas about decent work? Did that then make the analysis consistent and coherent? Are coherent analytical standards now being kept throughout the analysis? I don't think so, as there are still plenty of places where I am trying to have it both ways.

Take the analytical point I make where I say that policies around precarious work and labour exploitation are not taking full account of the lived experiences of the workers. To replace these accounts, I then provide an analysis that draws out how the main concern of workers is with how to deal with the devastating impact that work has on their lives.

I arrived at this notion about work in different ways. A lot of academic research on post-work, anti-work, work alienation, etc. could align with parts of the experiences I had in the field. However, it was not just a distant analytical rationale that informed that analytical direction; it was also based on the visceral emotional responses and the traces that living and working in the field left on me. Memories of the ever more sunken faces, the violent anger in the eyes and fists of people, the exhausted tears, the lifeless bodies erased by work into shadowy outlines of former selves would still flash up from time to time, ready to tear up eyes and analytical views of the world.

That the experiences in the field and some validated research supported the notion that work was inherently problematic did not mean that the analysis was entirely consistent or coherent. The unfolding, messy, entangled flow of people's lives would always escape any possible analytical delineation that might be applied, even at a highly regimented place like Iroha or the call centres.

For example, the issue of social relations was something that I left largely untouched. Laughs, jokes, acts of kindness, and people's fascinating stories could also be part of a working day and, yes, it could technically be seen as a coping mechanism that made work more endurable, but it seemed to be more than that. When some people were fired or left, it was followed by a distinct melancholic feeling. Like Shahu said on the last day before most of us were fired from Iroha:

J:	Hi, how are you?
Shahu:	I'm not so good.
J:	Why? What are you doing?
Shahu:	SBC,[26] but I am sad because all my friends are leaving.
J:	Yeah, I guess a lot of people are leaving.
Shahu:	My friends are the only reason I ever come to work. When I get here I don't think, oh I am going to Iroha, I think I am going to meet all my friends . . .
J:	So are you looking for another job?
Shahu:	I think so, but now I don't want to find a job with friends because it is too sad when everyone is leaving.

I could have tried to stretch my analytical categories related to anti-work so that they could encompass mess and experiences that transcended their explanatory boundaries, but I am sure that there would be other parts of the lived experiences that would then not be containable within them. There are countless other moments, memories, and notes from the field that could easily trouble the categories on which my analysis was built.

What my analysis has therefore done is to criticise some analytical perspectives on decent work for not taking into account the lived experiences of the workers. To replace these simplified and singular views of what role work plays in the life of people living in precarious circumstances, I have drawn up new sets of analytical perspectives that if examined closely could again be seen as presenting a simplified and singular view of the experiences of work that people encountered. Or in the words of the feedback, I end up 'playing the same analytical game they are only in mirror-image'.

My sense is that this is not just an issue with my analysis. I have a hunch that if any of the academic references I use to support my argument were approached with a Derridean-inspired deconcentrated exploration of their borderline and marginal areas (Derrida, 1988: 44), it would result in the revelation of ever more inconsistencies and points of having it both ways.

As an example, would my conceptualisation of resistance as having dialectical properties survive a full exploration of the analytical claims upon which it is built? In Part I, I use Mumby (2005) as a key reference to support my argument that resistance and control are in a dialectic co-constitutive relation to each other.

In the text, Mumby argues that critical studies on resistance have approached it with 'an implicit duality of resistance and control' and that 'a dialectical approach better captures the notion of resistance and control as mutually constitutive' (Mumby, 2005: 20). Mumby bring up Kondo's ethnography of a confectionery factory in Japan as 'perhaps the most sophisticated in its effort to examine the relationships among discourse, identity, and organizational relations of control and resistance . . . [that] framed resistance as a shifting, contextual, and contradiction-laden feature of everyday organizing' (Mumby, 2005: 34).

Kondo's approach to resistance is complex. In places, like the quote below, it does seem like Kondo's approach to resistance aligns with that of Mumby:

> In a setting like the Satō factory – indeed, in any setting – it thus seems suspect to talk of a pristine space of resistance. A term like resistance, when considered in all its living complexity, seems inadequate at best, for apparent resistance is riven with ironies and contradictions, just as coping or consent may have unexpectedly subversive effects. (Kondo, 1990: 224)

The reason why Kondo aligns with this conceptualisation of resistance is in an attempt to move away from traditional monolithic notions of pure domination and resistance:

> Our starting point for a politics of meaning should not be a monolithic category of hegemony or domination countered by a grand, utopian

> space of pure resistance, especially if the forms of that hegemony or resistance become foundational categories which can always be known in advance. (Kondo, 1990: 225)

To replace these foundational categories that can always be known in advance, power is introduced as a concept that turns out to be inescapable, no matter how romantic at heart the people and readers of the study may be:

> People like my coworkers and the shachō', in the Satō company may rearrange power relations as they appropriate and redeploy cultural meanings, but they can never escape to a romantic place beyond power. (Kondo, 1990: 224)

There might be some utopians who, without an ounce of romanticism, still had hopes of space beyond power, but again Kondo has bad news, hidden in a positive message:

> Arguing that there is no utopian space beyond power does not necessarily entail political paralysis, the chaos of meaninglessness, inability to make judgments, or nihilism. (Kondo, 1990: 225)

In other words, Kondo is replacing resistance and hegemony as one set of 'foundational categories which can always be known in advance' with power that is so foundational and knowable that no amount of romantic utopianism can escape its hold. This is not too dissimilar to what I do in Part I, where I argue against the foundational categories of decent work versus precarious work and to replace them I use the imposition of work versus resistance to work. Just like Kondo, I replace one set of foundational categories with another set, and similar to Kondo, the rationale I use for this is that they are better at reflecting the complexities of the lifeworlds I describe.[27] However, Kondo has not given up on resistance entirely:

> For perhaps it is not a matter of some utopian space of resistance as such – though this notion could be invoked *strategically*,[28] for particular purposes. (Kondo, 1990: 225)

It could perhaps be argued, along the lines of the feedback I received, that Kondo is trying to have it both ways. Resistance is inadequate as it simplifies lifeworlds, except when it is invoked strategically, where it then turns out to be adequate to illustrate a key pattern. Kondo subsequently also uses resistance in its more traditional meaning. For example, in the historical analysis of gender and work in Japan that traces women's acts of resistance against management discourses that sought to frame the company as a 'family', Kondo describes some of the acts of resistance against this discourse as follows:

> In view of these moving songs of resistance, the high rates of labor turnover, the outbreaks of strikes and slowdowns, and the ultimate form of protest-suicide... management attempts to impart a sense of 'company as family' seem at best a mockery. (Kondo, 1990: 272)

Is Kondo's strategic use and critique of resistance problematic? Does this and other sets of contradictions and 'have it both ways' arguments by Kondo start to unravel Mumby's arguments and thereby the analytical points I make in Part I? Maybe not by themselves, but I wonder if there was time enough to explore all references in Mumby's analysis, and whether similar kinds of contradictions could not be found in them all. Perhaps the foundational grounds of all types of analysis, no matter how robust they claim to be, are vulnerable to careful examinations that can expose the precarious grounds upon which they are built.[29]

That all academic analysis and the methods they use might be vulnerable to being revealed as more inconsistent, contradictory, vague, and complex than they claim to be is perhaps not surprising if we look at Law's argument that traditional methods 'are complex, but also that most aspects of that complexity are denied' (Law, 2004: 145). The ease with which my analysis of precarious work and living in London relatively quickly could be drawn into a discussion about the ins and outs of Nihonjinron and the particularities of a Japanese confectionery factory in the 1980s is perhaps one illustration of that complexity and how it is mostly denied.

What I want to experiment with is to see what happens when the denials of methodological complexities are scaled back and when questions that highlight the problematic nature of my framework are welcomed and made visible within the text. I don't know what the effects would be, but I am curious to see whether this will leave the analysis more vulnerable and open for apprehending something else about a precarious world, or whether it will have other conflicting and contractionary consequences. I believe what consequences this kind of method has will depend on others, which is why I want to leave it unresolved (as far as possible). Or is that in itself just another way of having it both ways?

Notes

1. This notion of multiple selves could also be linked with parts of Kondo's (1990) work that show how there are no purely disentangled selves separated from messy entanglements of power and resistance (although that argument, like any other argument presented here, is problematic).
2. The average top EuroMillions prize.
3. I feel a slight academic horror of using this factual unreliable, unreadable, disorganised, methodologically weak site systematically biased in terms of gender, race, and nationality, and shaped by corporate campaigns and 'clique behavior, social stratification between a guardian class and newer users, excessive rule-making, edit warring, and uneven application of policies' (Wikipedia, 2020, top of page). Perhaps it says something about the differences between academia and Wikipedia that these criticisms are all on display for free and upfront in a dedicated Wikipedia entry, whereas any criticism of academia always seems to be hidden deep inside other headline entries and spread sporadically across endless academic articles.
4. See, for example, Miyazaki's (2006) examination of how Japanese businessmen use of Excel impinges on their hope and planning out of possible futures, and Latour and Woolgar's (1986) work on laboratory life and culture where inscription devices play a key role in performing realities.
5. For a more in-depth discussion about the role of authorship, see Foucault's (1979) analysis from a more historical and literary point of view, and Graeber's (2004) short discussion about the relationship between hierarchical ideologies and the focus on the individual.
6. See, for example, Mol's (2002) work on the body multiple.
7. See, for example, the 14-page-long notes to 'contributor' for a prominent journal in the field of sociology of work (WES, 2024).
8. It is perhaps still too early to say how the growth of AI tools to assist in the research process will exacerbate or change these dynamics. Can AI be used as a tool to better survive, wreck, and undermine absurd academic matrixes, practices, and norms that entrench gendered, racial, colonial, classed, cultural, and linguistic patterns of exclusion, exploitation and privilege? Or will it lead to a further intensification of exploitative academic production practices that concurrently enable new regimes of automated control that in a millisecond can label and punish people who transgress the expected academic norms and social positions?
9. This is not to say that technologies determine anything outside their social context, but the material aspects do perhaps play some role in how things come together and unfold.
10. For example, all the edits on the 'Social Research' entry can be traced back to 20 November 2003.
11. In relation to the specific websites, apps, and technologies I refer to here, I am not claiming that they are unproblematic and that using these technologies will lead to singularly beneficial results. However, they can perhaps bring out something else about the world than the linear and fixed texts academia tends to produce.

12. And similar aggregated search tools. A warning – this fragment ended up being somewhat allegorical.
13. A very rare achievement for me personally and when it has happened, it has been close to 100% skim-reading and 0% understanding.
14. Calculated assuming I could read ten works a day.
15. This dynamic also reminds me of other work situations. At Iroha, it was well known that the targets were always moving. First, you might be told to count sixty boxes in an hour, but once most people had reached that target, the goalposts moved and we were now all expected to count seventy an hour, and when people had reached that target, it was raised again. Within a month, most people stopped worrying about targets as something that could be beneficial to achieve. In academia, I now never quite know what to feel when friends successfully publish their work. Should I celebrate their success? Or should I point out that now the goalposts for all of us has moved just a bit further away?
16. I tried, but probably not entirely convincingly, as a line of the feedback said: 'Ha, I'm not so sure about the former – it's more like a rhetorical fall guy – but I take the point.'
17. As explored by Malinowski (1922).
18. Even after teaching theory to first and second-year undergraduate students, I still feel like I am transgressing into dangerous territory if I try to recirculate classical theories as part of publishable academic analysis. It is as if their spirit, as Mauss (2002) in a slight mistranslation might have called them, is more sacred than other possible academic gifts, especially when they are exchanged in more high-stakes circumstances like an academic article.
19. For more details on this, see Lila Abu-Lughod's work on writing against culture (Abu-Lughod, 1996) and more recent work on everyday bordering and regimes of belonging (Youkhana, 2015; Yuval-Davis, 2010; Yuval-Davis et al., 2018).
20. Several works highlight the politics and 'screening techniques' (Ahmed, 2013) of citation practices that reinforce gendered, racial, colonial, classed, cultural, and linguistic patterns of exclusion, exploitation, and privilege in academic writing (Ahmed, 2017; Badenhorst et al., 2022; Bekar and Fay, 2020; Canagarajah, 2002; Chakravartty et al., 2018; CLEAR, 2021; Kubota, 2022; Todd, 2016).
21. In a darker reading, this gift exchange might take on a more macabre character. What is being exchanged, in social science at least, is artefacts from the very life of 'the others' that are being excluded in the process. Perhaps to borrow another anthropological metaphor, we don't just exchange shell necklaces and armbands, but like the Amazonian Shuar (Rubenstein, 2007), the shrunken heads of someone else's life(worlds) and perhaps like the Ilongot, another old headhunting culture, this is partly because we need a place that can carry our rage and anger after being exposed to the (social) injustices of suffering and death (Rosaldo, 1993).
22. Nakane's work is one of the most influential and cited books on the anthropology of Japan (Ryang, 2004) and it might incidentally also present a valuable lesson about the importance of resilience when the messiness of the

world threatens to undermine your analysis. Despite having to deal with student occupations and month-long violent battles between Molotov-throwing students and up to 8,500 police officers (Steinhoff, 1999) at her Tokyo University campus, Nakane still impressively managed to proceed undeterred so that she could write a comprehensively researched analysis where, with academic authority, she convincingly argues that Japan is a well-functioning hierarchical society free from any troubling conflict and disorder (the student revolts are explained away by comparing them to a child's tantrum) (Ryang, 2004: 144–45).

23. There might be an argument that knowing the details about where certain claims come from is not that important as long as they have been academically verified and therefore can be considered stable and solid. Unfortunately, the rubber stamp of peer-reviewed data doesn't always seem to protect against problematic claims being repeated and brought forward. See, for example, Ryang's work, where amongst other things she traces out how one piece of research with an unfounded claim about the link between toilet training and a supposed Japanese national psyche ended up informing academic studies for decades (Ryang, 2004). That these studies used a problematic citation to support their analysis does not make them useless, but it does expose their claims to comprehensive knowledge and authority as being precarious and vulnerable.
24. In case some nonacademic readers should ever read this text, it is perhaps worth mentioning that in this process, it is mostly (if not always) fellow academics who validate the analytical realities. The people directly involved in the lifeworlds that are being described and that are used as fodder for the analytical explorations rarely play a part.
25. Regardless of whether that is data gathered from participant observation, surveys, or some other traditional delineated method.
26. The work task Shahu normally preferred.
27. Kondo shares many of the same concerns that I had when writing this research. There is no space to give full justification to her complex concerns about how to grasp the complexities of the field in written form, but see, for example, pp 47–48 (Kondo, 1990), where she argues for the problem with making distinctions between style and theory.
28. The italics are in Kondo's original text.
29. Deconstructive nondeconstructive, nonmethods methods certainly seemed to indicate the possibility of exposing vulnerabilities of any analysis, no matter how much analytical strength it tries to display (Maley, 2007). Even the way I have here selectively picked out parts from Kondo's brilliantly nuanced, vivid, and thoughtful work in order to support my own (attempted) coherent analytical point that says that there can be no coherent analytical point without contradictions could perhaps be seen as being inconsistent and 'having it both ways'.

Part III

Fragments

Arrival

It is never quite possible to tie people down to a particular past or to uncover an exact calculated reason as to why they arrive in this place. Traces of people's circumstances can come up and become the topic of momentary conversations seeking to uncover what is going on, but they never succeed in solidifying anything. There are hints of all kinds of circumstances, half-known or unknown or implied or understood for why people might end up staying here. It might be planned, a temporary step until they have settled into life in London or, perhaps, they are always moving in and out of the city, so a temporary place like the hostel will do. For others, it might not be a choice they would have wanted to make, but one they had to make in the wake of broken relationships, money running out, landlords throwing them out, debt to be escaped, losing jobs or never having a job in the first place. You hear different stories and sense different circumstances, and no matter how hard you try to extricate the facts, there is always an element of uncertainty and tension embedded in anything you think you might know of why someone is here. But whatever it is that has led them here, when they first arrive, they suddenly find themselves alone setting out to try to live in the hostel.

You can sometimes see their anxious and cautious look when they are first brought in. They don't know what to expect. Some might have never heard of the hostel before and have just booked it on a generic hostel platform because it is cheap or near a convenient location for them. For others, this is just another hostel that they occasionally move between. For those who are new to the hostel world, they can seem uncertain about whether they are the odd ones out. They may entertain doubts about whether everyone else here is just a happy tourist playing their way through London's attractions, while they themselves are still trying to get a grip on their circumstances.

Yet, once they start to hang around, they will notice that the hostel as space is different from the glossy pictures on the booking website depicting happy backpacking youths lightly traversing the world and no matter what convoluted backstory you might have, you will not stand out. This is a place for all kinds of people: people fluid in ages, genders, nationalities, jobs and most importantly personalities; people revelling in big groups and people more comfortable in the shadows; people who can chat for days on end and people who hardly say a word; defensive people, who see any encounter as a potential confrontation and an opportunity for a fight, and easy-going people who won't get angry even if they have been woken for the nth time by someone slamming the doors.

There are people who will effortlessly manoeuvre between different spaces and gatherings of people settling into the expected conversational rhythms and movement, and then there are people who at seemingly random times will shout out loud accusations to the world or fall into mumbles or whisper to themselves or hidden others; people who for weeks on end can seem like all light and movement have left them, unable to mutter a word until they – from out of nowhere – will be nothing but exuberant words and gestures.

This messy picture also manifests itself in how people connect and become part of the rhythms of the hostel. Some will almost immediately throw themselves into most streams of conversation they come across, and they will draw and be drawn to concentrations of social moments and chatter. For others, they rarely approach people by themselves and they will seek to avoid most situations where they have to make their way through conversations with people. No matter how people settle in, they will soon become part of the place's temporal flows and as they do how you and other regulars move about, feel and become part of the hostel changes as well. Soon you and others will also come to know the patterns of their daily rhythms, when they get up and go to sleep, when they fiddle around with their luggage, how much space they and their stuff take up, their sensitivity to the noise they or other people make, and when and how they like to talk – if at all. Some people will enter into few if any conversations. But their presence is still felt.

So, when Elin is here, you and the other people in the room will quickly learn that she goes to bed early. Thus, as a gesture of goodwill, you try to avoid turning on the light after 8 pm and go quietly about what you are doing, and similarly you will learn to recognise that the carefully muted sounds at 3 am are from her getting up ready to work. When getting up and making your way down to the kitchen in the morning, you will expect to see the same people sitting and moving about. Sometimes tired morning conversations will flow and other times there will only be a quick exchange of greetings and facial expressions anticipating the daily trepidations of work. In the common room coming back from work, you will hear the sound of Peter typing away on his laptop, Juan laughing out loud to his Argentinian comedy, or Matt meticulously rolling up a joint before bedtime. It might not seem much, just the beat of people's ordinary presence, but when they leave the hostel, it feels like a little rupture, like something is not quite how it is supposed to be. Traditions have room to form quickly here and when they are disrupted, they leave small traces of nostalgia for a time when the weight of a person's presence was not absent and things were how they used to be. But soon their absence merges into and becomes part of new unfolding patterns of people, their things, movements, and felt presences.

Making Beds

The bunk bed is at the centre of how to settle in. When you first come into a room and if you haven't lived in a hostel before, you will choose your bed largely at random and make rudimentary arrangements by putting on the sheets you have received from the hostel at the same time as you try to find an empty locker in which to put some of your stuff.

Soon you discover that not all beds are equal. Maybe with every turn you make, the bed squeaks, grating on you and others, disrupting precious moments of sleep. Perhaps you learn that the bed is on one of the more busy paths people use to make their way to their beds, lockers and in and out of the room (or to the toilet in the rooms that have one). And as storms, rain, frigid winter calm, and humid summer nights pass through the hostel, you will notice that some beds are hidden away and forever trapped in stuffy air pockets, resisting any outside change, while others feel like they are caught in the middle of London's unsteady seasons.

You will also learn that the people in the beds below, above or around you also matter. How loud and consistently do they snore? Do they talk and whisper to themselves awake or asleep? What time do they get up and when do they stumble back to bed? And when leaving or settling in for their sleep, do they swiftly arrange their things or do they pull out and rummage through all of their plastic bags to find that one thing they need? Do you take the peaceful bunk bed where no one else is staying, but risk an unknown force when the room fills up? Or do you share the bunk bed with one of the regulars whose rhythms are mostly expected and known?

There are many factors to take into consideration and it is not a perfect science. The rooms change with new seasons, people, set-ups, tempos, and atmospheres, and with all of it, your own preferences might change too. Finding the right bed takes trial and error, and more than a little patience, particularly if you have your eyes set on a bed to try out that is currently someone else's home. Once you have found your bed, it is time to settle into it and the room. There are all kinds of ways into that. Some mark out their presence in the room through meticulous arrangements: the bed made neatly every morning, luggage compartmentalised and boxed in, work clothes hanging crisp on the hangers on the bed. For others, it is a more dispersed affair. Clothes, slippers, and stuff spread out and make their way to all corners of the room; beds made up only by the sudden impact of having to get up in a rush; food forgotten, lost and rediscovered in the inner reaches of a fridge.

No matter how you approach settling in, it takes some initial effort and time to embed yourself into the patterns of the room. Although it is a process that never finishes and never really stabilises in terms of things staying the same, like some imagined catalogue picture of home frozen in time, the dorm, this patch of bunk beds, stuff, and people's movements, will enwrap you so that when you come back from work, open the door, set out your things as they should be, chat with your roommates, and lay down in the bed, at that moment, with no promises of future commitments, it feels like home.

Hostel, London

There can be a ghostlike quality to people. You might know there is someone there. You see some of their luggage or clothes on the floor, or you sense that someone is sleeping behind the sheets that people hang around their bed to provide some privacy. You might quickly pass by them whilst running to work or you will hear their footsteps as they rush out to somewhere else. The night manager who comes around every now and then to collect rent from people will sometimes come and ask a group of us if we have seen so and so. Sometimes someone will have an idea of who they are talking about, but often all we will have is a free-floating name that doesn't seem to attach to any person or face that is part of the hostel that we know of. On other occasions, you will hear small snippets that indicate that these people are more than just elusive shadows:

> And then G said . . .
> Who's G?
> What do you mean 'Who's G?', he has been here for like months!
> Never met him!
> He is the guy who sleeps in the noisy bed by the window.
> Ahh, yeah, I never met him.

And then suddenly they will disappear after a day, a week, or maybe even years of staying in the hostel. Some people never become more than ethereal beings that might leave small traces behind, but never embed themselves fully in any of the moments and rhythms of the life of which you feel part. Some of the people you see, talk, and hang out with all the time can suddenly and without warning evaporate. Maybe your schedules have changed. They started a new night job, or the job they are doing just turned into a job that devours all hours of the day, or maybe they just had other things to deal with. And sometimes they just leave, with no one knowing exactly why. Maybe they were thrown out, maybe some debt collectors came looking for them, maybe they found someone to live with – no one really knows, but possible explanations are sought out with stories and rumours circulating until those traces also disappear from your everyday life and thoughts. The hostel is a big house, but still just a house. Maybe there are around fourteen to sixteen rooms in all. And at its most busy times, maybe there can be fifty people all in all, though most of the time there are perhaps around twenty to thirty people at any one time. Despite this, you never get to feel like you have a 'full' solid sense of the hostel and the people who come and go; people and space only seem solid as they come together in sporadic moments, before disappearing into traces of passing movements and small talk stories. It is not only at the hostel – it feels like most of what is going on slips through your fingers before you can get any sense of it being something solid, something that can be grasped, contemplated, and studied as a whole. At work you only ever see fractions of the place; sometimes all you get to see is your PC screen and the call centre landscape you can observe on the way to the toilets. Other times you might have some sense of miles and miles of warehouse shelves, but only as you encounter them through the particular kind of work you do and the group of people you work with. Sometimes the people and spaces at work will seem like all you ever experience, like they are the main part of your life, but once work suddenly ends, everyone dissipates into other tenuous patches.

Evening Chatter

It is evening. People are starting to come into the common room in the hostel:

Rafael what are you doing?
  I'm a negotiator.
What's that?
  I'm negotiating contracts for companies. So looking for the best products for the cheapest price. It is alright, but it gets too much. It is always the same, we have to look for cheaper suppliers and better products. And when we find one we always have to push the price down or look for someone else.
But when you say 'negotiator', it sounds interesting.
  It does but. . .
What about your work colleagues?
  What do you mean?
Are they nice? I mean for me at least, whether I enjoy a job or not depends a lot on whether I have good work colleagues.
  That is true . . . but in my last two jobs I have been unlucky . . . People are afraid, they have fear . . . for . . .
Unemployment?
  Yes . . . they are afraid of being . . .
Fired.
  Yes! Fired. It is like they have this atmosphere . . . like they don't want to lose their job so they don't want to help you.
That's not great.
  No, and in my old job it didn't use to be like that.
Is that why you want to find a new job?
  Yes . . . But it is very hard to find a job and people know this. I have applied for many jobs, but there is always a big competition for the job. You always have to prove you have to be the best, the best negotiator, the best administrator, the best worker, always the best the best. I don't want to be the best. I just want to be normal. I want to have a normal life, spend time with my family and friends and work a bit.
I know, but it is going like this in many places in Europe.
  Yes, and it is ourselves that do it. We keep on looking for the cheapest price. For the best deal. And we create this system where we have to work harder and harder for less and less. Like, my current job, it is almost half of what I used to earn. Half. And I have to work harder and people are full of fear.
And it doesn't have to be like this, we have more money than ever.
  Yes, and the money doesn't go to us. My grandmother was richer than her mother, my mother was better off than my grandmother, I

was better off than my mother, but my son he will be worse off than I was.

It is the same here in the UK, there are even three generational houses now.

Yes but it is also because it is not the politicians that control it. It is the banks the multinationals . . . the what do you call them?

The elites?

Yes the elites, they control everything. Politics is just a front. They don't control anything.

Ranvid has come into the room in the meantime and now joins in the conversation:

I think it is all about confidence value. It is all because we humans, we manage to fool ourselves. We think up values that don't exist and which can disappear at any time. Like with the stock market. Everything goes up and down. They hear something and everyone gets scared and things fall apart. That is why the rich want to get more and more because it is not real value and they can lose it at any one point. So they keep on getting more and more money and value because they know what they have all come down to the confidence people have in their value and at any point [clicks fingers] it can disappear.

Rafael and J nod with attentive expressions:

You also see it with houses, the price goes up and up but for what? It has nothing to do with what is real. And it can disappear at any moment. So the rich can never rest because they have nothing and the rest gets less and less. That is why the rich get richer and the poor poorer, but in the end, we are all poor because we have nothing. I think this is how it all ends. The poor will have had enough and will kill everyone. This will be the end of the human race. That is also why . . .

Thomas comes into the room. Ranvid smiles and asks:

Thomas, what do you have in that bottle?

Oh I have a little bit of expensive stuff and some coke.

Expensive stuff?

Yeah too expensive for you [he says smiling with a big sparkly grin].

How much do you put in there?

Only a little bit [he indicates around one-twentieth of the bottle].

Is it good?

You know, just a little thing is good. I come home, change, make a little drink, and then I am happy.

Happy?

Yes, just you know, happy, in a good mood.

That is good, but everything in moderation right?

Yeah but just a little bit, to make you happy you know? To just feel alright.

Mahmud pops his head in and with a big smile asks:

Do you like chilli? [They all nod] Good, good, I have made some tuna pasta. Very good only a little chilli.

Mahmud disappears back to the kitchen and soon returns with some plates full of food. He asks some of the other people in the common room if they want something. Some people seem to indicate that they are already full and others seem hesitant to accept the food from a stranger. Seeing the food, Rafael says:

Wait, I have a few beers I hid in the room.

He disappears and comes back with them. Mahmud takes some mugs. Rafael asks:

Why mugs?

We have to hide it from [points upwards towards the surveillance camera].

I thought they didn't work.

They don't, but if Antonio sees it we will be in trouble.

Sometimes he doesn't mind as long as he knows us and we don't get too crazy.

They all sit down and start to eat. The conversations become more blurry and the voices sometimes emerge into a crescendo of noise and at other times almost unintelligible whispers. There are a few conversations that for whatever reason stand out in the noise, clearer than others. At one point, Mahmud's voice stands out:

You know, I told you before I can talk with animals. This guy here [points at Thomas] he didn't believe me until I showed him this picture. Here have a look.

He shows a picture on the phone.

I was in my friend's room and there was this butterfly that he couldn't kill and I told the butterfly I'm not going to kill you I will just set you free. And then it came and landed in my hand like this picture shows.

It's right man, and the weird thing was that just when Mahmud told me that story a bee came buzzing into my ear and this was March and there are no bees in March man [Thomas says this with excitement in his voice].

It is true, and ever since I have been a child I have been able to talk with animals, we used to have budgies flying around and I could call them and they would land in my hand. I don't try to call them making their sounds, but they can feel if you want them any evil.

The voices flow into each other again. Some of them go out to smoke, and the echoes of the laughter can be heard in the rest of the common room. They come back in and another strand of conversation starts. Thomas tries to contain his laughter and attempts to start another story:

There was this guy . . .

Mahmud interrupts:

Listen, it was this Spanish guy who sat meditating all day and night until the physio would call him to do some work. He would control the light, the light belonged to him. Whether it was switching it on or off, he would do as he pleases. And if we changed it, he would just go up and change it again.

I mean man, I would come home at 8 and it was already dark. And I would be like man, I need just a bit of light you know?! I mean if he asked nicely about it, it would be ok. It was like the other day when you had to work early, like 8 or 9.

After 10.

Yeah so a bit to 10. I mean but you asked nicely and I was like, no that's fine. But this guy he just did whatever he wanted to do.

Yeah he was crazy, you know about the cheese? Oh, it was Rosario who had asked everyone to clean out the fridge and then she removed what was left. And then one week later he comes back and asks where is my cheese?!

And I'm like I can vouch for everyone in this room because I know you Mahmud, and there was another guy also called Rafael at the time so by the process of elimination I said the only person I didn't know was this guy from Taiwan. I didn't know that Remi had emptied out the fridge.

That's why I said are you accusing me?

But we fell out over it, didn't we Mahmud?

Because you didn't want to hear anything more about that cheese!

Mahmud comes over to me and says 'You know what?'

> And he goes like 'No I don't want to hear it!' and all I wanted to say was that we should put posters of the cheese up and ask if anyone had seen it, you know like those of missing cats.
>
> I had heard so much about that fucking cheese all day so I just couldn't take it anymore.

Everyone laughs.

The conversations continue for some time and later on it turns into an impromptu karaoke session with songs by, among others, the Bee Gees and Barbra Streisand. Towards the end, Thomas and Mahmud end up in a heated discussion about how the US President is elected. Mahmud argues it is the system, but Thomas believes it is the people. Rafael, Ranvid, and J give up on trying to settle the argument and say some half-heard goodnights, leaving Thomas and Mahmud to sort out the state of democracy in the United States.

A Sense of Work

How do you give a sense of work? Not the abstracted and condensed form that flattens and makes things bearable, but the weighted grinding flow of time seeping ever so slowly through you. How do you give textual form to the dreary slow-paced movement that will engulf you and relentlessly tear into your body and joints? How do you share the surging feeling that builds up through the minutes, hours, days, and months that no amount of small tactics, tricks, and subterfuge will ever be able to save you from this place?

There is no textual form that can do it true justice. To get a small, abstract, and disembodied sense of the dreariness, try perhaps to read through the textual movements of work below. Try to say it out loud or whisper it silently. Take the time and see how long it took you. Subtract it from 10.5 hours. The time left is how long you would have to continue doing this activity before you are let go for the day:

> Look down at the scanner, look at the number for the shelf you need to scan, take one step to the right, find the number, scan it and start to count: one, two, three, four, five, six, seven, eight. Put 8 into the scanner. It beeps. The number is not what the system expected so a recount is needed. Take each item out of the shelf and put it on the trolley that you push around, then put the items back in, piece by piece: one, two, three, four, five, six, seven, eight. Put 8 into the scanner. The scanner asks for confirmation that the 'wrong' number is correct. Push yes. A new number shows up. It is a shelf that is a box on the ground. Find the box and sit

> down on the grey plastic stool that counters like you are allowed to carry around with them. Pull out the box and start to count. one, two, three, four, five, six, seven, eight, nine, ten, eleven, twelve, thirteen, fourteen, fifteen, sixteen, seventeen, eighteen, nineteen, twenty, twenty-one, twenty-two, twenty-three, twenty-four, twenty-five, twenty-six, twenty-seven. Put 27. Pray to the system that the number is what they expect. It is. A new shelf number turns up. Move on to the new shelf three steps to the right. Look, scan, one, two, three, press number, error, one, two, three, press number error, confirm, look, move to the side, scan, error wrong bin, look, scan, one, two, three, four, five, six, seven, eight, nine, ten, eleven, twelve, thirteen, press number, correct, look, sit down, scan, one, two, three, four, press number, correct, look, stand up, scan, one, two, three, four, five, six, seven, eight, nine, press number, correct, move to the other side, scan, one, two, press number, look, put stool on the ground, stand on it, scan, 0, error, 0 error, confirm, stand down, put stool on trolley, look, go to the side, sit down on stool, scan, pull out box, one, two, three, four, five, six, seven, eight, nine, ten, eleven, twelve, thirteen, fourteen, fifteen, sixteen, seventeen, eighteen, nineteen, twenty, twenty-one, twenty-two, twenty-three, twenty-four, twenty-five, twenty-six, twenty-seven, twenty-eight, twenty-nine, thirty, thirty-one, thirty-two, thirty-three, thirty-four, thirty-five, thirty-six, thirty-seven, thirty-eight, thirty-nine, forty, forty-one, forty-two, forty-three, forty-four, forty-five, forty-six, forty-seven, forty-eight, forty-nine, fifty, fifty-one, fifty-two, fifty-three, fifty-four, fifty-five, fifty-six, press, error, one, two, three, four, five, six, seven, eight, nine, ten, eleven, twelve, thirteen, fourteen, fifteen, sixteen, seventeen, eighteen, nineteen, twenty, twenty-one, twenty-two, twenty-three, twenty-four, twenty-five, twenty-six, twenty-seven, twenty-eight, twenty-nine, thirty, thirty-one, thirty-two, thirty-three, thirty-four, thirty-five, thirty-six, thirty-seven, thirty-eight, thirty-nine, forty, forty-one, forty-two, forty-three, forty-four, forty-five, forty-six, forty-seven, forty-eight, forty-nine, fifty, fifty-one, fifty-two, fifty-three, fifty-four, fifty-five, press, error, stand up, move to the side, scan, one, two, three, four, five, six, seven, press, correct, move to the side . . .

Were you bored? How long did it take? You have now counted nine bins. You need to count eighty an hour with no errors. Your workday is 10.5 hours. How long do you have left before it all finishes?

Stakeholders

With a big smile and assurances of the importance of the work being done by all the government agencies, the business community, and the charities in tackling the crime of labour exploitation, the inaugural national conference of the newly established Gangmasters and

Labour Abuse Authority (GLAA) is officially finished. At the very same moment, the conference DJ moves into action and starts up the music with Calvin Harris' 'Feels', one of the big summer hits of the year.

The cheery voices of Pharrell William and Katy Perry fill out the hall. Police officers and government officials from across Europe, representatives from business communities, distinguished academics, and delegates from charities start to get up from their seats, greet a few colleagues, and make their way home after another long day in the fight against labour exploitation.

The day has been packed with speeches from stakeholders giving talks about the ingenuity of the criminal elements that exploit people for their labour; about how these criminal masterminds manage to infiltrate decent hardworking businesses, and how only through a comprehensive partnership between businesses, government, charities, and the main unions can the hidden blight of labour exploitation and modern slavery be made visible and eliminated. The talks have gone well, the conference food has been enthusiastically received, and the tea and biscuits have been readily flowing to keep people fuelled for the fight. All in all, it has been a successful first conference for the GLAA, the UK government's much-lauded new enforcement agency on labour exploitation.

When I come home to the hostel in London where I am staying for my fieldwork, I talk with Traian. He is in his late thirties and is from Romania. He has been in London for years working in places with noxious chemicals that gave him headaches and in factory lines that broke his back, but he is now in a good warehouse job where the main benefit is that you can take a break when you want to without being hassled too much by management. Some of his friends are amongst the people who every morning at 5 am stand outside a nearby hardware shop waiting to be picked up by a new employer to do a day's worth of work in construction, cash in hand and no questions asked. These people are amongst the favourite images brought up when labour exploitation stakeholders talk about people at risk of being exploited. Traian's friend has told him that the work is OK, there are good days when they hardly have to do any work and bad days when they are forced to work hard. The jobs pay between £80 and £120 a day, more than Traian in a 'proper job' gets after paying tax.

I tell Traian the story about the conference and how the government and all the stakeholders are trying to tackle these highly organised criminal crime groups that are behind all this labour exploitation going on. He looks at me with a despondent expression and shakes his head: 'They are all like Jehovah's Witnesses or something. Ridiculous.'

A Future of Tears

Most of the time, people's tears are kept for other places. Tears tend to belong at home, in the hostel. They can be found in the dark corners of the common room, in the quiet conversations away from everyone, in the far reaches of the garden, and in the middle of the night when a quiet sob can almost be hidden in the deep sleep of others. Just by being there, you will stumble upon breaking voices, distant stares, and the small drips of tears. Tears can be pierced out in many ways. A compassionate but distant phone call from a worried ex, a sister who's started to cut herself again, a friend whose heart suddenly stopped, the last picture of long-lost daughter ('she was only two but already a genius'), memories of lost children who were taken and given like it was nothing to someone else. Tears are not strange, they are not uncommon, they are part of the tapestry and you care, but they are ordinary and in a place where they and you feel they might belong.

But this time it is tears at work, in the rest area of the call centre where you have all worked for three weeks trying to interview the head of purchase for public kitchens in a 20-minute-long interview about their supplier satisfaction on a scale from 1 to 10. The tears suddenly, without much warning or sound, start to drop from Lise's eyes. She is a hopeful documentary maker who has been in the United Kingdom and London for years chasing her dreams of one day filming and telling the world. So far most of her time in London has gone with working on 'projects' like this to pay for another week or two of living in a shared room that with her bus pass takes hours to get to each day. 'Er du okay?' (are you OK), you ask worriedly.

There are other people, but your conversation seems private as few speak your language and few know each other outside the projects they work on:

> It is just . . . you know Karl?
>
> Yeah.
>
> I just talked with him. You know about how he used to have everything? Travelling all over the world, having family holidays in his summerhouse in Switzerland, being the owner of his own company, and living the life until he suddenly lost it all.

Yeah he told me that too.

I mean it is just, what is he? Sixty-two? And he is still working here J, he is still doing this shit job you know. Calling stupid phone numbers all day. J, When will it stop? When will all this shit stop? I just imagined that when I was his age everything would be settled you know. No more things to worry about . . . but will it ever finish? Will we ever be free from this?

You both know that there is no answer and all you can say is a half-hearted prayer of salvation: 'We will be fine.'

Karl will never complain about the job and the stories he tells about his past are not told to imply that he deserves better than this. It just seems like the sheer magnitude of happier memories is too great to keep out of most of the words he speaks.

No one dreams of futures like this. In our minds, this is a stopover, a temporary divergence on the way to something better. It is in the belief in a fleeting present that it is possible to keep hope and endure, and it is because of the future possibility of something better that our tears are kept at bay.

The break finishes, Lise's tears have stopped, and as you go to the phone and sit next to Karl, he whispers with a big smile and in a voice overflowing with optimism: 'Only two hours until we are free.'

Winter Day

I don't get a good night's sleep, but a bit better than yesterday. When I come down into the kitchen, Gloria, Matt, and Abbas are sitting there. Gloria says: 'J you got your hair cut!'

I smile but have to hurry to the toilet. When I come back, Gloria is gone and Matt says that Everton is looking to get Giraud:

Wow, really?

Yeah apparently they want to sign him, but I wonder if he wants to go there like no European football for one season at least.

Yeah, I don't know.

I start to prepare breakfast by washing up a dirty cup and bowl. Gloria comes back into the kitchen:

I must not have seen you since Saturday when I got my hair cut.

Yeah? What day is it today?

Wednesday? . . . No Tuesday.

Matt says:

No no, definitely Wednesday man, if it was Tuesday I would die.
Hahaha.

I then ask Gloria:

What are you doing for Christmas?
I will stay here [said with an unhappy grimace].
Yeah?! That's great!
J! You are not listening.
No no that will be great, we are one, two . . . seven people then who will stay here! That's good! Are you going to cook for us [many people cook for each other in the hostel, but Gloria like me is not one of them]?

Gloria gives me a 'no way look' and replies:

But I like salmon with tzatziki.
What is that?
It's salmon on toast with a bit of tzatziki.
What is tzatziki?
It is some yoghurt cream or something with some cucumber.
Ah yeah, I know what you mean.
I like that.

I say whilst looking at both Matt and Gloria: 'So you eat salmon for Christmas?' That seems to wake Matt up, who dozed off for a second after another night shift. He says with hope in his eyes: 'You have salmon?'

Some conversation about salmon ensues and Abbas, who has been sitting working on his laptop, tries to make a joke about selling us all some salmon.

Somehow the conversation moves on to Antonio, the night manager who has a radio show here:

Gloria: I think it is true I have seen the video.
Yeah me too (I nod).
It is easy to get on the radio you know?! (Abbas interrupts and Gloria rolls her eyes).
Yeah I guess there are free internet radio.
Everyone can do it, even Matt could do it.
Aw thank you man (said half-sincere half-ironic). Have you ever been on a radio show?

I have, I called in once.
To voice your opinion? (said half-laughing).
No for a Lord of the Rings quiz because I am a huge fan of Lords of the Rings. I have watched all the movies and read the books. It was to win a DVD box set but I already had the box set you know? (Abbas says laughing).
So did you win it?
No it was cheating.
So were the questions hard?
No they were easy, man. It was about the characters and easy questions.
So why didn't you win?
Because there were like 20 people calling in and they all got them right so they drew something to determine the winner.
That's shit, that's not fair.

A bit later, Abbas ask me with a keen expression:

Did you say there was free internet radio?
Yeah like you know free YouTube online streaming.
Ah so online radio.
Yeah internet radio.
We should start our own hostel radio! (Gloria says half-excited).
We could sell the idea. Like man, we have an idea we know you want (Matt chips in).
Yes and I could be like the presenter like in reality TV.
It would all be about someone who left their stuff here or didn't wash up.
Yeah it will be great.
It could be like the next big thing internet radio.

It is a random conversation at 5 am on a Wednesday, but it cheers me up and makes me feel less miserable about going to work.

Later at Iroha

We are told to go to a briefing at 4:30 pm. We all kind of know that it will be about winning the 'power hour'. We come to the briefing area and all the leaders are dressed up as medieval characters because the theme of the competition is based on *Games of Thrones*. Besides the leaders of the Quality Assurance (QA) department, we also have Leonardo the manager of the whole warehouse and a UK national manager.

Connor, one of the many managers we have, talks first, congratulating us on the highest-ever peak performance and how we as a team can be proud of ourselves. Then the head of UK operations says something similar and how glad we must be to beat our rivals in Milton Keynes to the title. A trophy is handed first to Connor and then to Saaf, one of the regulars who was the highest performer during the power hour. Some more vouchers are distributed to other high-performance people and pictures are taken for the Iroha newsletter. Leonardo does his best politician impression and gives a speech about how proud we can be now that we are the best in the country. We then go to the canteen where there is pizza, sweets, chocolate and Pepsi waiting for us.

On the way out, I again talk with Viktoria about how slow we worked and how we didn't really deserve this award.

In the canteen, the mood is boisterous amongst the temps, but a lot of the regulars have stone-hard faces. Midway through the celebration, Shahu somehow falls down from his chair, spilling Pepsi all over the place. Everyone laughs around him while we and the high leaders help him up. Apparently, he was losing balance for quite some time and tried to get someone to help him, but we were too busy eating pizza, so in the end he grabbed the table, but let go when it was too light and therefore found himself falling over in slow motion.

Shahu seems surprised and there is a mixture of laughter and worry, but when it turns out that he is OK, most of us start to laugh uncontrollably and the mood gets even more silly and boisterous. You can see the bosses starting to feel uncomfortable. They start to clean up the floor. Sadia and I start to help out a bit. Afterwards, the national boss of QA ask meekly if he can have some coke as if he was out of his comfort zone.

There are loud comments on how shit we were doing power hour and how we did not deserve this. When preparing to take the group picture, amongst all the noise you can hear clearly audible talk about giving the 'fuck finger' when the picture is taken and in between the laughter, there are loud shouts of 'fuck you'. The full-time associates are quiet and look generally unhappy, but do not do much during the séance. After 20 minutes there, we are told that they only have managed to get 30 minutes off for this event, so we have to be back at work at 5 pm.

We head back and I do a few bins, but soon head to the toilet for my second 'free' post-2 pm break. I meet Ibrahim there and we talk a bit about the reward thing and how it was alright to get pizza and stuff. He then gets a message saying that there is a briefing at 5:50 pm and that he should not be late. I have already logged out of my scanner so I don't get any messages. I hurry to the toilet and then log in, and I get the same message telling me to log off and return the scanner before going to the briefing.

I can't find anyone nearby me to discuss what this message is about, so I do a few more bins and then start to walk around a bit. I then come across Ibrahim's cousin Fahim, who asks what time I will go there and if we should meet at the stairs. I agree, do a few more bins and then head towards the stairs.

There I come across Saaf and I ask him what the message is about, as it seems like he also got it as he is heading towards the QA area, and it is only 5:42 pm, so it is too early for him. He says he doesn't know. I then wait a bit for Fahim, but when he doesn't turn up, I start to head to the QA area. On the way, I meet some of the regulars who I follow towards the inbound briefing area as I am unsure where it is.

It is packed and I find some of the people I know there. No one has any idea what it is about. Finally, some outbound manager comes and tell us that on Christmas Eve we will only work until 4 pm but will get paid until 6 pm, and that the embargo on taking holidays on Christmas Eve has been lifted, so if we want a day off, we can stay behind and ask the human resource people about it. Then we are told to log off and go home. I have already heard the thing about Christmas Eve before, as have most QA people, so it is only the people who are put on picking or packing assignments who don't know. Malik comes over:

> What did they say? I didn't hear anything.
>
> Oh nothing new, just that if we work on Christmas Eve we will only work until 4 but get paid until 6.
>
> That's alright!
>
> Ah, you didn't know that?
>
> No!
>
> Alright, were you not at the briefing?
>
> No, must have been picking that day.
>
> Ah, I didn't realise that, but yeah that is good. And then they said that the embargo on Christmas Eve was lifted. That is all.
>
> OK.

We go to the log-off area, but because it is 5:55 pm, people are reluctant to log out. There is some debate about whether we can log off without getting a penalty:

> They said just log out and then go home, we will sort out the pay.
>
> No, they just said log out, but nothing about doing it early.

Most people end up not logging out until it gets to 6 pm. In the meantime, I talk with Ibrahim, who has started to get a headache again and looks quite unwell.

Malik gets tired of waiting so he goes and sits on some boxes, but then he moves over to take one of the chairs that are meant for the Flow-Team (higher-end people, but I don't know what they do). We laugh at him and when Denisa, one of the managers, comes by and appears to give him an evil look, Fahim says:

> Oh oh, you are in trouble now innit.
> Un-uh, I'm doing picking innit. I won't get in trouble.

The time finally gets to 6 pm and we log out. At some point, I ask Sadia if she is coming in on Christmas Eve and she says she will. Viktoria asks if I will do overtime and I say 'overtime, as if they would' and both she and Emma laugh out loud sarcastically.

Later I found out from Shahu that Viktoria, Emma, Eli, and Ahmed had all requested overtime, but that they were called down to the QA desk and told that they could not get it because they had too much time off task. Shahu, who is always talking and not doing much, did manage to be given overtime. He says that he never takes more than 3–4 minutes off at a time.

Going out of the canteen, I remember joking with Shahu about how now every boss and everyone else will remember him as the guy who fell over when the bosses were there. Earlier we also joked amongst all the temps about how it is us who have been the most productive at counting during power hour. even though clearly none of us worked hard at all.

Emma says: 'We tried our best to sabotage it.' She laughs out loud sardonically. Viktoria replies: 'So did we all! Ha ha!' We talk loud as we walk towards the canteen. The bosses are around but we don't care. Shahu says: 'I think we need to have some breaks in this job. You can't count all the time! It is too boring. You need to talk a little bit.'

Later, Tarun, in another conversation, also says: 'It is not normal to just count. You can't do that all the time.' I reply 'Yeah it is like a lecture said to me, we can only concentrate on a task for 20 minutes at a time'.

I remember Viktoria talking about how the Hungarian couple were shouted at by Denisa for talking for one minute together and how they had then complained to HR. Denisa was then really nice to them in the briefing when the head of QA was there because according to

Viktoria, she wanted to give the impression that she was being nice to them in front of the people who dealt with their complaint. Viktoria told me that the Hungarian couple had left one of the previous days (Tuesday or Wednesday).

Shahu had seen some virtual reality glasses:

> They look really good! I want to try.
> I know, it is interesting.
> But it is too expensive.
> Yeah?
> You know if an item gets broken a bit Iroha will try and sell it with a discount. So one day I tried to break open a box and remove a little thing from it. And the next day Iroha was selling those glasses for a discount! Haha!
> Wow, really?
> [He nods] I didn't buy them, but maybe next time [he laughs].

Shahu has also started to get back pain: 'In the last few days, my back has started to hurt. I thought about getting a massage for it.' I tell him about foam rolls and how I have read that it is not good to massage the back directly, but that I am not sure. He replies:

> I did not know, that maybe I will try that.
> Do you go to the gym?
> I go sometimes, but I am so tired afterwards and my muscles ache so much. However, I like swimming.

He then goes on to tell me about how he has learned swimming from watching YouTube videos and nothing else:

> How can you do that?!
> I just watch the YouTube video a few times and then I remember it and then I try. It is OK.
> Wow, I'm impressed
> You can learn anything from YouTube videos. Whenever there is something broken in my house, I just go to YouTube and look at how to do it. People ask me how do you do it? And I just say I look at YouTube ha ha!

Throughout the day, we talk about how boring the work is. Counting is so boring and time goes so slow. I remember Eduardo saying back in the hostel:

> This time is hard for me. I used to celebrate Christmas with my mother, but now I don't have anything.

> You have us now.
>
> I think about stuff and my mum, it was always with her we used to celebrate.

I talk with Malik. He says that regular jobs pay less, but then you know that it is secure, whereas temp jobs pay more, but you can get fired at any time. There seem to be some Lidl openings in Shepherd Bush. We talk about how Lidl, Aldi and Morrisons pay well, but he is not interested in working there. He doesn't want to have to deal with customers all the time: 'If I'm tired right, I don't want to have to be all nice to people you know? It is too exhausting. I can't do that.' I reply: 'When I worked in a supermarket it was alright. I mean sometimes I had to work with customers, but most of the time I was just putting stuff on the shelves or working in the storage area where there were no customers.'

I talk with the picker who worked for Alpha (a recruitment agency) again:

> There are so many rumours here man. You can't trust anything unless it is written down. One day you hear one thing and the other another thing. You never know until it is written down. I used to work for this company and they would put us in a circle and we had to whisper one sentence into each other's ear and at the end of it, the last person only heard one word! So it is like here. I once read that Napoleon or something at a battle sent a message to advance, but at the time it had arrived, it had turned into Dance or something like that. So you can't trust it until it is written down. Like with the buses, like you say maybe they will stop them, but I heard that they will continue with the buses. But I also heard that they will increase the prices to £3.50 – who knows what is going to happen. Maybe they will fire us soon or maybe they will keep us until the end of January. I will just take it as it comes

At one point during the day, I hear a group of the regulars talk:

> For fucking six months they put me on Single Bin Count (SBC), what the fuck. I used to do problem-solving and now all the fuck I am doing is SBC. Fucking fuckheads. What the fucking fuck.

At one point last week when I and Viktoria talk during the power hour, Peter the boss walks quickly by and he shouts: 'Count!!' Viktoria rolls her eyes. At another point, Sorina interrupts me and Shahu when we are talking during power hour. 'It is power hour, what are you doing?' she says, to which Shahu with a proud smile responds: 'Talking.' She gives us a disgruntled look and we stop talking. But later Shahu says that he saw her talk. He shouted 'Stop talking, it is power hour!' and she was laughing.

I come across Malik at the end of the shift. He looks absolutely exhausted:

> Man you look knackered.
> I am so tired, I have not been sitting down all day!
> You should have come and sat down on one of our chairs.
> I know, I keep on looking for you guys, but I could not find any of you.
> We were on V3 all the day doing SBC.
> Ah man, that is why.

Tejas overhears a conversation with John where he discusses all the ways we can get an error that is not our fault – like stowers putting things there, pickers taking the item, someone misplacing an item in a box we have counted, someone consuming the item, or maybe the item just falls in between the cracks.

I talk with Tejas and Adam:

> There are so many items that are stolen. Like I came across this box where there were a bunch of silver rings that had all been stolen. It was like maybe fifty or so that had been taken. I then looked up how much they all cost and it was like £50 for each of them so that is like £2,500 just for that. And you know silver is not detected by the security gates, I have a silver necklace and it doesn't beep whenever I go out.
> Really?
> It is something with the carbon content of it. I think things like silver and gold are not really metal so it doesn't go off because they don't have as many carbon molecules in them.
> Right, what about diamonds?
> They will go off, I think.
> Right.
> I heard that someone got away with stealing £100,000 worth of goods a few years ago.
> They never caught him, so he got away with it (Tejas say).
> Wow.

I tell them the story about the person who smuggled stuff out through the toilet. The toilet in the secure area was connected to the toilet in the canteen with an open space in the wall. The person would put the stuff and in that way smuggle valuables out until they were finally discovered. It was Martin, a regular from the local area who told me about it.

Later I meet Shahu who says:
Denisa always comes whenever I am not working. I don't know how she does it!.
Maybe she can smell it when you don't work.
Haha, maybe.

Earlier in the week, Lucio said he doesn't like the job anymore – later in the week, he changes his mind and starts to like it again:

What do you mean!! Of course, I don't like it, man! I need some sleep man. Now I only get like five hours of sleep because I come home so late man. And the breaks. I think the main thing is the breaks. I just want to sit down and relax a little you know?
Ah OK, because I thought you kind of liked it here.
Pff, of course, I don't like it. My brother works in security and he might be able to get me a security job.
Where?
What do you mean? In security.
But I mean where in security?
Just security.

At some stage, Lucio talks about how he needs proper clothes for the security job. At other times, he talks about how he wants to gain a crane certificate to earn some good money.

Losing It Alone

You come into the room late in the evening after work. Eduardo is talking with a new person you haven't met:

Eduardo: Your headphones? What those cheap ones? No, I haven't seen them.
X: But I gave them to you!
Eduardo: Man, that was like months ago. I don't know where they are now [he huffs]. I can buy some new for you if you want. They are like a couple of quid.

The new guy is looking angry, but doesn't say anything else and continues to take some stuff from under the bed; soon, he leaves. Later on, you come across other flows of conversations talking about the incident:

Mahmud: Did you see the guy who we looking for his stuff? He was upset because they had thrown out his stuff despite him paying, but it was just because he was in the hospital for a long time that they threw it out. He had gone to an England game at Wembley and had started drinking and he knew that when he started drinking, he couldn't handle it. But he drank a lot and when he came home he drank some more until he couldn't control himself and he ended up in the hospital for several weeks. I told him that he can't worry about all the stuff he lost, that he has to forget about it and move on.

J: It is harsh though isn't it?

Mahmud: That's what they do, they wait until he pays and pays, and when then someone complains, I'm not saying who, they also go through his stuff and take whatever it is that they like. I tell myself that is what happens when you have no one in your life. It is not like the poor people in Egypt, there the poor help each other. If someone is in the hospital they help each other out take care of what needs to be taken care of. Not here though . . .

J: But didn't he tell people to take care of his stuff?

Mahmud: No, he doesn't have anyone's number. He hardly speaks to people! So how can he get any help like that? People often ask me to look after their things or receive a package for them and I always make sure I look after their things, so they never lose it. Never.

He says with the intensity of a TV lawyer closing a case full of righteous conviction.

The Key Moment

There it is, the moment I have been waiting for. Finally, the policies on labour exploitation have a direct impact on the lives of workers that I am here to research.

It is the first day of an introduction to a warehouse job at a global media company. As part of the induction, we have to fill in pages of information related to health and safety, personal details, compliance signatures and so on. There are also several mathematical questions and questions to test our language abilities. We get 10 minutes to fill it all in because we are running out of time before the training begins. The staff from the agency goes out for errands whilst we fill in the forms.

There are eight recruits in total: some speak with a distinct London accent and some have trouble saying much in English. We are supposed to do the tests by ourselves, but it quickly turns into a group exercise where we give the answers to each other.

We all sit and fill out the forms. Individually we might struggle to fill in the correct answers, but as a group the questions are easy. English grammar questions are answered by Charlotte, a native English speaker, while the math questions are quickly provided by Kobi, who used to be the best in maths class back in Ghana. No matter what the test throws at us, there will always be someone in the group who knows the answer we are all looking for.

There is one set of questions that we have to fill out that gives me a sense of excitement. It is a paper designed by a group of key stakeholders who work on labour exploitation. It asks questions such as 'Did you have to pay money to work here?', 'Did someone take your passport against your will' and 'Do you feel you can leave your job at any time you want?' We are running out of time. Most people just tick the 'no' box without reading the questions, but Julianna, a Polish woman in her forties, asks the whole group: 'What does this mean?' The woman next to her, whose name I don't get before she leaves later that day, asks Julianna: 'If you want to go, can you go?' Julianna laughs: 'Yes, of course, but who will pay me?' 'Then just put no', she is told.

It takes perhaps 20 or so seconds to fill in the questions related to labour exploitation. Those few seconds are the only point over 18 months of fieldwork where the politics of labour exploitation have a direct bearing on any of the workers' lives. A few seconds of ticking a row of no boxes with difficult worded questions that are barely understood. The endless amounts of policy work that I examined before the fieldwork and that were going to be one of the main focuses have resulted in 20 seconds of cursory impact. It might have taken hundreds of thousands of hours of work by large groups of policymakers, charity advocates, and frontline practitioners to create the conditions for this particular moment, but I am still left wondering to myself: 'How do I write a research book about 20 seconds?'

The Luck of Existence

Endri has been here for a few weeks. Whenever he speaks to you, he comes as close as possible with only a tiny membrane of air to separate you. When he first arrived, his stare was intense and he spoke with conviction and urgency about wanting to take a Ph.D. in political science. Today he comes home with a tired look, drained for any sign of presence. How did it go with the bank? Someone asks and he shakes his head. A few of you gather around to hear what happened, but the story he tells is not unique: the bank did not believe in him.

Providing enough proof to convince a bank that you exist is a journey that involves skill, effort, and most importantly, luck. The journeys people take to convince a bank that they exist is never the same. Some will get theirs almost immediately. They will walk into random bank branches sporting their nicest-looking clothes and big youthful smiles until someone shows mercy and gives them a bank account. For others, it can take much longer. They will gather more and more documents, their passport, National Insurance applications, job contracts (if they have one), receipts for online parcels, bank statements from other countries and any other thing that can help them convince the bank that they are someone whose presence in the world is worthy of recognition.

The banks will have clear and easy rules to follow. You just need to prove your identity and address. It is national policy. Nothing they can do about it. They need to do it to prevent money laundering, organised crime, and terrorism. Just look at the Money Laundering, Terrorist Financing and Transfer of Funds Regulations from 2017 – it is all there in black and white, they will say. The fate of the world depends on it.

People are sometimes mistaken. They will feel that all they need to prove their identity is this embodied self, which luckily they always bring with them. They will also misunderstand that the place they live is the same as the bed they tug themselves into night after night. But in this part of the world, addresses and identity can only ever be found in carefully crafted documents and bright friendly smiles.

Endri has already tried for several weeks to get a bank account, but so far he has never even been close. We all give him advice. 'Why don't you go to the Santander Branch down at KB road? Ask for Gabrielle, she is friendly to foreigners', Pedro would say. 'Or why don't you try this online bank?', Lilou would shout from across the room behind her laptop working on another app. Antonio will ask his Philippine friends if they can help and Alessandro will offer a new sharp haircut that might overcome the sceptical stares of the bank clerks. We all chip in, but this time no amount of collective effort can convince any bank that Endri exists.

The frustration of being told you don't really exist, that you in truth are not valid as a being, impacted on Endri and everyone else for whom the process dragged out. Tears, angry shouts into the air, fists slammed into the table and walls, deep puffs of cigarettes and joints, sleepless nights, comforting hugs and conversations, small and large amounts lent and given to get some invisible person through another week were pressures whose ripples could be felt through the hostel.

Endri tried to hang on. Without a bank account and with a body that could only walk slowly and use one arm, his options were limited. Late in the evening, you would often find him coming back soaked and disheartened by the meagre earnings he managed to make standing all day in the rain handing out free pamphlets and newspapers to people rushing to work. In the end, something happened – no one knew what, but one day he disappeared without a trace from our sight as if the banks had been right all along.

The State of Help

I have arranged to meet with Aurora after work. She has an appointment with the police and wants me to tag along. I stand to wait outside the ticket barriers at Angel Station when she emerges from the escalators looking slightly confused. She spots me, but has to stop up at the ticket barriers to look for her travelcard. She finally finds it and comes out of the ticket barriers:

> J!
>
> Aurora!
>
> You are not going to believe it. It is not possible. Today at work, this bitch, my manager comes over to me and I have been sorting these clothes for hours and the bitch comes over and says why are you folding it like that. Because no one has told me how to fold it, so I just fold it and the bitch says ha, no that is completely wrong . . . aw, look at that bird . . .
>
> What?
>
> The . . . what do you call them?
>
> Pigeon?
>
> Yes, this old man just tried to feed it and the pigeon was like no I do not want your trash, I'm better than that, I have been in London for too many years to just take anything . . . J, today at work there was this beautiful girl and I was like ooh how I'm in the same world . . .

Aurora's talk takes a plethora of directions and is always full of unexpected jumps interspersed with taking on the imagined voice and character of other people, animals, and things. She only stayed in the hostel for a few days, but we initially bonded over a poor little dead mouse inside the cupboard that she promptly made up and played out a tragic heroic background story for. She left the hostel soon after because there was another mouse in her bed.

The place where Aurora lives now has single rooms or shared rooms with just one other person. The reason we are going to meet the police is that her next-door roommate often goes crazy (when he is off his head on something) and tries to force his way into her room. She has already talked with the police who have arranged a time for her to come to this police station to report the incident.

The police station is not too hard to find, and we end up being five minutes early. We go in. To our right, four people are waiting. To our left, through some windows and doors, we can see a policeman talking with someone. There is a reception area, but no one is there. We stand hoping that someone will respond to our confused stares. After 15 minutes, a police officer walks through the area behind the reception desk, but doesn't look in our direction. After a few more minutes, we decide to sit down.

After another 30 minutes with nothing happening, we get to talk with some of the other people who are waiting. They have already waited a few hours. At some point, a police officer comes out and looks in our direction. The person who has been here the longest goes up and is taken into the room we can see through the glass windows at the other end of the room. Another hour or so goes by and a person comes in and looks at the people waiting. She asks how long we have been here. I reply: 'Two hours I think.' She responds: 'I was here yesterday and the day before waiting for hours, never got to be my turn.' She sighs and leaves.

We wait another half hour and then Aurora looks at me. 'Let's go', she says.

Aurora manages to find a new place to get away from the crazy person. But one day she is in the wrong place at the wrong time and is trapped in a police raid. She loses most of her valuables in the raid and has to come to the hostel for one night. Normally you can't turn up unannounced, but I talk with Antonio the night manager, who agrees to have her come without letting the office know. In the middle of the night, he comes over to bring the bedsheets for her. She never gets her things back from the police and a month later she flies away to another city, leaving London without her stories saturated with colour.

Knowing and Letting Go

The alarm rings at 4 am on a Friday morning. I'm working 55-hour shifts in Iroha because it is peak season in the run-up to Christmas. I'm exhausted but manage to convince myself to not call in sick. I grab my bags with food and go down to the hostel kitchen to have my breakfast. There is no one but me in the kitchen at this time. After a few minutes, someone is hammering on the front door of the hostel. There are no staff to let them in, so I disgruntledly get up and go over to open the door. It is Charles. He has not been here for long, maybe a week and I have only talked with him a few times. He seems to be on something – not weed, probably something like amphetamine or coke. He starts a hectic explanation of how he lost his key, but I don't have the mental ability at this time to process any of the things he is saying. I make my way back to the kitchen table to finish eating my breakfast and he follows me and sits next to me.

He tries to make conversation, but by this time I'm too tired to become part of any conversation. He starts to complain about how quiet it is and asks: 'Where is everyone? It is so quiet. It used to be so much more fun last time I was here. There is hardly anyone now . . . Where is everyone?' He sighs.

I remind him that it is 4:30 am and that most people are either at work or sleeping, but he doesn't pay much attention and continues to lament the loneliness of the place. After a while, he gets a surge of energy and bounces out into the garden. Whilst he is away, I pack up my food and go to brush my teeth in the toilets that are right next to the kitchen. After a short while, he shouts something about where I went. I groan back that I'm in the toilet. There is a brief moment of silence before there is a loud knock on the toilet door. I open the door with my toothbrush in hand. 'What?', I say annoyed, but my sour tone doesn't seem to affect him:

> You know that you left your stuff behind.
>
> Yes.
>
> Just be careful you never know where people might take stuff.
>
> It is OK, there is nothing of value. Sorry, I have to go soon so I need to finish.

I then slam the door shut. When I come out of the toilets, I go to pick up my jacket and my backpack. I feel the pockets of the jacket to see If I have my travelcard. It is gone. I check again all my pockets and

I start to roam through my backpack and I double-check my wallet. Empty. Nothing there. 'For fuck's sake', I exclaim. I run up to my room to double-check if I have my travelcard there, but no luck. It is time to go, so I make my way back down the stairs to the front door, which is now wide open. My thoughts immediately race to conclusions. 'The bastard took my travelcard and went out again hoping to cash it in. I don't need this!'.

I run to the train station, get a new travelcard and take the bus to work. Work is more horrible than usual and although everyone sympathises with my story, the anger lingers.

When I come home, I am tired and still seething. Gloria, one of the ethical and moral sages of the hostel, is also back from her sales job and is sitting in the kitchen watching a reality show she likes. I have known her for a few months now, but in the eventful hectic temporal flows of the hostel, that feels like years.

Gloria sees me as I come in, takes out her headphones and shouts across the room: 'J!' I go over to the table and sit down. 'What's the matter J?' In streams of semi-connected words, the story of what happened falls out of me and I end with: 'I'm sure he took it, arrgh.' 'But J, you don't know', she says. I look at her suspiciously. She continues:

> When did you last see your Travelcard?
>
> Yesterday I guess.
>
> Anything could have happened. You could have lost it anywhere. Going back from the tube or down the stairs. You might have forgotten it somewhere. Like the other day I found a wallet in the toilet and you know I was a bit like hmm . . .
>
> You could've run for it.
>
> Yes, but I just went around asking people whose wallet it was and I found the owner eventually. But not everyone is like that. Someone else might just have taken it. Or you just lost it. Or maybe it is still in between your sheets in the bed. J you don't know.

As always, she is right and I calm down. This is far from the first time she has mellowed someone's urgency for truth and determination of guilt. In the rolling swirling flows of the hostel, nothing ever seems to stay in a predictable place or character. Remote controls will go missing, only to emerge weeks later in the fridge. A bundle of cash locked in steel cabinets imitates Houdini and breaks free, never to be seen again. In a single encounter, someone can go from a suit-wearing and hardworking entrepreneur to a debt-ridden gambler working the slot machines. It can seem as if nothing is ever fixed or in place beyond an unfolding present that always leaves us at the mercy of something that is felt, but never quite there.

At times, out of nowhere, pressures will suddenly surge into piercing anger and demands of clarity about the world. Someone will lose a month's wage and will demand we all empty our luggage, which we do as an act of care. There will be heated discussions and chatter that tries to nail down the trustworthiness of someone who now seems to owe half the hostel money. Why do they keep on borrowing money? Is it really for their children who always seem to get new kinds of illnesses or is it for gambling? In these moments of pressure and intensities, questions are asked, answers demanded, and accusations and threats charge the air with cold lonely suspicion.

It is in times like this that someone or something else is needed that can soothe, recalibrate and warm the situation. In this particular moment, it is Gloria who is there to diffuse my anger and drain any desire for a mock trial with me as the judge, jury and executioner. In other patches, it might be Ranvid who in between puffs of smoke always seems to be able to provide warm and insightful words that can cool down furious attempts to define and judge a person solely on unpaid debts and made-up children. Or maybe it will be Lilou with her jokes, Matteo with his yoga and weed, Himari with her inquisitory steel, Antonio with his humorous stories or someone else who with their presence can disperse suddenly surging intensities. It is not always the case that there will be someone to mellow the situation and if the concentrated tensions with their attraction to clarity and defining verdicts are allowed to linger, something will be ripped apart with unknown consequences.

'You are right', I say to Gloria, 'I don't know.'

Summer Day

It is morning and I am in the kitchen with Primin. He is making his food, which is always an arduous process. After a while, James, the hostel owner's son, comes in:

James: I'm sorry but you have to move room up to 14 today. We have a big group coming in.
Primin: OK, that is fine.

James leaves and Primin turns around to me looking happy:

Primin: You know I just booked online for a very cheap price and normally they would tell me to move hostel, but I guess now

I can stay here! I am supposed to be in 14 for weeks now – I just haven't moved yet

J: That is good. But I think some people are going to be angry

I know that this has happened before – that we are suddenly told with hardly any warning that we will have to move rooms. A lot of people are already at work and their stuff will be moved by the staff.

A few minutes later Josephine comes down:

Josephine: Arrgghh, I can't fucking believe it. They are doing it again. They woke me up and I have to go to work soon. How the hell am I supposed to move all my stuff with this little warning!!

Primin: I know, it is ridiculous.

Josephine: And they always send these innocent staff to tell us the message. They are all nice, but it is not their fault. It is all about communication. They say somebody forgot to tell us yesterday, but is one day enough! Are they saying that they only got the booking yesterday?! Come on!

Later on, I talk with a Tahiro who is leaving today. Whilst talking with him about buying extra luggage for all his stuff, Gloria comes in:

Gloria: J, I can't do this anymore. It is too much.

J: I know, they are doing it again.

Gloria: I can't do it. This is supposed to be my day off. And then they come like this in the last minute. Why? Why do they have to do this?

Me: I don't know. Why don't you move into the same room I am in now? (it is on the ground floor which she prefers).

Gloria: I don't know, is there anyone snoring?

J: Yeah, there is one now, but not as bad as Eduardo.

Gloria: How many beds are in there?

I open the door and start to count, but then Juan waves me in: 'Who is in that bed?', he asks me and points to the bed below me. I reply: 'Tahiro.' He says: 'We are too many people. Don't ask more people to come here, I can't sleep.' I say that we will get someone no matter what, so it is better if it is someone we know. Juan disgruntledly accepts. I finish counting the beds and go out to Gloria:

J: There are three beds free.

Gloria: And anyone with both free?

J: No.

Gloria: Pff, I don't know.

Yesterday Luz the cleaner was stressed. The room I am in is dirty and smelly, and there are clothes spread all over the floor:

Luz:	People in your room are so dirty. They spread it all over the floor. It is that guy Juan, he is too much!

Lilo, who is also in the kitchen, laughs: 'Too much'. I smile:

Lilou:	I mean he is a good guy, but he used to be in 14 and it was too much.
J:	Yeah, I know.
Luz:	Too much and when I told him to clean up, he cleans it up but then 10 minutes later it is all the same again! Too much!

We all laugh.

I talk a bit with Fabian. He has stayed here for two months. He says that he really doesn't like the cleaner – she is so rude:

Fabian:	One time she came in and told me to clean up. And I start and then she comes in with the vacuum cleaner and just slams my things around.
J:	Yeah it is like that sometimes here. I once had all my stuff moved without any notice. When living here, you have to sometimes be like . . . [I take a visibly deep breath and he gives a little smile].
Fabian:	And I lost so many things here since I came. My shoes, laptop everything has been stolen.
J:	Oh yeah, I never leave my valuable stuff around.
Fabian:	But no one told me! And I lost it in many different rooms. And I think I know who it is. There is this guy who has stayed here for a long time and I think it might be him.
J:	Yeah, there are some who are suspicious about that guy and there are some who think it is old residents who still have the keys to the hostel even though they don't stay here any longer. They sometimes drop by so it might also be them. Did you hear about the girl who lost. . . [Fabian interrupts before I can finish the sentence].
Fabian:	Yes I have heard it all now, all of it.
J:	It is not great, you really do need a lot of patience here. Like now every time I leave my phone behind I get nervous so I try to bring it with me everywhere.
Fabian:	Yeah yeah, me too.

I talk with Primin about his project. It seems like one of their investors has taken them to court in order to try to not pay up the money that they have committed to the project (a building material project). Primin trusted the guy who is now bringing the lawsuit and he says that 'it is really evil things that they are saying. They are just making stuff up. And that is very hard to take especially since we are not like that. We never lie like that. Chloe [his US-based business partner] is also in shock'.

We end up talking about dodgy ways of making a living like through tax evasion:

Primin:	I know this person and she is this lawyer who specialises in tax evasion and I once asked her, don't you ever feel bad about what you are doing? And she said: 'What do you mean? I am rich and it is interesting what I do, like trying to figure out how to move the money around so that they don't have to pay any tax.' But you will end up with nothing. You just get consumed by all of this money and that is all you ever have. Like there was this guy (the same who is now suing them), he made millions, but then suddenly there is a tax evasion case against him and he stands to lose everything and then his wife also decides to leave him and she takes everything she can and he is left with nothing. And that just makes him worse which is why he is trying to screw us over now.
J:	It must be hard having to deal with all that shit.
Primin:	It is very difficult especially for Chloe who is not used to this kind of thing.

A few days earlier, Primin tells me that he has finally got his US visa and initially he says he will leave in a few days, but in the end, he is still here and he tells me he has postponed going to the US.

It is Antonio the night manager's birthday and with a few days' delay, me, Gloria and Josephine buy him some perfume and chocolate. We wait for ages for him to finally come around. When he comes he says that he had to go to three different ATMs with this guy who could not pay the rent. In the end, there is no money in any of the accounts and another person in the hostel ends up lending him £75 to get by for a few more days.

The Time We Have Left

Max is sitting outside in the garden smoking. You sit down next to him.

How are you?
I heard bad news.

> What?
>
> It was someone I knew in Cambodia who died.

His face sinks in. He looks more tired than usual.

> They are all dying now. One by one . . . but this one was young. Younger than me.
>
> That's shit.

Max is working 100 hours a week. He is starting to look like a burned wretched image left behind in reality. He used to run marathons, but now he smokes for the stress instead.

Don't work yourself to death (you mutter and pat him on the shoulders). He says there is good stress and bad stress, and what he is experiencing now is bad stress where things don't get solved. He worries about his age: 'I got ten years left as I see it. I'm fifty-one now so ten years left before I have to find another way of making a living until I die.'

Max continues to talk about how it is possible to work those crazy hours in the restaurant because, at the end of it, you create something beautiful, something that is worth it: Why would you want to do something else? At least that is what they think especially when they . . . when I was young.' He finishes his second cigarette:

> Everything has also got more intense. Like out in South East Asia it used to be that it was only a small group of people who would consider going out there and get a job, but now even the young ones think 'Why not?'. Like it used to be that you could get a job because you knew about the conditions. I got my job in Egypt because of some contact I had in Namibia. Like at that time you couldn't get what you wanted. You had to have it flown in from Europe and when you ran out, you ran out for good and there was nothing you could do. Now you can get everything everywhere so it is not such a big deal to go somewhere else.

You ask him why he can't reduce his hours since he will quit anyway and he says that it is because if he does, things won't get done – there are orders that will not get in, machines that won't be fixed, and it will all come back to bite him, so things will be even more difficult in his job. He is hoping to leave in three to four weeks to go back to Cambodia. 'What is it about Cambodia that you like?' He says that he knows that he is in a privileged position because he can leave anytime he wants and he has healthcare and economic resources. He says that if he didn't have those things, it would be different. What he likes about it is that it feels more free and laid back, although it is changing now that the big Chinese companies are coming. But still, if you want something done and you have the resources to do it, you can get it done – no law or anything will restrict you.

Max tries to light another cigarette, but you tell him that he has put it in his mouth the wrong way round. He looks at you with a sad distraught expression: 'My brain is only half-working.' He gives up and says he will go and watch a murder crime drama: 'I started to really like them. I think because they make me feel so relaxed. Everything fits neatly together and gets solved in the end.'

He gets a text whilst we talk saying that someone cancelled their shift:

> And I had looked so much forward to watching a film and get some sleep [he says this with a despairing face and half-fake crying].
>
> Couldn't you just say no?
>
> No there are some good people on the shift today. If I don't turn up to help they will have even more shit to deal with.

His weary figure makes its way across the garden and disappears into the kitchen, and for weeks all there seems to be left of him is the worn-out cigarette buds on the ground.

Where It Ends

You have been back for four months and time has been taken away by teaching and trying to write acceptable lines of words. The phone rings. It is Ranvid:

> Ranvid how are you?
>
> Good, where have you been?
>
> Still at uni.
>
> So they are still making you work?
>
> Yeah.
>
> When are you coming down here again?
>
> I wish I could go today, but I don't have the time and money. How is everyone?
>
> You know, the same. Max is still working like crazy, Eduardo is still here doing what he does, Lilou still working on her apps, Antonio still trying to collect everyone's money. Like the other day, he came in at 2 in the night, put on the light and start to ask for this Irish guy. I told him: 'Antonio, the Irish guy left days ago, what are you looking for?'

Hahaha.
Can you believe that guy?
I know.
Just got to let it flow. You can't do anything about it.
Yeah we can try.
We had the Christmas party again this year.
Yeah? With all the Filipinos.
Just like last year.
That was the best Christmas party ever. Did it have all the food, games, and karaoke?
It was all there, else it wouldn't be a Philippine hostel Christmas right?
Did Eduardo sing 'Sweet Caroline'?
Aaalll the night, everyone knew every single word of it at the end.
Hahaha, did you sing it with him?

Ranvid starts to half-sing the chorus. You applaud:

I wish I could have been there.
You should've. So when will you come down here again?
I don't know when I can, I got to somehow finish this Ph.D. first.
You got to do what you have to.
Yeah I guess.
We all need to take care of ourselves.
And each other.
Yes, but in the end, you only have yourself you know. No one is going to come to do it all for you. No one will come and take care of you. People will always come and go. All you ever have is yourself.
Yeah, but I hope to see you all soon.
When you come maybe we will make some dinner and have a drink like old times.
That would be great.
I got to go, but see you around.
Definitely, take care and say hi to everyone.
You too, bye.

The sound of the fridge echoes through the room. The footsteps of others can be heard, but are never seen. Muffled voices from the television next door are still celebrating the beginning of a new year. A page is open on Word, blank and waiting.

Postscript

Blank Pages and Q&A

If I asked you to write something on the blank page that is waiting, what would it be? The different textual fragments I have provided throughout the book have in a very small way been part of your life for a certain period of time. In what way they have become part of your lifeworlds I cannot say.

Perhaps you have been turned off by the lack of a linear succinct structure, with no clear instructions to reveal the intentions and purpose of these haphazardly gathered texts. In this confusion, maybe the different textual parts have left little to no impact beyond the fact that reading them has taken up some of your time. Perhaps the only lingering feeling left behind by it all is a desire to finish it and move on to something else, something better. I feel like that myself often and if 'Finally finished' is the concluding remark you want to leave for this moment, it is as fitting as any.

Maybe there are some small parts of the text that in one way or the other have left more visible and lasting traces in the reader. Could it be that the short mention of Kondo's work sparked some interest so that you have now read one of her books yourself and discovered their brilliance? 'Kondo is brilliant' is as fitting a conclusion as any.

There are perhaps longer underlying textual tones and registers that resonate with your concerns. Maybe fragments that seem to indicate the hardship of work are something you feel compelled to use and build on. A cry of 'Abolish work' or any longer-lasting desire of planning and organising the end of work are all as fitting sets of conclusions as any.

There is no way for me to know how the textual fragments I have presented here have impinged on you or any other reader. Have they become part of any of your analytical thoughts and explorations?

Have they played into any sensual and emotional registers? How have they been made sense of? What has been forgotten without a trace and what has lingered on for longer? Are there fragments that initially seemed irrelevant and unimportant that suddenly in the right context have taken on unexpected significance?

It might seem like I have plenty of questions, but very few answers. This might not seem very appropriate. After all, in academic books shouldn't the author attempt their utmost to present themselves as academic beings that are fully capable of providing answers and new groundbreaking insights that can change the world? Leaving the reader stranded with a concluding blank page with no clear answers and nothing but blank questions is surely not the way to imbue academic competence.

I believe that this book could stand alone and be made sense of in multiple creative ways, as it is without any clear guidance from me the author on what it all 'really' should mean. The idea of portraying divergent and conflicting realities written in the voice of complex and uncertain authors is nothing new and when we encounter it in literature, poetry, movies, and everyday stories, it is nothing out of the ordinary. However, when it comes to academic writing, it is perhaps less common to come across enactments of different realities and it might therefore cause some unease when books like this experiment with precarious methods that are full of uncertainties and entail a multitude of divergent realities.

This section is written in the hope of addressing some of the questions and concerns that people who expected a more traditionally written academic book might have. The section is conceptualised as a sort of written Q&A session where I, the author, try to answer some of the questions that I can imagine the reader might have. Although the questions are somewhat ordered, it is possible to jump ahead to any question that might resonate with your particular concerns. As will also be made clear in the answers, this should not be seen as the definite way to understand the 'real' meaning of the book, but rather just one perspective from an author who tries to make sense of a research process and written output full of contradictions, uncertainties and multiplicity. The questions can be read and skipped in any order, and you should only feel obliged to read questions that might be of interest to you. However, just like with other interviews of figures that seek to project authority, whether that is other academics, film directors, or politicians, I can't promise that the answers I give won't be full of longwindedness, contradictions, secrecy, repetitions, and a barely hidden self-indulgent belief that my answers are important and insightful. I do however promise that I will do my best to answer the questions in a way that at least makes these dynamics somewhat apparent.

Questions & Answers

I Don't Have Time and Energy to Read It All: What Is the TLDR?

This book experiments with precarious methods to enable more vulnerable ways of apprehending and surviving wrecked worlds. Drawing on ethnographic research in a London hostel for precarious workers, it explores the political, analytical, and practical limitations of using traditional methods when trying to make sense of life in precarious worlds. It argues that it is necessary to experiment with precarious methods to apprehend and enable multitudes of conflicting and uncertain political, analytical and practical potentialities.

Precarious methods are characterised by context-dependent and ongoing experiments with ways to:

- enact survivable methods to create room for immediate survival tactics and move towards other ways of being in the world;
- make the text precarious, vulnerable, uncertain, and unfinished to open up for more diverse analytical apprehensions, political reimaginings, and collaborative potentialities;
- unsettle divides between academia and precarious worlds to facilitate a more intra-dependent exchange of methods, tactics, and survival skills between people in precarious circumstances;
- resist authoritarian knowledge by bringing forward and exposing analytical uncertainties and inconsistencies to disrupt academic and political desires for certainty and control and beliefs in glorified individual geniuses.

Precarious methods are a response to concerns with the wider political, analytical, and practical implications of relying on traditional methods to study precarious lives. The book outlines how using traditional methods assumes a singular underlying reality that can only be exposed through rigours and internally coherent analysis. These assumptions in turn underpin political and academic practices that frame vulnerable precarious lives as being problematic and in need of robust stakeholder interventions. Concurrently traditional methods are rooted in practices that emerge from privileged social positions, and the enactment of these practices is deeply entangled in the very processes that create the conditions for precarious lives.

Precarious methods are constituted and moved by changing and overlapping motives that refer to the entanglement of shifting circumstances, forces, registers of hope, intentions and desires. This book's experiments with precarious methods were shaped by motives of wreckage, survival, and vulnerability.

Precarious methods grew out of wrecked worlds characterised by precarious jobs, insecure housing, disrupted communities, reconfigured state interventions, and entrenched border regimes. Whilst this wreckage entailed shattering disruptions to people's lives, it would also enable affective registers and sudden surges of care and resistance filled with unexpected emancipatory potentials. Precarious methods sought to explore ways that could encompass these shifting potentials of wreckage to wreak havoc on people's lives whilst also enabling emancipatory practices.

Survival was an underlying motif that shaped the everyday practices of people in the field and pushed the methods towards exploring how to encompass survival as an immediate and ongoing practical concern. Rather than relying on the exclusive focus of traditional methods on creating more survivable worlds in distant futures, precarious methods approach survival as an immediate and ongoing concern with implications for how methods are continuously enacted.

Precarious methods sought to move away from political and academic approaches to vulnerability as a property of 'the weak' that mark them as ripe for heroic analytical and political interventions. Instead, precarious methods experimented with ways to make the text itself precarious in order to explore how vulnerabilities were interconnected in unexpected ways across different worlds and to facilitate more collaborative, interdependent, and multiple ways of apprehending precarious and vulnerable worlds.

This particular experiment with precarious methods resulted in the crafting and juxtapositioning of three different sets of precarious realities, each imbued with various constellations and enactments of precarious methods. In Part I, traditional methods are used to explore how people living in precarious circumstances sought to minimise the impact that work had on all aspects of their lives and that these practices played into ever-changing dynamics of resistance and control. In Part II, scribbles from a messy and precarious research process are drawn out to highlight how a messy academic research process outside the field shaped what kind of realities could be portrayed in Part I. Part III experiments with fragments that seek to apprehend something about an unfolding weighted present, whilst giving some fractured sense of how people survived vulnerably in wrecked worlds.

What Are Precarious Methods?

The precarious methods I use in this book are shaped in relation to the circumstances I encountered during the research process. It is tempting to say that these methods were all carefully planned and executed, as this would align with dominant narratives about academic expertise and foresight. However, I think it is more appropriate to say that the way in which the methods came together should be seen as a somewhat desperate attempt to try to make sense of, stay afloat, and impact the turbulent ebbs and flows of the precarious living and work conditions I experienced. Therefore, the shape that precarious methods took in this book emerged out of and were inherently entangled in particular situated circumstances that cannot (and should not) be replicated. As such, precarious methods are perhaps inherently situated, implicated, and reacting to the lived experiences of a precarious world. This also means that they cannot be reduced to the application of particular techniques grounded in single theoretical paradigms. Any attempt to try and write a set of instructions on how to design and enact precarious methods is therefore doomed to be futile, as that would require a foresight of countless unfolding interlinking and contingent practices and circumstances.

What I can try to do is to write about some of the different aspects that have shaped my research process and that have resulted in this particular enactment of precarious methods. I have tried to provide answers on various aspects of precarious methods in a way that can speak to a range of interests and concerns. I don't think it is necessary to read through all of the questions and please do not consider these answers as a comprehensive description of precarious methods. I don't even consider this to be a comprehensive draft. At best, it is a beginning, an attempt where I do my best, given the circumstances of it all.

What Was the Background for Studying Precarious Work and Living?

My first contact with labour exploitation as a distinct topic that could be separated, studied, and politicised was working as a social researcher in the UK civil service focusing mainly on modern slavery and labour exploitation issues. Before, during, and after that period, the issue of how to tackle labour exploitation and abuse had received considerable attention from policy makers and had resulted in a number of government and parliamentary initiatives that were trying to understand and deal with the issue.[1]

These policy initiatives had created a flurry of activity amongst so-called stakeholders, a policy term often used to describe the networks of people and organisations that come together to work on solving the issue through the everyday practices of policy making and being on the imagined 'frontline' of the fight against labour exploitation. The types of stakeholders and activities were everything from civil servants drafting policy papers; the police investigating organised crime groups involved in modern slavery; the local council looking into potential victims at 'houses of multiple occupation' (HMO); medical staff reporting suspected labour abuse; charities providing support to victims; unions providing intelligence to the new labour enforcement agency; business reporting on labour exploitation in their supply lines; and Immigration Enforcement coming across cases of labour exploitation during raids (Home Office, 2014).

At the same time, although not necessarily directly connected with these government-centred policies, there was increasing unease with a set of work practices that were seen to be particularly adverse to the wellbeing of the precarious workers in question. Media reports, often involving excited undercover journalists, described controlling working conditions, people not being allowed toilet breaks, working too long hours, being fired for being sick, getting paid less than the minimum wage, and getting no holiday pay (Goodley, 2016; Selby, 2017). The debates would occasionally centre on particular aspects of 'the problem', such as the increasing number of people working on zero-hours contracts (Monaghan, 2017).

The so-called gig economy, whether in the form of Deliveroo, Uber, or Amazon Mechanical Turk, was another flashpoint for these debates. Did new digital developments mean a brave new world where everything would one day be divisible, flexible, and monetized at will for the seller and buyer (Green, 2016)? Or was it a return to Blake's Dark Satanic Mills, with workers slaving away under Victorian conditions far away from the benevolent places of stability, certainty, and personal growth that modern work should be (Harris, 2018)?

Academically, a range of research was carried out exploring a plethora of issues relating to precarious work, such as the impact on subjects' self-identity (Armano and Murgia, 2013); the mobility strategies of precarious migrant workers in London's hospitality sector (Alberti, 2014); the everyday geographies of precarious workers living in precarious properties (Ferreri et al., 2017); and the emergence of precarious work and its consequences for the labour market (Kalleberg, 2009).

What I wanted to do initially with this research was to get the perspective of the people who were working and living in precarious circumstances. Having worked for a short time in policy and stakeholder worlds, my impression was that there was very little information on the actual lived experiences of people in precarious jobs that filtered through to the people working on 'tackling' the issues. I therefore set out to conduct some ethnographic research where I would live and work with people in precarious circumstances.

Why Did You End up Using Precarious Methods?

Before starting my research, I planned to write a very straightforward kind of book using traditional academic methods. There would be chapters on different aspects of the things I observed and participated in during fieldwork, and those chapters would be flanked by methodological and theoretical considerations at the beginning and a conclusion at the end. As the research process progressed, it became harder and harder to maintain that vision. I found that the 'precarious' part of the topic I studied in different ways resisted this way of writing an academic piece of work. It was not any kind of 'eureka' moment that made me realise this; rather, it was a slow process informed not only by analytical considerations but also by moments of emotional unease with what I was doing.

What was it that was troublesome about precariousness? There is no one way to write about it that will encapsulate all the different entanglements that created this sense of unease, but if I had to delineate it into particular aspects, I would say that there are political, analytical, and practical elements.

Politically, the 'precarious work and living' I studied had been at the centre of attention of a range of government institutions, political movements, and actors. The way in which this 'precarious work and living' was framed, repackaged, dissected, and applied resulted in a narrow field of possible conceptualisations and policy practices that were often disconnected from people's lives. Much of this analytical work and many of these policy practices were shaped by assumptions that precarious work and living were a problem belonging to groups of vulnerable people and that this problem could only be solved by congregations of policy makers and stakeholders. Furthermore, it was taken for granted that the dynamics that shape precarious lives were separate and unconnected from the policy and stakeholder worlds that sought to know and solve these 'problematic' lives.

This approach to precarious work and living had similarities to academic approaches that mostly considered precariousness as something that belonged to particularly vulnerable groups that were calling out for research interventions that could map the dynamics that shape their lives. The implied hope in these kinds of research was that by conducting an academic analysis to understand the dynamics that create the conditions for precarious lives, it would be possible to pave the way for future policy interventions that could rectify the problem.

The issue I had was that these particular political views and academic approaches to precarious lives could end up closing down the voices and lived experiences of the very same people they sought to understand and 'help'. This also meant that the issues of what the problem was, who it affected, and how to 'solve' it were largely predetermined and remained unaffected by the diverse, complex, and unfolding lived knowledge and experiences of the people dealing with precarious work and living. During the research process, it also became apparent that there was a great disconnect between the policy and academic worlds' efforts to address the issue of precariousness and how these issues were experienced by people living and working in precarious circumstances.

How to analyse and make sense of precariousness was the second aspect that caused troubles during the research process. I found that the kind of methods that were used in academic and political analysis of precariousness were characterised by attempts at ordering messy precarious life into a singular reality by applying assemblages of analytical techniques, concepts, types, categories, and structural frameworks.

If you want to give a sense of life in precarious circumstances, a life supposedly characterised by fragmentation, fluidity, contradictions, incoherence, instability, and vulnerability, is using methods that seek to portray the world as a single unentangled reality the best way to do that? Academic research is to a large extent premised on and evaluated against criteria of analytic coherence, the robustness of its categories, the logic and stability of its arguments, and its ability to project a sense of strength and structural integrity that can survive the critical gaze of its peers. In other words, academic research is striving towards becoming everything that precarious life, at least as I saw it, was not. As I still have some kind of ambition to give a sense of how life was as I was involved in it, that was surely at least somewhat problematic and should raise questions about the different methods we could use to bring that type of reality into view.

The final aspect that caused issues was what I call, for want of a better phrase, practical precariousness.[2] This is something that emerged as a concern once I returned from 'fieldwork' to my imagined academic home. Whilst it is normally imagined that there is a clear distinction between the phenomena you study in the field and your academic home, for me this was never the case. Academia, at least in the United Kingdom, is heavily shaped by the same processes that seem to shape the lives of the people I lived and worked with during my 'fieldwork'. Precarious working conditions, increasing workloads, and the fragmentation of social life were not things that I somehow left behind in the 'field'. These precarious conditions were, and still are, very much part of the academic life I am living now. Furthermore, the work and research practices that you, as a budding academic, have to manoeuvre to have a slim chance of progressing your academic career in order to achieve some sense of imagined order and security in your life are themselves problematic. The performance of universities, departments, and individual academics is increasingly being measured and evaluated based on selected key performance indicators like research output, teaching excellence, student recruitment, retention, and satisfaction.

In an academic world like that, premised on creating measurable and ordered research products to enhance performance whilst being ever-more dependent on a precarious workforce, trying to write in a precarious way that fails these standards and that seeks to resist analytic order and coherence might be seen as problematic, but perhaps it is also politically important to do. So, to completely cut out how the precariousness of academic practices and life shaped my research on the precarious life and work of 'others' didn't seem appropriate, especially when you take into consideration the other political and analytical tensions that my study of precariousness raised.

What Academic Texts Inspired You When Writing This Book?

I would like to highlight five particular academic inspirations for this book. I don't want to claim that I can fully understand and make sense of these scholars' work, but when reading their work, they sparked something and propelled my analysis and writing in particular directions. This might have been based on imperfect and debatable understandings of their work, but nonetheless, these unsettled understandings of mine mattered in terms of how I ended up writing the book. Trying to untangle how other readings have impacted the book is always a somewhat arbitrary endeavour and there were probably countless other academics I could have brought forward as key inspirations for this book.

One thing I do want to point out is that although the book has been influenced by these and many other academics, the greatest influence on the whole research process is the countless people, most of them non-academics, that I lived and shared experiences with. The way in which they navigated this world, the methods they used to get through it all, the connections they established, the words they spoke, and the silent gestures and movements that provided support, care, and revolt more than anything have helped shape this book and its analytical, methodological, and theoretical directions. How they influenced this book is not easy to recognise within the peculiar writing practices of contemporary academia that almost exclusively favours staunchly written and purely disentangled academic text as suitable for theoretical recognition. It is therefore difficult to embed in the text a full appreciation and perhaps even celebration of how different people through my shared lived experiences with them have shaped the book. Without experiences such as Gloria's cutting ethical analysis, Ranvid's expanding philosophy muttered in verbal and material puffs of smoke, Ibrahim's ingenuous and insightful work avoiding practices, Aurora's exploring, probing, and polymorphic stories, and all the other weighted and shared moments I spent with people, the theoretical, methodological, analytical, and enacted practices of this book would not have been possible. I hope that some of this influence at least becomes partially visible in the different fragments of this book, but I also know that this in no way does enough justice to their significance.

Butler's Precariousness

Judith Butler's work on precariousness (Butler, 2004, 2009) helped me to explore the consequences of how precariousness was framed and to move away from viewing precariousness as a problem belonging exclusively to particularly vulnerable groups. Her approach to precariousness is complex and I will not claim to be able to 'frame it', to use Butler's own terminology, in a comprehensive way. What I saw as one of the central links with this book is how Butler views precariousness as the very condition of life. She argues that we all are vulnerable and interdependent on others, and without this precariousness, there can be no recognition of life. Precariousness is therefore a condition of the world and our lived lives. To approach the world as precarious is to apprehend that we are embedded and depend on others we may or may not be aware of.

This does not mean that Butler ignores the political factors involved in what she defines as precarity,[3] which in her terminology refers to the 'politically induced condition in which certain populations suffer from failing social and economic networks of support and become differentially exposed to injury, violence, and death' (Butler, 2009: 25). However, how things are framed and how they end up becoming recognised also have political and normative implications as any given 'frameworks both to preclude certain kinds of questions, certain kinds of historical inquiries, and to function as a moral justification for retaliation' (Butler, 2004: 4). When it comes to precarity, this moral imperative to seek out some political entity like the nation state to retaliate or intervene is inherently fraught, as each intervention brings with it potential new ways of being subjected to the violent workings of the nation state.

Given these potentials, what paying attention to our shared precariousness can do is break open the frame and unsettle and reshape our comprehension of the world by apprehending our mutual vulnerability and interdependence. Furthermore, by unsettling the frame, the workings of power also come into view as 'taken-for-granted reality is called into question, exposing the orchestrating designs of the authority who sought to control the frame' (Butler, 2009: 12). As a consequence, 'other possibilities for apprehension emerge' (Butler, 2009: 12) and these can serve to upset the processes of normative purification and boundary making implicated in dividing those cared for from those who aren't (Butler, 2009: 12).

Butler's considerations of precariousness and precarity are a good starting point to try to move away from framing precarity and precariousness as a problem belonging exclusively to particularly vulnerable groups. Whilst a lot of the so-called 'rescue industry' that promotes the issue of labour exploitation as a global problem in need of urgent interventions (Agustín, 2007) seems to be informed by the underlying hierarchical moral question of 'how can *we* save *them*', Butler's approach to precariousness opens up for other types of questions that are more fragile and have a more tenuous connection to hierarchical political framings of the issue. The nature and focus of the questions, and in this context the 'research questions', we need to ask therefore also change. Instead of setting out to explore 'how can we/the state/charities help *them*?', the question becomes more along the lines of 'how can we help each other?'. And instead of asking 'how can we, the academic and political knowledge producers, get a better understanding of *their* lives?', the question becomes 'how can apprehending shared vulnerabilities help unsettle fixed framings and understandings of the world?'. Finally, perhaps the research problem is not 'how can we bring social order and security to precarious lives?', but 'how can apprehending the precariousness of the world help us disrupt the violence of the social, political, and economic orders we live in?'.

This approach to precariousness not only helped me in terms of opening up space for asking new types of questions, but also allowed me to reconsider some of the key underlying assumptions about what a research book should look like, and how this relates to the wider ontological and epistemological practices and norms of academic research and writing.

Law's Method Assemblages

Reading Law's (2004) work on messy methods assisted me in creating an analytical leeway to explore how to enact more precarious methods. Law traces out how methods in social science are often underpinned by a range of assumptions about what constitutes proper science. Some of these assumptions are that there is an external reality that exists independently of our practices; that this external reality precedes us; that it is made up of forms and relationships that are definite; that this reality is singular; and that it is constant. These metaphysical assumptions also underpin assumptions about what methods are and what they do. In a world that is conceptualised as singular, external, and constituted of unchangeable forms and relationships, the role of methods is therefore to discover what the world is in its 'real form'. If the results we find using traditional methods are riddled with contradictions, multiplicities, and vagueness, this is treated as the result of 'faulty' methods that have not managed to uncover and represent a singular and coherent world as it is supposed to exist externally of these methods.

Law considers these assumptions to be problematic, as methods are never just a technical matter, but are performative and 'help to produce realities' and social arrangements with political implications (Law, 2004: 143). To make these processes visible, Law approaches methods as 'method assemblages' that are constituted by 'a hinterland of realities, of manifest absences and Othernesses, resonances and patterns of one kind or another, already being enacted' (Law, 2004: 143). In traditional method assemblages, the end research product (the research findings, the finished academic product) is usually favoured, as 'method is imagined as a means to an end for knowing better' (Law, 2004: 152). However, if we consider that method assemblages can create patterns of presence and absence, then method assemblages that notice 'the practicalities of making realities' (Law, 2004: 152) and examine 'the various ways in which they generate realities on the one hand, and condensates on the other' (Law, 2004: 152) become useful. Furthermore, by acknowledging that method assemblages both bring out and silence realities, we need to be reflexive about the researcher's 'complicity in reality-making' (Law, 2004: 153).

When it comes to traditional social science method assemblages, for a book there are often underlying expectations of definiteness and singularity concerning the arguments advanced – i.e., that the different parts of the book will be strongly linked together and tie into a strictly coherent and definable argument. This is true even where there is an understanding that in practice, research is messier than this allows and that the reality that is presented does not attend to most of the richness and complexity of life as lived (Abu-Lughod, 2000). Yet, if we open up for other ways of doing social research or for other types of method assemblages, we should perhaps also allow for 'realities that are indefinite . . . [and] appreciate that allegory, noncoherence, and the indefinite are not necessarily signs of methodological failure' (Law, 2004: 154). And instead of seeking to present visions of singular realities, perhaps it 'becomes important to think through modes of crafting that let us apprehend that multiplicity' (Law, 2004: 152).

The way in which this book has been constructed is an attempt to bring out different types of precarious realities that are not necessarily aligned with some of the traditional expectations of coherence. If this book is approached with expectations of finding clearly definable and visible overarching arguments of a singular world, it might be considered incomplete, a failure of methodology. It might be seen as too fragmented, too messy, and with connections that are too partial and precarious to truly qualify as something 'real'. If, however, it is understood in alignment with Law's approach, the precarious realities that are brought out in this book are not less 'real', they are just constituted in ways that seek to bring out some of the multiplicity of precarious presents that are normally hidden in traditional methods.

Tsing's Rush of Stories

To find textual forms that could attend to the messiness of the experiences of which I was part, I tried to take inspiration from Tsing's (2015) work that explores survival in a precarious world. Tsing's notion of precarity is similar to Butler's as she approaches precariousness as 'a state of acknowledgement of our vulnerability to others. In order to survive, we need help, and help is always the service of another, with or without intent' (Tsing, 2015: 29)[4]. Tsing puts this understanding of precariousness up against 'dreams of modernity and progress' (Tsing, 2015: 20) with promises of neverending capitalist economic growth and scientific advances that in terms of employment would 'fill the world . . . with jobs, and not just any jobs but "standard employment" with stable wages and benefits' (Tsing, 2015: 3). However, Tsing notes that these promises have not materialised and we now live in a world that is both precarious in terms of the destructive environmental effects of modernity and in terms of capitalist developments that have resulted in circumstances in which 'almost no one has what we used to call a "regular job"' (Tsing, 2015: 3). She argues that precarity is often considered 'to be an exception to how the world works' (Tsing, 2015: 20), but suggests instead that 'precarity is the condition of our time – or, to put it another way, what if our time is ripe for sensing precarity?' (Tsing, 2015: 20).

To try to sense this precarity, Tsing utilises a 'rush of stories' as a method whose 'research object is contaminated diversity; its unit of analysis is the indeterminate encounter' (Tsing, 2015: 37). The effect of drawing together these types of stories 'cannot be neatly summed up. Its scales do not nest neatly; they draw attention to interrupting geographies and tempos' (2015: 37). These types of stories place emphasis on the disruptive potential of the art of noticing in a way that does not conform to 'modern science, which demands the possibility for infinite expansion without changing the research framework' (2015: 37). For Tsing, it is 'in listening to that cacophony of troubled stories that we might encounter our best hopes for precarious survival' (2015: 34).

This rush of stories seeks to notice how survival hinges on diversity, collaboration, and contamination, something that stands in contrast with more traditional scientific and capitalist methods of engaging the world that rely on ideas of self-contained entities, whether in terms of capitalist notions of the self-interested homo economicus or evolutionary notions of selfish genes (Tsing, 2015: 28). This idea of a rush of stories helping us to notice the precariousness of the world interlinks well with Butler's call for ways of apprehending the precariousness of the world and Law's call for method assemblages that do not seek singular bounded realities. Furthermore, it allowed me to start experimenting more with different ways of apprehending and approaching precarious worlds.

Stewart's Disparate Scenes

I also drew inspiration from Stewart's work *Ordinary Affects*. This 'experiment', as she calls it, sought to 'provoke attention to the forces that come into view as habit or shock, resonance or impact. *Something* throws itself together in a moment as an event and a sensation; a something both animated and inhabitable' (Stewart, 2007: 1). Stewart seeks to notice an emergent present that cannot be summarised and described by 'the terms neoliberalism, advanced capitalism, and globalization that index this emergent present' (Stewart, 2007: 1). She considers her work or method as:

> an assemblage of disparate scenes that pull the course of the book into a tangle of trajectories, connections, and disjunctures. Each scene begins anew the approach to the ordinary from an angle set off by the scene's affects. And each scene is a tangent that performs the sensation that something is happening – something that needs attending to. From the perspective of ordinary affects, thought is patchy and material. It does not find magical closure or even seek it, perhaps only because it's too busy just trying to imagine what's going on. (Stewart, 2007: 5)

In another short work on precarity, Stewart argues for using this type of writing to approach precarity as:

> [It] hones attention to the way that a thing like precarity starts to take form as a composition, a recognition, a sensibility, some collection of materialities or laws or movements. Writing culture through emergent forms means stepping outside the cold comfort zone of recognizing only self-identical objects. (Stewart, 2012: 518)

For Stewart, the emergent presence of precarity 'can take the form of a sea change, a darkening atmosphere, a hard fall, or the barely perceptible sense of a reprieve' (2012: 519), and writing about precarity as an emergent present 'can raise the question of how to approach ordinary tactile composition, everyday worldings that matter in many ways beyond their status as representations or objects of moralizing' (2012: 519).

Writing academically about how to write in ways that are not susceptible to traditional methods is problematic, to say the least. The forms, contours, and sensibility of the texts are more troublesome to summarise and are more difficult to narrow down into the confines of academic coherence and singular meaning making. Nonetheless, I took inspiration from Stewart's experiments with ways of apprehending and noticing precarious worlds.

Breeze's Resisting Imposters

Breeze's work on imposter syndrome as a public feeling helped me to seek out the tensions and potentials of exposing analytical vulnerabilities and actively failing to comply with the ever-increasing demands of neoliberal academic life.

Breeze uses traditional research methods to expose how imposter syndrome is not solely an individual feeling, and that it is linked to neoliberal informed patterns of inequality in higher education. However, she merges this traditional analysis with short autoethnographic moments where the text becomes more vulnerable and less focused on trying to establish hard academic truths and deep theoretical understandings. From my particular position as a precarious academic, this enactment of vulnerability also allowed for a sense of emotional commonality and potential for interdependencies in a precarious world, even though the social position of the author and the patterns of inequality and exploitation she was exposed to were very different from mine.

However, Breeze also explores the tension between performing the part of a neoliberal academic whose knowledge production can be recognised whilst seeking to produce knowledge that resists neoliberal ideologies and practices that link individual 'achievement' with hierarchical positioning and status. It is in this tension that Breeze argues that feelings of being an imposter emerge and that this tension can also serve as an 'avenue for negotiating the ambivalence of being "within and against", of trying to play the game and change the rules of the neoliberal university' (Breeze, 2018: 211). From this imposter position, academic success also starts to look different and she tentatively suggests that a:

> feminist version of 'academic success' might look like failing to meet (some of the) established – and patriarchal, colonial, classed – definitions of academic excellence. Failing (inevitably) to live up to standards that are impossible to meet . . . and doing so strategically, collectively, and publi-

> cally, offers one way of critiquing, and rejecting, institutional conditions of competitive audit cultures and compulsory self-promotion. (Breeze, 2018: 211)

I did not end up using the imposter as a key analytical motive in this version of the book; nevertheless, how my experiments with precarious methods played out drew on Breeze's work on how best to navigate and survive tensions of resisting vulnerabilities and pressure to comply in a system that you are within and against.

How Did You Try to Research Precariousness?

In the beginning, I thought that the premise for my research was simple. I wanted to explore how people in precarious working and living conditions made sense of the world. A simple-sounding premise maybe, but like other neatly defined things, when faced with the sublunary multiplicity of this world, the simplicity quickly evaporated.

The first issue I encountered was who and what exactly I would study. Even within 'stakeholder' policy and academic assemblages working on labour exploitation and precarity, this was not a simple issue. There are extensive debates about who 'the stakeholders' were supposed to be helping, what practices were supposed to be the target of stakeholder action, and how to separate the 'real victims' from the less fortunate who did not fall within the scope of stakeholder policy and mercy.

A constantly evolving set of questions were asked, such as 'What is a potential or real victim of human trafficking for labour exploitation?' 'What is forced labour and how does it relate to slavery, modern slavery, and labour exploitation?' 'What is the spectrum of decent and exploitative work?' 'When are you self-employed and when is it all bogus?' 'And how do you differentiate patterns of exploitation in the labour market from other types of social and economic exploitation' (Andrees, 2014; Di Nicola, 2007; Hussein, 2015)?

To answer these types of questions, a range of 'objective' methodological practices were used to build up hierarchical and binary types of categorisations so that the 'right' kind of people and practices could be made visible and delineated from other social practices. The problem was that these brittle 'objective' terms, these carved-out ideal types, always failed to fully capture the complex pattern of practices and meaning making of the precarious social worlds they were trying to order and make visible (Davidson, 2010; Pearce, 2011).

On top of these issues connected with chasing the right definitions, there was the issue of the supposedly hidden nature of precarious working and living practices. From the viewpoint of government-centred policies, exploitative labour practices were omnipresent, yet always hidden from view (Bradley, 2014). Dark figures around the number of victims may have been calculated (Silverman, 2014), stakeholders may have gathered to shine a light on the dark patches of our society (Stop the Traffik, 2017), and the public may have been educated on how best to uncover the murky criminal practices that took place in broad daylight (Home Office, 2014), yet the phenomena of exploitative and precarious work and living were still imagined as being hidden away and hard to uncover.

Looking at debates around precarity, the prospect of finding and studying these practices did not look any brighter. The precarious labour market was drawn out to be in constant flux; with new businesses emerging and disappearing, new technologies dismantling and reshaping work practices, and people being in a constant precarious state of floating from place to place in search of the next paycheque (Armano and Murgia, 2013; Chan, 2013; Johnson, 2013). If I had taken these visions of the issue at face value, as accurate descriptions of what was going on, how would I have even tried to find and engage with these hidden and elusive people and practices? Worse still, if I wanted to approach life, the sheer multiplicity of life, as always becoming, always partial, with patches, processes, ideas, and meanings flowing about, how would I find a starting point to examine that?

As Law (2004) has pointed out, social research, even when it takes an ethnographic form, might still have remnant yearnings for the researcher as a detached, separate entity who with a cold, observing stare gathers empirical data from a spot chosen for its ability to provide the optimal point of observation. However, the way in which the research ends up unfolding is often very different and based more on the particular histories, links, and assemblages that the researcher has engaged with and has access to.

For me, to get a sense of this great hidden unknown that I was going to research, I started with what I knew: London. I had previously spent years in different parts of London. When I first arrived in London, I stayed in hostels for the first few months with other workers and, through various employment agencies, I had been working a range of different call centre jobs on zero-hours contracts, as they would be called now, to make a living. Although I had not stayed in any of these hostels for six years, I decided that it might be a good starting point as there might be a chance of getting to know people who were moving from job to job and from place to place. At the same time, I would apply for short-term and low-paid jobs that in some stakeholder contexts would be seen to be problematic.

Over the next 18 months, I stayed as much as possible in London hostels whilst working odd short-term jobs that came up. I had teaching obligations in Liverpool as part of the studentship I received, so during the semesters, I would make my way back to the University, but for a full semester I didn't teach and whenever there was a break, I made my way from my quiet Liverpool flat to the bustle of the hostel. This meant that my stay in London was sporadic and patchy. Sometimes I would come to stay for only a few weeks and at other times I managed to stay for several months in a row.

In those 18 months, I was constantly moving between worlds: the academic world of teaching, marking students' essays, and fulfilling the administrative demands of the university on the one hand, and the world of the hostel and my different short-term work on the other. Throughout the research process, I also attended union conferences on precarious work; the Gangmasters and Labour Abuse Authority's National Conference; labour exploitation events across England; and I even made it to a few business-oriented gatherings on the ever-expanding potentials of the gig economy.

During my fieldwork, every day, I would take notes of the things I experienced as soon as I had an opportunity to do so. Most of the time I would take notes on my phone or laptop and I would try to write as much detail of my impressions and experiences as possible – though, on some days when my work swallowed up most of my time and energy, I would only muster a few reminders that I would try to write out in the days I was not working.

It is an impossible task to try to untangle exactly how and to what extent my everyday actions were shaped by the fact that it was part of a research project. Were my conversations and actions shaped by what I thought my research was about? There might have been some kind of attempt to keep the conversations focused and my practices relevant and connected to my research, but mostly, whether I wanted to or not, I ended up being engulfed by the everyday flow of life that resisted any attempts to conform to whatever narrow research endeavour I may have had.

When I came back from the field, I ended up experimenting with precarious methods. This also meant that I tried to experiment with methods that could unsettle the analytical boundaries between the field and my academic 'home'. So instead of only steering my methodological vision towards the 'field', I had to start noticing the hinterland of practices and norms of life as it unfolded in academia. To do this, I drew inspiration from autoethnographic work that as a methodology 'seeks to describe and systematically analyse (graphy) personal experience (auto) in order to understand cultural experience (ethno)' (Lean, 2015: 72).

For this research project, maintaining a distinction between the 'auto' and the ethnographic elements was always problematic. Even when I conceptualised this research purely as a study of precariousness in 'the field', it had autoethnographic elements. Trying to write and grasp a world that is in constant flux, whether at the hostel or in the myriad of jobs I did, is difficult without including the only constant: myself. In life at the hostel and work, there would be long stretches of time, sometimes days, where the presence of others only materialised as hurried distant steps through the warehouse, as background chatter on the phones in a call centre, or as ghostly presences in the hostel. To try to grasp something about this kind of lifeworld I had to be reflective and notice the world through my own experiences. Failing to do that would leave out most of what was going on.

This also meant that when I realised that my research focus needed to transgress the boundary between the field and my 'home' academic life, the practice of what I was doing didn't change much as I would continue to take notes about my experiences in a similar way as I had done for much of my fieldwork. Where there was some difference was that I started to reflect on processes that I had previously thought would be outside the remit of the research. This is not uncommon in autoethnographic research that often involves practices that 'retrospectively and selectively write about epiphanies that stem from, or are made possible by, being part of a culture and/or by possessing a particular cultural identity' (Ellis et al., 2011: 276). Therefore, I did not put a temporal border between what memories and epiphanies to include and exclude. Instead, I sought to select moments in terms of how they could bring out particular aspects of precariousness and vulnerability.

Vulnerability is another key element that is often highlighted in autoethnography. Autoethnography often seeks to 'present an intentionally vulnerable subject' to explore the 'dialogic relationship of self and culture' (Holman Jones et al., 2013: 24). The way this is conceptualised is in terms of disclosing personal information that makes the author vulnerable. Although there is much merit to this approach, the focus in these particular experiments on precarious methods is more on making the *analysis* precarious and vulnerable.

There will be some personal disclosures when it relates overtly to precariousness, but large parts of the personal will still be left out, even though it might also have had some considerable influence on the timings and flows of this book.

What Motives Informed Your Experimentations with Precarious Methods?

The method was more shaped and moved by the lived and changing circumstances in which I found myself during the research process than any kind of forcefully executed plan of the author. So it is difficult to separate any kind of intentions with the methods from the situated contingencies from which they emerge. To capture this dynamic, I think it perhaps makes more sense to think of how precarious methods have been informed by particular clusters of motives. In this context, I understand motives to refer to the entanglement of intentions and aspirations and the key themes, forces, forms, and motifs that shape the methods.

It could perhaps be argued that any particular enactment of methods is informed by different clusters of motives, whether that is natural science methods emerging from and perpetuating motives of race, patriarchy, and imagined objectivity (Haraway, 1989), social science methods implication in the formation of rational nation states (Savage, 2010) or anthropological, literature, and area studies writings getting entangled in and enabling colonial discourses and practices of exploitation and oppression (Said, 1979; Thomas, 1994). However, what precarious methods try to do is to make some of those motives clear in terms of the methods that the author seeks to use. What motives inform precarious methods will be contingent on the ever-shifting circumstances that engulf the research process and they can therefore not be predetermined. These motives will most likely be inherently interlinked, overlapping, and constitutive of each other, as well as shaped by other clusters of motives that at different points in the research process can take on more weight and significance.

For the experiment in precarious methods, what motives I have considered to be important have shifted and changed countless times. The motives I will discuss here should therefore not be seen as the planned, definitive, and coherent set of motives that have informed this experiment in precarious methods. That I ended up discussing these motives should perhaps rather be seen as a temporary and arbitrary settlement of a multitude of shifting understandings entangled as much in memories of a past research process as the weighted immediacy of the present where I have sought temporary relief from unaffordable heating bills in the warmth of my university canteen.

Wreckage

It was in the wreckage left behind by immediate and continuous disruptions of lives that precarious methods emerged. Whilst traditional academic methods often seek to keep analytic distance from our damaged worlds, precarious methods were a set of experiments that tried to give some sense of wrecked worlds in all their conflicting messiness. This also meant that rather than trying to disentangle wreckage into predetermined paths of analytical and political certainty, I sought to keep the wreckage imbued with some of the multitudes of uncertain potentialities so that the implications of this wreckage were left open to be explored and determined by others.

Initially, wreckage was a background setting for the research. It was part of a wider academic justification for why the research was relevant. The argument was something like this – in order to understand the lived experiences of people in precarious circumstances, it was necessary to notice how these lives had been wrecked by the intertwining forces of unsettled employment patterns, migration regimes, worsening housing crises, and the withdrawal of the welfare state. Looking at the academic literature, it was possible to draw up a canvas that could give a robust yet distant view of social, economic, and political forces sweeping through people' lives.

There were outlines of how Fordist visions of work had been torn up. Notions that standard employment models, unions, and the welfare state would raise people out of poverty and bring increasing economic stability, and wellbeing for workers had turned out to be at best a short-lived moment in history (Breman, 2011) and at worst an ideal that has always been far removed from the lived reality of workers (Gambino, 2007; Neilson and Rossiter, 2008). Instead, work was characterised by low-paid, insecure, and short-term jobs with limited rights, high levels of surveillance, and work stress and pressures that encroach on and shape all aspects of social life (Kalleberg, 2009; Weeks, 2011; Woodcock, 2017). These working conditions together with changing welfare provisions resulted in growing numbers of working poor (Andreß and Lohmann, 2008), increasing levels of food insecurities (Jenkins et al., 2021), and consistently high levels of income and wealth inequalities (Advani et al., 2021).

Concurrently, it was possible to draw out how there was an ongoing international housing crisis causing financial upheavals, making urban housing increasingly unaffordable, resulting in the creation of generations of renters and increasing homelessness (Byrne, 2020; Fields and Hodkinson, 2018). This happened at the same time as gentrification pressures continued to displace working-class communities, whilst past disruptions of deindustrialisation are still palpable (Atkinson and Bridge, 2004; Lees et al., 2013; Morris, 2018; Strangleman, 2017). As the housing situation became more precarious and more people ended up being on the move through endless short-term rented places, there were concerns that these developments unsettled long-held social stabilities (Bone, 2014).

Politically disarrangements could also be brought into play. Previous dominant ideas that competent welfare states could gain popular support by steering societies towards ever more secure and wealthy lives could no longer be maintained. Instead, governments gained legitimacy by managing and minimising the political fallout of increasing precarity by preventing any credible political alternatives (Lorey, 2015). This politicisation of precariousness tied in with the rise of populist movements that sought to 'take back control' in a world where power was seen to be slipping away from idealised homogeneous nation states to diffuse and uncertain forces that threatened the notion of deep-rooted communities of belonging (Kallis, 2018).

These dynamics could also be weaved into the emergence of increasingly restrictive migration regimes that were supported by new technologies of 'everyday bordering' that attempted to order and control diversity (Yuval-Davis et al., 2018). Furthermore, increasing migration flows of low-wage workers had been facilitated by global neoliberal economic policies that through the deregulation of employment and the labour market had created conditions that made it necessary for many to migrate to find work and survive (Wills et al., 2010). This interaction of restrictive immigration policies and neoliberal upheavals creating low-paid migrants interacted to create the conditions of hyper-precarity where migrant workers with few rights were forced into exploitative and unfree labour (Lewis et al., 2015).

This canvas of havoc and wreckage drawn up by traditional academic methods and analysis was not wrong. Yet as life became entangled in the research, it was no longer possible to view it with the privileged knowledge that it was just a distant background picture that could easily be disengaged and forgotten. Instead, you increasingly found yourself living in worlds that had been wrecked and where the havoc never stopped. In these worlds, people had been lost to you and more lives were taken away through it all. Your homes had been ruined and new ones continued to be crushed. Work had torn down who you used to be, and relentlessly it haunted you through every waking and sleeping hour. Your naïve expectations of a presence full of life with all its twists and turns had been flattened into a ceaseless hunt to make it through just another moment and your' vague dreams of future change were being smothered against ever more narrow possible horizons. You found yourself like debris being crashed into places you never wished for and any delusion of transcending these currents to trespass into safer grounds evaporated against towers of ever more violent borders and impossible demands. Yet amongst this wreckage, you lived, and life unfolded into a multitude of confusing, uncertain, interdependent patterns. In these unsettled worlds, you were thrown together with unknown others and in these shattered conditions, you found new forms of living, belonging and being part of wrecked worlds and others.

When I went back to my academic home, the wreckage never stopped, yet I found myself being drawn into telling stories and trying to make sense of this wreckage as if they were not part of unfolding worlds and lives. As I tried to tell these stories, I also started to doubt what the purpose of my particular attempt at research could and should be. I was lost and I didn't know how to move on. At the time I wrote down these thoughts about some of my frustrations:

> I'm talking with a friend about life in the field. The 50 hours plus work week, the chronic lack of sleep, my slowly crumbling body, people fainting, getting into ambulances, smoking themselves into weed zombies, mumbling conspiracy theories through the night, going days without food. I catch myself talking like I'm performing a drama, like telling lines from an apocalyptic W.B. Yeats poem:[5]
>
> > Things fall apart
> > The centre cannot hold.
>
> The fieldwork stories of distilled despair are the ones that elicit the greatest response. I can sense how they invoke a surge of empathy, of pity 'the poor things', 'what a life to live'. These tales of darkness also invoke a glimmer of hope for heroic paths we could take. The stories trace out the contours of new and old causes to fight, causes to change and save the lives of others. One way of life, our way of life, saving another. A chance to bring them from the dark into the light. A path to shine a light on the issue, as one of the anti-trafficking charities would say.
>
> When I tell these stories I'm not telling lies, per se, but I'm invoking a drama, a calling for our emotions and intercession, an overture before the intervention. Something needs to be done. This darkness, this misery

cannot stand. Else the centre cannot hold, and mere anarchy would be loosed upon the world. And we can't have that, can we?

At other times the stories I tell take another shape. These are stories of resistance, grit, and hope. About how people drag their feet, ignore orders, cleverly dodge work surveillance, play the hostel system to their advantage, and through their everyday activities challenge an overarching capitalist system. I have a greater personal affinity with these stories, who doesn't like people punching up? 'But does it matter?' is a question that quickly comes up within conversations and my own musings. Can these small acts of resistance really change anything? And can they be scaled up? Can they be ordered, reined in, and used to push through wider national or global social change? Whether those changes are framed as a wish for greater and more powerful unions, a change in parliamentary power, or maybe even imagined as a singular revolutionary path out of capitalism, they all seek to appropriate, control or at least nudge people in the right direction. Like people are nothing but unfinished revolutionary heroes waiting for a vanguard, a new leadership, a new group of people to manage and direct them towards a better world.

I tell other stories too. Stories that create more confusion than clarity. About how I hadn't had a proper night's sleep for months since leaving the hostel to come back to my university flat, the lack of sound from other people keeping me awake; how trying not to work with my colleagues at my warehouse job was more fun than I ever had in a well-paid middle-class civil servant job; how the sociality of hostel life was scattered with moments of creative poetic joy; and how the regular well-paid office job that some of the people in the hostel found didn't bring them one step closer to the life they wanted to live. It doesn't get better when I start to tell vague stories that are closer to the messiness of everyday life, where things are not separated out and assembled into neat narrative lines and tensions. Stories where there are no angels giving us guiding lights; no victims covering in the dark; and no working-class heroes flying free after overcoming the impossible odds of this world. Stories where people did not stick to the script, did not conform to purified expectations of how they ought to behave, where all we are left with is a mess of people still being human through it all.

These stories tend to receive a more muted response. They don't carve out a clear path to salvation. They don't set out a clear course of action for change that can bring us to an imagined state of equilibrium where the saintly victims have been rescued and revolutionary heroes have been led down the righteous path to a world where the centre holds and everyone is as one common world spirit, and surely that would be better, right? And are some of these stories I tell not just romanticising brush strokes used to cover real suffering people who need our help and guidance for the good of everyone? And if we can't get that what is the purpose of doing this research in the first place? Should it have an impact? Should

> it help make the world a better place? Should it shape policies? Could it steer the actions of the state in the right direction? And should that impact be evidenced? Has the impact started when it is being mentioned in parliamentary reports? Or has the impact started once the civil servants take it up and bring the findings to the attention of the minister? Or is research a self-defence weapon that can be yielded to fight against oppression and carve out better futures by revealing the inherent contradictions and power dynamics of our world (Morrow and Brown, 1994)? Is research about opening up windows to other worlds and future possibilities by translation and creating communicative links between different worlds (Asad, 1986)? Or is it perhaps a collaboration? One community of scholars bringing their time and analytic resources to a community, as a resource to wield however they like, as a gift with all its possibilities and doubled-edged responsibilities (Graeber, 2004)?

My experiments with precarious methods were tied in with these uncertainties and anxieties. They were a series of attempts to find ways that could give a sense of the implications of living in wrecked worlds in ways that did not solidify into predetermined analytic patterns of sense making, whilst also doing research that had some implications, however undefined and messy they might be. Wreckage was a growing motive that informed these experiments both in the sense that they grew out of and were entangled in wrecked worlds, and also in terms of trying to keep some of the disruptive, rebellious, and perhaps even emancipatory potentials that wreckage could also entail. Lives were continuously wrecked by the havoc of economic transformations, unsettled labour markets, housing crises, and restructured state interventions, yet as life unfolded across hostels, warehouses, and call centres in some social moments, this wreckage could be used to throw together barricades that could disrupt, diverge, and protect against these devastating forces. In the rubble that was left behind, people also continuously probed and sought out ways to use the debris to build up and explore new forms of life and socialities that would not have been possible otherwise. Whilst I had no illusions of ever being able to give a full sense of these aspects, the precarious methods were an attempt to give some sense of how this wreckage unfolded throughout the research.

In some ways, this idea of considering the potentialities of wreckage to create transformations overlaps with Beck's arguments about climate change and the 'positive side effects of bads' (Beck, 2015: 79), where global risk creates normative horizons filled with potential emancipatory effects. Wreckage, if understood in terms of seeking to cause disruption, block powerful processes, intervene in patterns of oppression, and instigate transformative possibilities, has also played a part in much academic analysis. This use of wreckage can perhaps be seen in Marxist attempts to integrate analytical, theoretical, and critical perspectives to pull apart oppressive ideological practices (Celikates, 2012); in feminist theories that seek to interrupt and reconstitute historically contingent political and social practices that maintain the incarcerating of lifeworlds into a binary gendered iron cage (Butler, 1999; Haraway, 1989); and in postcolonial endeavours to disrupt discursively enacted processes of ordering and othering the world into hierarchical ordered cultural units of purity and differentiation (Abu-Lughod, 1996; Said, 1979).

Where my experiments with precarious methods differed from these approaches was perhaps that I tried to be more hesitant about predetermining how to make sense of and guide the disruptive and emancipatory potentials of wreckage. Instead, by maintaining and holding up different wrecked realities, I sought to give a sense of some of the multiple, incomprehensible, and contradictory implications that wreckages could have. I wanted to give a sense of how wreckage could fragment and shift across unfolding moments of traumatic social, political, and economic ruptures tearing life apart; affective calls for everything between revolutionary change and pitiful interventions; and haphazard gatherings of wreckage where lonely tears, screams, and silences were wrapped in the sudden surges of care and comfort of others. What I tried to do was to maintain the wreckages of which I was part during the research as undetermined artefacts that were imbued with a multitude of potential implications that were inherently interdependent on the lives of unknown others – unknown others, like you the reader.

Survival

Survival emerged as a motive in all aspects of the research process. In the field, how to make it through another day at work and move towards more survivable worlds created patterns of experimentation, innovation, hopes, and practices amongst all the people I lived and worked with. Similarly, when I came back from the field, my own personal concern often centred around the possibility and practice of surviving life in academia. As the research process unfolded, it also became clear that this attempt to survive in the worlds of which I was part was inseparable from what methods it was possible to use and therefore also what types of realities could emerge from the writing.

The motive of survival was therefore integral to how precarious methods emerged. There are multiple different ways in which this was expressed, but there were some particular registers of survival I found important. First, how to survive emerged as an immediate concern in a complex and ever-unfolding present. By that, I mean that survival was a constant question about how to make it through another moment, another hour, another day without being pulled under and apart by the onslaught of upheavals, pressures, and impositions that work and life threw at you. The immediate concern was therefore how best to manoeuvre and minimise the impacts of these pressures. Another key register of survival was how best to move towards other more survivable worlds. The motive was not only how to make it through this moment in time, but also how to envision and move towards other ways of being and surviving in this world. These motives hinged on shifting hopes that it was possible to reconfigure your place in the world in order to become emancipated from current oppressive and overwhelming modes of survival.

In the field, I encountered a variety of entangled practices, strategies, and hopes that sought to deal with these different registers of survival. As described in the main parts of the book, how to make it through another moment at work was a concern that spurned constant philosophising, innovations, experimentations, and exchange of 'best practices' amongst workers. Similarly, when seeking more long-term emancipation from precarious work and life, multiple avenues were explored. Some had aspirations of becoming part of entirely different lived realities, whether that took the form of winning the capitalist lottery and becoming included in the billionaire class or the creation of postcapitalist worlds. In other instances, more survivable worlds were sought in a reconfiguration of the self and its relations to what kind of worlds it was part of. Embodied philosophical, religious, and scientific methods were explored to seek out paths towards more survivable worlds and at other times people would experiment with mixtures and usages of substances in the hope that they could bring about a new self that was better suited to survive the wreckage in which they found themselves.

These issues of survival also played out within academic worlds where increasingly precarious circumstances exacerbated patterns of inequalities and oppression with impacts across people's social and affective lives (Burton and Bowman, 2022). Precarious academics increasingly found themselves in a continuous present where the promise of a settled future never arrived (Bone, 2019). In the United Kingdom, where I was based during the research process, 54% of the academic staff were on precarious and insecure contracts (UCU, 2016a); wages in real terms had fallen by up to 17% since 2009 (Eyles, 2019); workload had increased, resulting in academics delivering on average two days of unpaid work per week, with part-time workers proportionally working longer for free (UCU, 2016b); and mental health issues were rampant, with indications of up to 43% of academic staff displaying 'at least a mild mental disorder' (Gorczynski et al., 2017: 2), with some initial research finding that 41% thought that workload had 'a lot' of negative effects on their mental health (UCU, 2018: 14).

During the research process, there were sporadic instances of strikes and people joining in pickets across university campuses. However, these instances were still uncommon and most of the time you tried to make your way through the everyday working life of academia. In this setting, one of the most common strategies that were used to make academia more survivable was to rely on the dominant methods of the discipline to highlight how patterns of exploitation and inequality were intertwined in academic practices. Ray's (2019) work, for example, uses this strategy by using a comprehensive understanding of sociological theory to reveal the disconnect between sociological theories and practices in relation to structure and individual achievement, whilst laying out how this disconnect helps maintain racial inequalities by hiding the fact 'that every "individual career" is ultimately a collective endeavor' (Ray, 2019: 4).

Similarly, Bhatt's research displays a comprehensive and deep understanding of sociological theory to draw out its historical developments and its relations to racism and inequality in order to establish how the 'Western sociological discipline concerns itself almost exclusively with white European and North American lives and, in that and other senses, makes and remakes itself as a white discipline' (Bhatt, 2016: 398).

There is also one of the great contemporary thinkers of sociology, Dorothy Smith, who in an expertly crafted, insightful, and intellectually exhaustive analysis explores issues of alienation of women in sociology. In her analysis she shows how sociological thought, methods, concepts, and subject area of study 'has been based on and built up within, the male social universe' (Smith, 1974b: 7), resulting in the subordination of the concrete particulars of women's experiences. This, in turn, results in alienation that:

> posits a relation between the work an individual does and an external order which oppresses her, such that the harder she works the more she

> strengthens the order which oppresses her. This is the situation of women in this relation. The more successful women are in mediating the world of concrete particulars so that men do not have to become engaged with (and therefore conscious of) that world as a condition to their abstract activities, the more complete man's absorption in it, the more effective the authority of that world and the more total women's subservience to it. And also the more complete the dichotomy between the two worlds, and the estrangement between them. (Smith, 1974b: 10)

Using dominant methods to bring out singular theoretically informed realities as a way to highlight how academic practices reinforce different patterns of inequalities and exclusion can be tremendously useful to move towards more survivable worlds, but I have some worries about relying solely on that strategy. My concern is that whilst this kind of research can expertly uncover hidden structures of oppression within academia, at the same time we can find ourselves in a situation as described by Smith, where the methods and practices we use end up reinforcing the very patterns of oppression and exclusion we seek to escape.

For me, I found that relying solely on registers of survival that focused on creating new future realities by utilising the traditional methods and practices of academia both risked making the present more unlivable and undermining my aspirations of more survivable worlds. Looking at it in terms of precariousness, the issue is that at least some of the dominant methods in academia have been carved out and maintained by nonprecarious lived experiences that through various kinds of financial, temporal, and spatial constellations have allowed for 'deep' theoretical engagement and thinking. The type of methods that are deemed to be more reliable and robust are also the kinds of methods whose production is reliant on a privileged intersection[6] of social positions resulting in, amongst other things, financial stability, greater amounts of free time to do conceptual work, and having to deal less with the disturbing mess of a nonconceptual world.[7]

When an academic from a socially more precarious position squeezes out some 'free time' by cutting away their weekend, holidays, and the hours they rest and sleep so that they can work for free, unpaid, on a conceptually deep analysis that might expose the very exploitation under which they are working, do they not at the same time help reinforce the very system that creates the conditions of their precarious situation? And does it even matter, then, if this work is done in the vague hope that exposing these inequalities will make a difference in some unknown future?

My sense – though this is not a strong conviction – is that it can be problematic to rely exclusively on methods that have been crafted in the furnaces of privileged social positions. Perhaps by doing so, we risk maintaining practices that reinforce academic divides between a privileged 'professor class' that through its social position is consistently enabled to reproduce deep and theoretically robust academic research, and a precarious academic class, whose social positioning in a messy precarious world makes it almost impossible to produce the 'right' kind of disentangled, deep, and insightful theoretical work that is needed to be deemed worthy of belonging to the privileged classes of academia.

However, our attachments to particular methods, even if they end up threatening our very survival, are perhaps also filled with hope and optimism about the kind of futures they are seen to be able to bring about. This can relate to how we use traditional academic methods in the hope that they can progress our careers so that we eventually will accumulate enough job security, wealth, and prestige to liberate us from the precariousness of the world and achieve the 'good life'. Similarly, we also attach much hope to how our traditional methods can help change the world by creating ironclad analysis that can cut through the mess. To shift hope away from traditional methods therefore also threatens to undermine the very optimism that keeps us going.

To experiment with precarious methods, it is therefore also important to recognise the cruel optimistic properties that our attachment to methods can have. As Berlant has comprehensively explored, cruel optimism is 'a relation of attachment to compromised conditions of possibility whose realization is discovered either to be impossible, sheer fantasy, or too possible, and toxic' (Berlant, 2011: 25). What makes these attachments cruel is that although they are detrimental to the wellbeing of the subject, 'the continuity of its form provides something of the continuity of the subject's sense of what it means to keep on living on and to look forward to being in the world' (Berlant, 2011: 25). I have a sense that for me and perhaps others, our attachment to particular methods is often shaped by similar dynamics. We hope that if only we hold on for just a little bit longer, if only we deploy the methods that we have dear in just the right way, and write long and loud enough truths, perhaps it will bring about the right kinds of insights, policies, and lives that we have so long been longing for. As such, reorienting hope or optimism away from the traditional methods we have been using also has implications for how we survive in this world. Precarious methods are therefore also an experiment in trying to find more survivable methods whilst recognising that much of the impetus that keeps us moving is tied in with particular disciplinary and academic methods, and the cruel optimistic hopes of present and future worlds they can bring about.

The motive for experimenting with precarious methods was therefore, amongst many things, an attempt to seek out new practices and methods that would enable new patterns of survival whilst navigating our tenuous and cruel relationships with the methods we hold dear. It was an attempt to enact research practices that could encompass some concern with registers of immediate survival and belonging. It was also done in the vague hope that experiments like this might play a small part in moving towards a palette of methods and research practices in academia that are more aligned with the multitude of lived realities and patterns of survival in an unfolding precarious world.

To do this, I took inspiration from how the people I lived with in the field experimented and probed to find ways of minimising the impact of the work regimes in which they were implicated. I tried to convince myself that trying to live up to the ever-increasing standards and expectations created for someone else's benefit would do me little good. However, at the same time, I also realised that in order to survive within academia, I needed to comply somewhat with the dominant patterns of how academic practice and methods were supposed to look like. Most of these experiments with how to survive did not leave any textual traces, just as most ways of evading crunching work pressures in the field worked best if they left no visible evidence behind. Even if I tried my best, I am not sure that I would be able to disentangle the process in order to present a neat story of how exactly I sought to enact more survivable practices in the research process.

However, I think that these attempts of enacting survivable precarious methods have perhaps left a few visible traces in the different parts of the book. Seeking out and following these traces could give some indication of how the figure of me as a precarious academic attempt to navigate the space between aligning with dominant academic methods that assume privileged social positions and the desire to use precarious methods that potentially can open up for other ways of surviving in a precarious world.

Looking at Part I, the figure of the precarious academic seems to be almost entirely absent and the methods that are used try as much as possible to align with traditional ways of enacting proper methods. The academic might not be explicitly mentioned in the text, but their presence is implied. The way in which the methods have been brought together is done in such a way that whilst it denies that the academic has any relevance to the 'findings' of the research, it concurrently also makes a claim that this piece of research should be a reflection of their individual abilities and competences as an academic. It can seem like the use of dominant methods is not only utilised to bring out the most accurate reflection of an imagined singular underlying reality but is also employed in the hope that it could portray just enough privileged academic 'depth' to the analysis so that the precarious academic can pass as someone who belongs.

In Part II, the research process that emerges is messy, convoluted, contradictory, and multiple, and it can at times seem deeply interlinked with the precarious unwieldy world that it seeks to describe as a separate entity in Part I. There are also traces that indicate that not only is the world complex and messy, but that it also takes time and effort to try to contain that world within traditional methods premised on singularity, coherence, and conclusive finality. The figure of the academic is exposed as an imposter who is not quite in the position of being able to produce insightful and theoretically deep academic work, yet tries to use a range of different tools, practices, and self-managerial disciplinary actions to create academic research that can make it seem like they do have those abilities. There are, however, also traces of ambivalence and outright resistance against these efforts to enforce self-compliance. In some moments, there are also indications that the precarious academic are exploring other ways of surviving and collaborating through the continuously wrecked worlds in which they find themselves.

Read in this way, the figure of the precarious academic that emerges in Part III is perhaps more ambivalent and fractured. There are indications that they are present as part of a research project that is premised on an imagined separation from the unfolding weighted present of life in the 'field'. Yet, in the multiple, confusing, unclear, and unsettled fragments that emerge in this part, there are perhaps also traces of other more interdependent and multiple ways of making sense of and surviving a precarious world.

Within these traces, amongst the fragmented chatter, unfolding socialities, and vulnerable sense of belonging, the precarious researcher that emerges is not only one who has ventured into the field in order to help 'solve' its problems with their fine-tuned, reality-grabbing methods. Instead, there are traces of *something* else that could indicate potential realities with other ways of surviving and approaching life in a precarious world.

How these precarious methods have been enacted has left many tensions unresolved. Whilst it tries to imitate nonprecarious academic methods with their accompanying measures of success, at the same time, this pretence is accompanied by attempts to undermine these methods by deliberately failing to meet all of the standards they require. Another tension is embedded in the contradiction of seeking hope and transformative potentials in the precarious social lives from which these experiments emerge, whilst also having clandestine hopes that one day it would be possible to belong to a nonprecarious academic class, even though that would perpetuate an academic social system that hinges on exclusion and inequality.

This experiment in precarious methods has been imperfect, faulty, and incomplete, almost regardless of what types of measure you can hold it up against. However, by allowing the methods to be shaped by motives of survival, it also created new potentialities for me to survive at least momentarily in new more liveable, interdependent, and collaborative ways. How exactly I tried to use precarious methods to survive is not possible to replicate. In a precarious world that constantly throws up new patterns of havoc, insecurities, and oppression, there is no single way to survive it all. If there is any significance to precarious methods it is therefore not to provide a pre-ordained roadmap on how to use methods in more survivable ways, but rather to insist that surviving the mess in which we find ourselves should matter, even if we were never meant to survive.

Vulnerability

Shifting, conflicting, and at times overlapping forms of vulnerability were troubled undercurrents that ran through policy documents, academic texts, and lived experiences during the research. Precarious methods were partly contingent on these currents, and the shapes that the methods took were done as an attempt to adapt to the changing forms of vulnerabilities.

When I was working on labour exploitation issues in the civil service, some variation of the term 'precariousness' might come up now and again, but 'vulnerability' was a more commonly used term. It was often used in the context of differentiation and labelling people who were considered to be more exposed to exploitation and unable to protect themselves from harm. It was therefore considered necessary for the government in collaboration with its stakeholder partners in local government, enforcement agencies, charities, NGOs, and academia, to design, implement, and evaluate policies that could provide the help and protection that these vulnerable people could not themselves provide. Who was considered vulnerable and what factors created this vulnerability could be issues of much contestation between different people and organisational factions. What role issues such as insecure housing, addiction, troubled families, abusive relationships, migration status, and country of origin related to the creation of more vulnerable social positions were debated, sometimes passionately in public and behind safely closed doors.

Despite these contestations, there was some common ground. Vulnerabilities were considered as something belonging to a limited group of people who due to this very vulnerability needed policy interventions and protection. This also meant that the questions that were raised, the direction of the policy gaze, and the bureaucratic practices that were planned and executed ended up being almost exclusively focused on vulnerable people however they might be defined at any particular moment. The effects of this were that the solutions that were created to address this problem tended to focus on the role of powerful stakeholder institutions and what potential interventions they could come up with to 'solve' the problem. This meant that in this political and academic vision of the world, people's vulnerable and precarious lives became associated with an unruly and disruptive part of the world in need of order and security.

When I initially ventured into the field, how I imagined my research would play out was at least to some extent informed by similar notions. When I chose to stay in hostels and work in warehouses and call centres, it was because I had some expectation that people would be more precarious and therefore also more vulnerable in those social settings. Sure, I wanted to get their views and I might have had a hunch that the policy narratives about their lives were disconnected from their lived realities and that they could have harmful implications. After all, the academic literature is littered with countless examples of how scientific, political, and social concepts, and categories in the nexus of patriarchal, nation-state, postcolonial and capitalist systems can have extensive and often devastating, impacts on the lives of the people exposed to these processes (Abu-Lughod, 1996; Butler, 1999; Said, 1979; Tyler, 2013). When groups of comparatively powerful people use particular terms to delineate and describe marginalised groups, we should therefore at the very least be careful, no matter what the stated intentions of those people are. Nonetheless, my thoughts were still informed by the notion that the people I would research were vulnerable, that this vulnerability was a key part of the problem, and I hoped that researching their lived experiences could help inform the creation of better ways to tackle the issues they faced.

However, as I went to the 'field', people pushed back against any notion that they needed rescuing by distant policy makers. Whenever I mentioned how some of the policies and initiatives that stakeholders, policy makers, and academics had cooked up, they were at best met with disinterest and, if there were any reaction, it was hardly positive. When I mentioned that government-centred stakeholders thought that exploitative labour practices were caused by organised crime that took advantage of vulnerable people (Broadbent and Green, 2017), the claim was met with disbelief and derision. The notion held within many policy and academic assemblages that more decent jobs could be an avenue for more secure and stable lives didn't fare much better. Rather than being seen as a promise of order and strength, it was often taken more as a threat that there would never again be a respite from the hardship of work.

Although this more explicit pushback caused troubles, what thoroughly fragmented and tore apart the notion that vulnerability was a marker of problematic life happened as I was slowly becoming part of the rhythmic beat of everyday life at work and in the hostel. For sure, if the visions of policy makers were applied, some of the people I lived and worked with could have been classified as vulnerable. Broken and abusive relationships, addiction, mental health issues, uncertain migration status, suffocating debt, and chronic insecure housing were not uncommon issues. However, what became clear was that within the social settings of fellow workers and hostel dwellers, this vulnerability did not manifest itself as a weakness that would be ceaselessly exploited; rather, in most cases being vulnerable became an invitation to care, a receptivity to be part of unfolding social lives in all their multitude, and a realisation that to make it through this wrecked world in which you find yourself, you have to rely on and be relied on by others.

When I returned to my academic 'home' and started my attempts of writing up the research, I found it difficult to use traditional research methods to grasp and convey something that related to the kind of vulnerable realities I had encountered. Initially, I tried to use methods that portrayed themselves as being solely concerned with presenting a singular underlying reality in the most robust and unquestionable way. However, I realised that the reality that emerged from these methods aligned more with how vulnerability and precariousness were portrayed within policy and stakeholder worlds than with how they unfolded amongst the people I lived and worked with.

I found that using traditional research methods whose values were evaluated against criteria of separation, strength, coherence, and singular certainties closed down the more vulnerable, messy, conflicting, and intertwined lifeworlds I tried to give a sense of. Although I might have tried to give the point of view of 'precarious people', I ended up using similar methods as other policy and stakeholders, and thereby created realities that aligned with the same policy views that were met with so much indifference and apprehension by the people in the field.

At the same time, other parts of 'academic life' started to become harder to ignore. There were long periods of strike action seeking to address the ever more precarious situation of working in academia and throughout the research process, there were tensions about the amount of free labour graduate teaching assistants and part-time employed people like myself provided to the university. These conflicts tied into perceptions of an academic sector that, at least in a UK context, seemed to become ever more precarious and exploitative. For me, living and being part of this academia also meant that precarious vulnerabilities were not something I left behind in the field. For a period whilst being employed as a lecturer, I suddenly found myself living in a hostel again and when I did find a flat, the mould and lack of heating impacted my health. Although things were kept under wraps, there were also hints that colleagues struggled with issues of food insecurities, lack of housing, mental health issues, fuel poverty, troubled relationships, addiction, and isolation.

However, these lived vulnerabilities in academia did not have the same implications as they had in the hostel and at the workplaces of which I was briefly part. To make sense of these differences it can be helpful to consider

> Sorry, this will be a bit of an academic interlude that will probably be edited out. When I was writing this part, I tried to find and grab onto a neat academic term that could somehow encompass these exact differences. At one point I thought about using the notion of reification to argue that vulnerabilities in academia in particular were reified into entities disentangled from the immediate, messy, vulnerable moments they emerged from. By reification, I meant something along the lines in the quote below which is a paraphrasing by Chari of Lukács approach to the term:
>
>> Reification is characterized by a lack of participatory involvement (Teilnahmslosigkeit) in soczial objects, whereby humans apprehend 'things' in the world as inert objects to which human consciousness merely conforms rather than actively constructs. (Chari, 2010: 589)

I also thought about clinging on to Smith's work on 'Theorizing as Ideology' (Smith, 1974a) to have a comforting analytical framework that could also give a veneer of academic credibility to the analysis and me. Drawing on Marx's work, Smith talks about how the process of making ideological representations is similar to the methodological tricks that are used to make theory. The three ideological tricks in Smith's version are:

> Trick 1. Separate what people say they think from the actual circumstances in which it is said, from the actual empirical conditions of their lives and from the actual individuals who said it. Trick 2. Having detached the ideas, they must now be arranged. Prove then an order among them which accounts for what is observed. Marx and Engels describe this as making 'mystical connections' . . . Trick 3. The ideas are then changed 'into a person', that is they are constituted as distinct entities to which agency (or possibly causal efficacy) may be attributed. And they may be re-attributed to 'reality' by attributing them to actors who now represent the ideas. (Smith, 1974a: 1)

Both of these approaches come to mind because I have taught them before, so they were more convenient to link up with than other potential theoretical frameworks. Maybe reification and theorising as ideology and the interrelationship between them could be used to make sense of how vulnerabilities had different implications in my academic home compared to the field. However, I am sure other analytical terms would be just as useful and perhaps there is also an argument that settling on one analytical framework to make sense of this misses the point. So I think it will be better to leave it undecided and open to be impinged on by others. Instead, let me try and describe some examples of how I thought vulnerabilities had different implications in academia compared to the field.

When I came back to my academic home, I noticed that despite the increasing work pressures, precarious circumstances, and a shattering pandemic that scattered people apart, there would still be the occasional moments where academic colleagues could share troubles and socialities.

When these sudden surges of social moments emerged, they would be filled with exasperated chats about the absurdities of management and university policies, overwork, discrimination, or some other immediate issue people faced. Now and again, these shared moments could build social bonds and allow for greater interdependencies just like at the other workplaces of which I was part in the field.

Yet often these chats would end up gravitating towards broader, more analytical discussions about university and state policies, and perhaps some academic research that was recently read would be brought into the conversation. As these vulnerable social moments unfolded, it tended to become less about how to face and live with this immediate and immensely messy shared moment, and more about how best to disconnect vulnerabilities from the shared entangled present moment so that they could be tackled as distanced more coherent and less volatile issues.

It was a subtle difference and I probably wouldn't have noticed it if I had not just come back from the field. There I had experienced how my academic dispositions to shift vulnerable moments and conversations into analytical safety were insistently interrupted by a barrage of practices and social relations that kept them thoroughly anchored in the present, shared, and messy lifeworlds from which they emerged. As I became part of these lifeworlds, my inclination to seek comfort in distant academic analysis receded. For a brief period of time, I felt that perhaps it would be better to just stay in these messy patches of life where you could only make it through by staying with the vulnerabilities of yourself and others. When I was drawn back to my academic job and 'home', these seemingly subtle differences in terms of how vulnerabilities were handled engendered unsettling shocks that instigated ongoing emotional re-adjustments and dreams of refuge.

Besides how vulnerabilities were handled in immediate social moments, I also found that how I tried to write about vulnerabilities could create troubles. This became particularly visible when I started to experiment with fragments that tried to apprehend messy, unfolding, and interconnected vulnerabilities of life in the field. These fragments did not cause much trouble when I showed them to people I knew through fieldwork and life lived outside academia. Sometimes they would not elicit much reaction, but at times they would resonate and play into the memories and rhythms of people's past and present experiences.

However, when showing these fragments to people in academia, they often caused trouble. One way in which these troubles could manifest was as pushback against the worlds they tried to portray. For example, when I at workshops and conferences presented fragmented texts that tried to apprehend something about vulnerabilities in all their divergent multitudes, a common line of responses was similar to this feedback I received in a workshop:

> What you describe sounds really nice, people are being kind, don't turn on the light if people are sleeping, and just getting along . . . where are all the ruins?'

This and similar comments stuck with me. Did my experiments with precarious methods end up romanticising life in the field? Did they end up being a reflection of my growing nostalgia for life in the hostel? A life where vulnerabilities seemed to enable mutual support and create patterns of sociality, rather than leading to increasing patterns of individualisation and self-punishing work patterns that I experienced in academia. I could not deny that this was the case.

Or were there maybe also other factors at play? Perhaps these fragments were considered problematic because they implicitly raised questions about some entrenched notions of what the relationship and power dynamic between academic research and their vulnerable research subjects should be. These fragments did perhaps give hints of realities where vulnerabilities unfolded in ways that were not ripe to passively receive robust academic analysis that could pave the way towards rescuing policy interventions or revolutions. Maybe these fragments also unsettled taken-for-granted visions of academia as the eminent creator and gift giver of insightful knowledge that could address the vulnerabilities of the world. By giving a few glimpses of how immediate and unfolding vulnerabilities could lead to unexpected moments of solidarity, interdependence, and resistance in ways that could not quite be encapsulated by traditional academic methods and practices, it perhaps implicitly indicated that in some circumstances, it was academic practices and worlds that were lacking and in need of vulnerable interventions from the field.

Another way in which these fragments created troubles was that for many academics, they didn't seem to make much sense. A common line of feedback was that the fragments 'did not integrate into any theoretical dimensions and therefore ended up standing on its own'. It seemed that without a reassuring theoretical framework to guide the academic reader, these fragments' vulnerable, wrecked, incomplete, and disorderly states of world making came across as senseless, isolated, and perhaps even slightly pitiful. When reviewers urged for the full force of insightful and orderly academic analysis to be applied, it was perhaps done in the belief that only this would enable these fragments to be rescued from their exposed seclusion and brought back into the community of comforting academic meaning making and practice. I might be overinterpreting things here, but these kinds of responses reminded me of how vulnerable lifeworlds were considered to be exposed, isolated, helpless, and in urgent need of robust policy interventions. So when these fragments created this urge for analytical intervention and order making, it perhaps played into the same emotional and analytical registers as when policy makers and stakeholders with rightful urgency seek to bring *their* order to vulnerable lives.

I also wonder if these interventions that tried to bring proper academic order to these messy fragments tied in with registers of concern and care for fellow academics making their way in an increasingly precarious academic world. If we consider that academics 'worth' largely hinges on whether they can use the right kind of methods to produce linear, strong, and robust research outputs that are publishable and citeable, then it can also seem like the only hope of ever reaching more secure life situations within academia is to succeed according to these criteria. When being exposed to vulnerable fragments that are unfinished, full of uncertainties, and riddled with contradictions, should a caring academic not try to remould them into 'proper' academic outputs? Are these editorial suggestions about how to steer the texts towards acceptable realities not just an act of kindness that can lend a hand to a fellow precarious academic so that they can move towards greater academic prestige, career progress, and stable lifeworlds?

However, I also fear that these registers of care can risk co-opting vulnerabilities into already highly individualised research cultures. As vulnerabilities are continuously remoulded in ways that disentangle them from the vulnerable social worlds from which they emerge, these vulnerabilities can become instrumentalised as a means to generate ever more publications and theoretical insights that can be attributed to individual academics caught in an everlasting isolated chase for security and stability that never arrives. So although I, like many other academics, found myself in increasingly vulnerable and precarious circumstances, the way in which these vulnerabilities unfolded within the particularities of academic worlds could end up exacerbating social orders that hinged on entrenched hierarchies and ever greater self-reliance, competition and social desolation.

To use traditional methods in those circumstances would have meant that the realities I could bring out would align more with hierarchical policy and stakeholder perceptions of vulnerability than what was happening in the field, and it risked processing my own vulnerabilities into the tools of my own oppression. So I started to experiment with precarious methods. What else could I do?

How Did You Experiment with Precarious Methods?

The first thing I tried to do was to make the text more precarious in the hope that it would enable more divergent apprehensions about vulnerable lifeworlds and their unexpected patterns of socialities, care, resistance, and interdependencies. To do that, I ended up juxtaposing different realities and methods in the three main parts of the book. I initially thought that just having a series of fragmented pieces of writing as in Part III of the book would be sufficient. Yet I found that if these fragments stood alone, they would not only be too easily dismissed as senseless by large groups of people steeped in academic traditions, but they also risked making implicit claims that the way in which they apprehended a precarious world was not only superior to other methods but also a reflection of the insightful competencies of the author.

So instead of having one singular set of realities and apprehensions, I gathered different methodological enacted realities that weaved across the research process with the aim of bringing forward and exposing how the research process was full of analytical uncertainties, inconsistencies, and multiplicities. Using methods that diffused and questioned the authority of the researcher could perhaps also threaten engrained yet rarely spoken notions of the heroic insightful academic who through rigorous methods uncovers vulnerabilities and bestows solutions to the problems in the world. By bringing forward and juxtapositioning different types of realities, I also hoped that this would make any tentative conclusions more brittle and engrain more explicit contradictions and uncertainties in the text that would enable the analysis to become more malleable, unfinished, and open to unknown collaborations and dependencies.

Given how vulnerabilities and precariousness were something that cut across and were intertwined in the different worlds of which I was part, I experimented with ways that could traverse these interconnections. This meant questioning the enforced divides and entrenched dynamics between the field and an assumed academic home. I tried to start to notice, question, re-examine, and write about my academic home as an integral part of the lifeworlds I was trying to make sense of. I explored whether putting fragments from life as it unfolded 'at home' and in the field could spark new interconnections and create space for apprehensions that went beyond sedentary notions of how lifeworlds across these settings related to each other. I hoped that by putting these different realities up against each other, it could perhaps counteract ever so slightly my own years of academic training with tendencies to valorise academic knowledge as inherently valuable gifts to a vulnerable world. By apprehending and implicitly contrasting different realities, I tried to bring out how vulnerabilities were not only intertwined across these lifeworlds but also had different implications that could not be condensed into simply binary narratives of strong rescuers and vulnerable victims, academic gift creators and unknowing receivers. What the relationship should be between academia and the world of which they are part is not something I seek to determine, but perhaps I at least want to question the wisdom of relying exclusively on strong robust academic analysis and practices to guide us through this mess in which we find ourselves without the helping and vulnerable hands of others.

What Characterises the Three Different Parts of the Book?

In Part I, I use more traditionally aligned methods to try to create a coherent, analytically robust, and academically convincing text that problematises the notion that the solution to precarious work is the promotion of decent work. I tried to draw on a range of academically verified sources, together with my selected and cleansed fieldwork findings, to support an analysis that argues that the concern with minimising the impact of work is one of the central dynamics that shape precarious work and life. Furthermore, I sought to illustrate how the desire to avoid the imposition of work plays into constantly changing and co-constituted patterns of everyday resistance and control.

I tried to present this analysis as a self-contained piece of work that described a singular reality with delineated dynamics and interrelationships. By structuring the analysis so that it came across as analytically robust and by framing the arguments in ways that aligned with academic disciplinary practices, I hoped that it would come across as a proper academic piece of work that might garner some interest from other researchers working on related topics.

Trying to convey this kind of impression meant that my role as a researcher was only brought up in connection with my presence in the field where I was described as a mere tool for data collection. By leaving out the practicalities of how the data analysis had been informed, it was implied that the only thing that mattered in shaping the analysis was my research findings from the field, and any discussion of what happened to that data between the time of collection and the finished product was irrelevant to the findings.

The type of reality and the particular analytical form I ended up portraying in Part I were not wrong. Yet it was the result of using methods that aligned with academic disciplinary practices and being part of social processes that all played a role in making a particular social reality visible. This also meant that the reality and analysis that was portrayed in the finalised version were just one out of many possibilities.

In Part II, I tried to pay attention to some of the things that are normally left unexplored in traditional methods. I examined how the analysis of Part I was not predetermined by the conditions of the field, but rather was shaped by multiple different factors. The different tools that were used, the kind of feedback I received, the particular patterns of work, and the authoritarian management techniques I sought to enforce upon myself all played a role in shaping the final analysis. I also sought to highlight how the finalised text had covered up how its conclusions, and its analytical argument were always in doubt right up until the finalised version.

Part II consists of more or less coherent scribbles that relate to the research process. These scribbles will take different forms. Some will be more analytical and directly guided towards the academic reader, some will be more explicitly allegorical in their form,[8] and yet others will be emotionally entangled in the moments in which they are written. Some will be more serious and dark in tone, and others will be more playful, ludic, and facetious. Most will be textual, but there will also be traces from the research process in the form of screenshots, software outputs, and other digital traces.

These traces and scribbles don't seek to portray a holistic narrative about how the research process 'really' happened; rather, at the most, they provide short flashes that briefly bring to light perspectives, moments, stories and entanglements from a complex and extensive research process. These flashes might not be able to make claims to a consistent narrative, but they can perhaps help to show that the robust and singular reality I created in Part I is built on ontologically and epistemologically precarious grounds.

Part III focuses on life as it unfolded in the field.[9] I try to let go of utopian research visions of order so that I can let things fall apart into more precarious, contaminated, and vulnerable fragments. The analysis was slowed down and I attempted to resist the ambitions of analytic coherence and order. It might come across as messy and vague, and it will probably be more difficult to make sense of for most people who are trained in academic customs. It is still endlessly distanced from the raw lived experiences of the field, but it has gone through fewer of the countless stages of academic processing and transformations that Part II describes. By stopping academic processing in its tracks, I hope to enable more spontaneous, fragmented, and vulnerable visions of precarious life as it was lived.

In contrast with the first two parts, a more diverse set of scenes and entanglements in the fragments are presented here. The reader might align some of the texts presented here with notions of 'work', but I imagine many parts of the texts will be hard to contain within any singular social and academic category. I wish I could have presented a more extensive array of textures that might have given a more weighted sense of how it was. However, no matter what amount of fragments, sceneries, and conversational flows I would have included, they would always have been arbitrary. What I experienced and how these experiences lingered or slipped away from memory and notes is never something that can be entirely planned out or delineated into coherence.

Most of the fragments are largely detached from the temporal ebbs and flows of how life is felt. In the field, some days hardly leave any impressions, traces, or notes. When you are in the moment, it might feel like something, but for some reason, it is not enough to linger so that it can leave notes and memories of a present that has already gone. On other days, the way in which things come together leaves more dense marks and will call back your attention to what life was like in these particular patches. How do you give a sense of that?

I was tempted to cut and paste memories and notes together so that they could be portrayed as a 'usual day' with occurrences evenly distributed throughout the day. However, portraying such a 'usual day' would actually be highly unusual. How the world comes together doesn't happen in evenly distributed intensities where a weighted present exerts equal amounts of pressure across temporally equivalent units of time. There will always be long stretches that, in hindsight, with our cultural-scientific inclinations, theoretically should be there with equal weight, but like dark matter are nowhere to be felt or seen. The way in which traces emerge in memories and written notes are also not bound by a temporal, sequential clock-time order. When sitting down to take notes and recall a lost present, there might initially be ambitions of keeping to a defined temporal order of the day, but sometimes something will trigger a memory that cannot quite be placed in a defined order.

To try to give some sense of these temporal aspects, I have chosen to insert some observational notes whose only unifying characteristic is that they were all written on the same day. Some of the leftover traces from a day might seem dense and extensive, but it still only captures a few blips of intensities engulfed in subdued unfolding presents that never left any noticeable traces. Keeping the notes together in one day is also a way to try to highlight all the things that are not there. Some of these notes taken in a day will have no mention of the morning, evening, or even work. Whilst many things are lost, there are also traces where even I sometimes wonder why I wrote in such detail about them. At the time, they must have seemed important and I have kept these parts, even though for me at this particular moment, they do not bring back any intense memories, cares, or concerns.

The texts in this part are far from 'raw' or unmediated. Weighted presents don't transcribe themselves into text without the guided help of someone. The fragments are built on quickly taken notes, impressions that happened to linger and find textual form, and memories that would suddenly surge and merge into textual flows, only to abruptly subside and disappear. The textual forms should therefore not be seen as more 'real' reflections of precarious worlds. As in the other parts, they have been ordered, drafted, and imbued with particular sets of aesthetic sensibilities and inclinations.

I imagine that in some ways this part will be the most challenging one to read for readers steeped in academic traditions. It might at first seem like an easy read as there will be fewer traces of theoretical or analytical frameworks to grapple with. If, however, the reader's experience of academic training has similarities to my own, they might have learnt to read academic texts in a way that uses the analytical and theoretical framework to propel them through and make sense of that text. When this framework is more intermittent or absent, maybe the journey through the text becomes more uncertain and feelings of being lost for direction and meaning might take hold.

At times, the reader might feel like a stranger thrown into the midst of conversational flows as if they had just arrived at a place where they don't quite know how to make coherent sense of the world and its people. Perhaps when reading some of this text, the reader will feel uneasy – as if some greater author(itarian) being has forced them into a troubling unfolding world without any steering on what is going on. The reader will encounter people who will only turn up in short flashing moments before they disappear, never to be encountered again. They will be thrown into conversations with a cacophony of voices that give a sense that there is something more, something that has weight, but is left untold and unexplored. At other times, the reader might feel that they drag along the thoughts and impressions of others that might make them feel alone and without much to hold on to.

The reader might at times think to themselves 'what does it all mean?', 'what's the point?' and 'why should I care?'. In some of the longer stretches of text, maybe the reader will feel apathetic, space out, be drawn towards thoughts about anything else, and look forward to the time when they can engage in something more meaningful. Other times, there might be something that for unknown reasons draws the attention, affection, and care of the reader. Perhaps there are patches where the reader feels that there is something that connects them to the fractured unstable and incoherent lifeworlds that unfold in front of their eyes. The reader might feel this partial connection because they can sense underlying patterns of meaning that, if explored further, could be solidified into something more concrete and lasting to hold on to before it all disappears. Or perhaps sometimes it is not entirely clear why something resonates with the reader at that particular moment. Some fragments might feel like they have more heft and are imbued with greater significance, but trying to delineate why that is by creating analytical categories of meaning will turn it into something else.

If the reader feels anything along those lines, this torn patchwork of texts has not been entirely in vain. For me, and perhaps for some of the people I lived and worked with during this research, there was no gentle author who sorted out and structured the world into particular sets of meanings that we could use as guidance. There was no comfort that it all made sense within a bigger holistic whole. There were moments of nothingness, frustration, nihilism, boredom, loneliness, irrelevance, joy, tears, care, and purpose, but it was never settled or predetermined. On a very small scale, I hope to give a sense of that to the reader, even if it means that the text might not always be enjoyable, comforting, or create a sense of interest and purpose. I do apologise to the reader if they at times feel frustrated with the incoherence, instability, fluidity, and meaninglessness of the texts I put in front of them. I just hope it does not leave them with too strong a wish to shoot the messenger.

How Does Your Experiment with Precarious Methods Relate to Other Academic Method Experiments (and What Discipline Does the Book Belong to)?

My familiarity with other academic method experiments is shaped by an unfolding amalgamation of too little time to explore; dwindling energy to go in depth; search algorithms that conjure up preferred search results; academic disciplinary situatedness that facilitates the circulation of some texts over others; and the shifting encounters with other academics who reveal new unknown bodies of literature to explore. My understanding of how this method experiment relates to others is therefore incomplete and partial, changing throughout the research process, and is intertwined with the different situational contexts of which I have been part. This is further complicated by how my academic training and thereby disciplinary belonging has also been partial and shifting across area studies, anthropology, and sociology disciplinary terrains. Depending on the standpoint of the reader and the context in which it is being used, this book can therefore be seen as belonging and being able to speak to only one, any, or none of the bodies of literature that shape, ground, and delineate these and other academic disciplines.

I do not think that this experiment is exemplary in ways that call out for duplication and imitation. Looking back at the research process, I feel that I mostly failed at enacting precarious methods that could better apprehend the vulnerable worlds of which I was part. This was partly because my experiments with precarious methods were not something that was planned, but rather something that occurred in relation to an unfolding research process. This meant that large parts of the research were carried out in ways that aligned with traditional ethnographic methods where I would be the sole author and the realities would be portrayed in textual forms. In the end, I was therefore limited to mostly textual modalities and although there are textual traces written by other academics, the vast majority of the text is written by me.

For some time there have been encouragements to experiment and to try new forms of writing that transcend traditional ethnographic writing (Clifford and Marcus, 1986). A multitude of experiments with writing, modalities, and design of ethnography has tried to open up and remould how to do ethnography (Marcus, 2007). Some of the textual experiments I touched upon when discussing what texts inspired the book, but there are many other experimental forums such as the magazine *Otherwise* and the journal *'entanglements: experiments in multimodal ethnography'* where textual and multimodal experiments take place that seeks to unsettle, fragment, and entangle different ways of knowing and sensing the world (Nolas and Varvantakis, 2018; *Otherwise*, 2023). At times I still believe that to convey something of how life was during the research, it would have been better if I had tweeted, Instagrammed, or livestreamed throughout my fieldwork. I also see great potential in experimenting with the design of ethnography, especially with experiments that try to ensure greater continued entanglements with the field throughout all phases of the research. I believe that had I embraced co-creative collaborations with the people I encountered during the research their para-ethnographies (Marcus, 2012) would have been better able to challenge ideas of hierarchical expertise and yearnings to represent the social world in a singular voice.

After most of the analysis was done, I also learned about the manifesto for live methods that seek to rethink, re-discover, and experiment with the crafting of sociological research that is 'equal to the new coordinated forms of social reality' and that 'provokes specific directions and highlights the capacities for the sociological craft' (Back and Puwar, 2012: 7). Some of the work emerging from live methods are moulded by similar concerns and circumstances that shaped my experiment with precarious methods.

My concerns with analytical processes and their implications for how we give a sense of unfolding lifeworlds resonate well with Back's use of live methods to explore 'how to account for the social world without assassinating the life contained within it' (Back, 2012: 21). My experiments with seeking to intertwine precarious life with precarious methods and the fragmented and vulnerable realities this can create overlaps with Gunaratnam's use of death as an inspiration to explore how 'following idiosyncratic fragments and the fleeting can bring us not only to the larger and longer lasting but also to the recessive, indeterminate and discontinuous qualities of life' (Gunaratnam, 2012: 108).

Finally, live methods seek to pay attention to how wider institutional and governmental circumstances influence the capabilities and temporalities of research (Back and Puwar, 2012) in a similar way to which precarious methods are perhaps inherently emergent from wreckages left behind by political, economic, and social transformations. There will be other live methods explorations that have other concerns and emerge from vastly different circumstances. Therefore, to what extent this experiment with precarious methods is encompassed within live methods and to what extent it is something else I will leave undecided and open for others to explore. What my all-too-late encounter with live methods can perhaps illustrate is that as my textual fragments become increasingly solidified and publishable, they not only risk becoming yet more 'epitaphs to a life passed in living' (Back, 2012: 21), but also close down the continued possibility of new live connections, capabilities, and affinities. To borrow from some of Gunaratnan's imagery (2012: 109), my hope is that even as these texts go stiff and withdraw from the unfolding life from which they once emerged, the care of others can bridge and make something else of their still suffering.

Isn't This Talk about Precarious Methods Just Some Self-Indulgent Academic Navel Gazing?

I fully understand if some readers[10] might have some concerns here. They might think that it is all very well that this book is experimenting with precarious methods, but isn't this just another form of academic navel gazing? Doesn't it just subsume the 'real' issues of precarity to highbrow academic concerns? Why should we care about the precarious circumstances of life in academia when there are people in real precarious positions? Why shouldn't I and other precarious academics just bite the bullet of our own minor troubles and moral conundrums, and go to work bringing to light the misery of others, regardless of what methods we use?

These types of questions are all valid and I can't say with certainty that they don't expose fundamental problems and flaws with these experiments with precarious methods. However, perhaps these kinds of questions are also informed by particular notions of precariousness as a problem of the weak in need of rectification by people in less precarious positions. This conceptualising of precariousness as a problem of the weak relies on the creation of a singular reality where people's lived experiences and practices are separated, ordered, and hierarchised within strictly enforced methodological boundaries. This is often justified by implied hierarchies of misery that seek to define, classify, and rank some people as passive victims without agency and insight, and others as active change makers who have the knowledge and power to make a difference and 'matter'.

The notion that it is desirable to make a hierarchy of misery and that there is an intrinsic value in delineating and classifying particular experiences that can be placed along this hierarchy so that resources can be focused on the 'right' areas of concern is not without its merits. After all, it would not be strange if you were more concerned with improving the life situation of someone who is barely able to afford food compared to trying to resolve the issues that a CEO of a company faces.

However, some problems emerge when trying to establish these kinds of hierarchies. If, for example, we look at the issue of labour exploitation and modern slavery, there are longstanding problems with how people who are classified as victims are implicitly and explicitly hierarchised along the lines of more or less deserving. These processes of classification can become entangled in gendered, classed and racialised discourses that inform practitioners' views on how to identify the 'real' victims of labour exploitation and modern slavery (Desyllas, 2007; Quirk, 2011). Labelling someone a victim is also problematic as it implies that they are without agency. This can end up steering policy responses towards a focus on rescuing victims from their enslavement and bringing them back to 'freedom', whilst ignoring the underlying complex set of reasons as to why they have ended up in that situation (Davidson, 2013). Relying on hierarchies of misery with their promises of singular truths risks sustaining policies and interventions that can end up having unexpected and devastating impacts on the people they set out to help (Aradau, 2016; Breuil et al., 2011; McCarthy, 2014; Weitzer, 2015).

These issues with the hierarchisation of misery are not only relevant to an analysis of government-aligned assemblages concerned with labour exploitation and modern slavery. Similar problems would emerge in an analysis of the life experiences in which I was entangled during my time in the field.

Take the example of Ranvid from the hostel. Ranvid was in his fifties. Every day, he would get up early in the morning to go to work. He would put on his suit and tie, quickly dash out for a cigarette, and then rush out for whatever office he would be working in at that time. He worked in information technology (IT) and had a couple of degrees. His work involved a mix of software development and the physical work of setting up office computers. At no point was he out of work and he never gave any sense that his job was insecure in terms of the hours he could work. When he was working, he would often not make it back to the hostel in time and would spend night after night sleeping on the floor in the office in which he was working at the time. He never disclosed his financial situation, but given the amount of time he was working and given he still sometimes struggled financially, I imagined his pay wasn't great.[11]

When work got especially intense, Ranvid's weight would slip away and his presence would become more ghostlike. His joking philosophical presence in the sociality of the hostel would fade, to be replaced with the repeated and worried question: 'Have you seen Ranvid?' During a particularly hard stretch of work, he came home at around 1 am, staggered through the dark room, and tried to climb up into the bunk bed. The strength in his arms had left him and he fell to the floor. Confused, he tried to get up and climb up into bed, but yet again fell to the floor. The rest of us had woken up and called out to hear if he was OK. He mumbled, confused, and tried a third time to climb up and fell down again. At this point, we realised what was going on and stopped him, put on the light, and sat him down on the floor. He didn't remember what had happened.

Ranvid did not seem to be drunk or on drugs (he rarely drank and didn't touch drugs). Instead, it was the exhaustion from work that seemed to have brought him to the brink. We convinced him that he was not OK and that we should call an ambulance, which he eventually agreed to. It took hours for the ambulance to arrive, at which time we sat up waiting with him. Eventually, it arrived, and the paramedics did various checks on him before determining that his condition was not serious enough to warrant a hospital visit and that all he really needed was some rest and to be more careful next time. He got one day of rest as the next day was a bank holiday, but after that, he was once again swallowed up by whirlpools of work that slowly but steadily drained more life out of him.

Does this kind of experience make Ranvid valid as someone who can be included in research on precarious work and living? After all, if we start to categorise, sort, and piece out his self-contained characteristics, this is a white-collar, highly educated IT worker with steady work that we are examining. These kinds of characteristics would make it easy to exclude his experiences as not being 'really' relevant, as there would be others whose disentangled characteristics could be defined as being more vulnerable and thereby more deserving of our attention and care.

Having been partially entangled in Ranvid's life and countless others with various characteristics across moments and patches of joy, laughter, philosophical explorations, and, yes, suffering makes it almost impossible to classify parts of those experiences as more or less relevant when it comes to precarity. Or at least before this separation and hierarchisation can be realised, it requires a leap of emotional disconnection and hard conceptual boundary work to separate out who 'really' belongs in conceptually pure and hierarchical categories of precarity and misery.

To say that there are issues with creating a hierarchy of precarity does not mean that we then should consider all experiences as being equal. People's suffering in a precarious world takes multiple, diverse, and fluctuating forms with different waves of intensity across temporal and spatial constellations. To say that these experiences cannot be grasped by singular and exclusionary notions of suffering and precarity is not the same as saying that all patterns of suffering should carry equal weight at all times and in all contexts. But how they could be said to matter is not something that can be predetermined, and explorations of such issues should be attuned to the messy, unfolding, fluctuations of social life.

From a theoretical perspective, this might sound vague, ambiguous, and ill-defined, but that is perhaps only the case if we insist on trying to create a conceptually pure theory of what precarious life looks like. If this idea of understanding precarity as a singular reality is abandoned, I think we would find that we are more adept at dealing with the complexities of a precarious world than we might think. Looking back at the London hostels I lived in, the issue of how to deal with complex, multiple, and undefinable layers of precariousness was expertly and adeptly dealt with by the people in the hostel.

For example, in the case of Ranvid, during the periods when the pressures of work tore away at him with visible intensity, people in the hostel quickly sensed this and adapted their behaviour accordingly. Free cigarettes would be given, food would be made and saved for him just in case he came home, and in the conversations with him, there was a greater focus than usual on providing emotional support and comfort. But equally, when the flows and ebbs changed and Ranvid found himself in moments of freedom and respite from work, he could spend hours carefully listening to and comforting others, and when money was tight for people, he would discreetly help because 'when we die, we can't take money with us anyway'.

The issues of separation and hierarchy also relate to the relationship between the researcher and the research object. Traditional methods often seek to make a clear separation between the researcher and the research object, not necessarily only in terms of creating a 'view from nowhere' (Haraway, 1991) but also in methods that acknowledge the position of the researcher, but that nonetheless maintain a clear separation between themselves and what they set out to research.

In terms of researching precariousness, there can be many good reasons to do this. If your methods rest on assumptions that there is a singular reality 'out there', that the singular reality is independent of the researcher, and that the role of the researcher is to uncover hidden patterns of inequality and exploitation that would otherwise remain hidden, there is not much reason to consider the lifeworlds of the researchers. This is especially the case since these methods are reliant on the assumption that the researcher lives a nonprecarious and relatively privileged life that enables them to conceptually uncover this singular reality. From that perspective, it could seem self-indulgent to not create and maintain a separation between an academic world of privilege and a precarious world of suffering.

However, seeking to create altruistic separations in order to focus on the 'real' issues of precarity can inadvertently result in the creation of hierarchical regimes of belonging and othering (Youkhana, 2015; Yuval-Davis et al., 2018). This has consequences for what types of voices and experiences end up being considered to be valuable and belong in particular social situations.

My engagement with labour exploitation and modern slavery stakeholders during the research process is perhaps an example of this dynamic. At the time of the research, the work that had gone into creating and maintaining a clear boundary between the world of stakeholders who study and 'solve' precarity and the people who suffer from precarity seemed to be almost perfectly implemented. I attended multiple academically and politically aligned stakeholder conferences. In addition, I read thousands and thousands of words about the issues of precarious work and living. Yet it was only on rare occasions that tiny fragments of sounds and patterns from any of the precarious lives that were the focus of all these activities made it through.

I say rare – that might be an overstatement. In total, I have probably attended several days' worth of conferences and speeches about issues with precarity, and in all that time around a total of 15 minutes was set aside for the voice of a single survivor. I wish I could recount her story of survival to give justice to some of the complex patterns of suffering she had experienced, but I can't because, at the time, I did what I imagine most other people in that room did: I started disentangling her stories into distinct categories. I quickly classified her as a female, Pakistani victim of domestic servitude (a category within the UK modern slavery framework) whose path into abuse was tied to kinship and relationship networks.

As she talked, her voice was already being silenced[12] by the instant analytical work I was doing. No matter what kind of expansive entangled multiplicity of suffering her story would have been able to bring out, it wouldn't have mattered, as the only way her story could be made 'real' and relevant was by becoming another disentangled case study to be dissected and categorised.

I imagine I was not the only one doing this instant silencing and dissection of her story. After her talk, the floor was open for questioning. There were one or two questions that tried to clarify some details of her story, but after a few moments of silence where the audience seemed to try to figure out what to do, there came an avalanche of questions directed at the male white stakeholder sitting next to her on stage. This stakeholder was one of the driving forces in a charity with links to government agencies and departments working on tackling modern slavery and labour exploitation, and his charity had been involved in providing support to her after she was rescued. He was seen as being part of the stakeholder world and it was perhaps not surprising that the questions quickly turned his way. After all, he 'belonged' to the same world as the audience. His language had the right amount of conceptual distance, which made it easy to process, and he knew about the 'real' problems in a similar way to the audience. In other words, he was one of the stakeholders and 'one of us'.

This dynamic, however, also works the other way round. The way in which traditional methods bring out singular realities about precarity was not met with open arms by the people it claimed to describe and relate to. When Traian, in one of the fragments from Part III, reacted by comparing stakeholders working on labour exploitation to a cult, I imagine that is hardly the reaction the thousands of stakeholders, academics, politicians, and charity workers might be hoping for. All their hard work trying to tackle the issue by disentangling the conditions of labour exploitation into pure conceptual categories that could form the basis for policy interventions that in their minds would improve the lives of 'vulnerable others' could nevertheless be unceremoniously dismissed as the work of madmen by one of these 'vulnerable others'.

Not everyone in the field had as cutting a reaction to academic-political embedded theories about their lives as Traian. As much as my courage allowed me,[13] I would occasionally bring up some perspective on precarity – not only the government-aligned view of labour exploitation but also other views about precarity that aligned with more academically liberal, left-wing, Marxist, and anarchist perspectives. Most times, the perspectives were met with polite shoulder shrugs before the conversation was changed to something more relevant and interesting.

At other times, the reaction was closer to how Attila reacted when trying to discuss politics and anarchist organising with him. Attila was a positive and often very enthusiastic and social person. He had more than a decade of experience working in all kinds of jobs, but when he was accepted as a trainee to become a chef at a four-star hotel, he was still over the moon and could not wait to learn how to create culinary dishes and experiences.

This delight was quickly dismantled by the heavy-handed management style Attila encountered. He had a strong sense of justice and what was right, which would often bring him into open conflict with work management as he would stand up to any unfairness he witnessed. After one such confrontation that had almost resulted in a physical fight because he had stood up for a colleague who was being bullied by the boss, I talked with him about politics, conspiracy theories, and the possibility of organising. I mentioned the more traditional unions and I also brought up anarchist methods of organising. His response was along the lines of:

> It's all the same. People want to tell you what to do. What the world is really like. Like saying everything is controlled by the 'deep state' or by some 'alien simulation' or that everything will be better if we only vote

> for this party (sighs with disgust) as if that has ever worked. Or they will come up with something like what you just said join a union or . . . be an anarchist and sunlight will start to shine out your arse . . . it doesn't matter, it's just people telling you what to think, telling you what to do . . . it's all the fucking same mate.

After that, I tried to meekly talk about how anarchism is different, as it was not reliant on dogmatic views of the world and was based on self-organising and consensus building. He would have none of it. It was still all the same to him. It was all about someone else telling him how the world 'really was' and that if only he did a, b, or c, things would be better. He might be an optimistic open-minded kind of person, but that kind of message was too far-fetched for even the most tolerant version of him to accept.

Across the different stages of this research, I would occasionally encounter and be tenuously involved in anarchist-aligned activities to self-organise workers. For the people I met in these settings, this type of dynamic was hardly any news. In the chatter amongst these anarchist-aligned work activists, the issue of belonging and how to create social connections was seen as crucial. Their everyday experiences of trying to convince and engage workers had made them recognise that devising ever more convincing and bulletproof arguments that would reveal the exploitative nature of work, capitalism, and the state meant nothing unless there was a shared social and lived reality with the people they were trying to engage.

How to create these moments of shared belonging was an underlying but constant part of their everyday struggle to make their own and everyone else's lives in these wrecked and precarious worlds more survivable. For them to address the 'real' problems did not hinge on the creation of an implied hierarchy of preordained problems and solutions arrived at by a conceptually and theoretically more astute ideologist; rather, in order for them to address the 'real' problems in all their multiple forms, they relied on a shared sense of vulnerable belonging and interdependence. This was never a case of 'them' solving 'other's' problems as they considered themselves to be part of a shared world with shared issues.[14]

This also relates to how methods are gathered. If the reality that is brought out is disentangled, purified, and plays a part in a boundary-making process that separates 'us' the researchers from our research objects, is it surprising that these 'objects' of our research concerns are not deeply enthusiastic about engaging with our findings as we generously let them trickle down upon them from our self-ordained place in the conceptual clouds?

This dynamic can also have implications for people in academia's ability to survive in a precarious world. To use methods that create a reality where 'we', the researchers, are the ones who address and solve problems, also means that 'we' deny ourselves the possibility of being vulnerable and of requiring support and solidarity. By seeking to constitute academics as the ones who have all of the solutions, we also eschew the opportunity ourselves to share in the methods people outside of academia use to make their lives more survivable.

I experienced this firsthand as I moved between and became part of these different patches of precarious life. When I was in the field, I felt like a novice who didn't know anything about how to make it through another day at work or how to settle into the fluid rhythms of the hostel. When people at work devised and shared various kinds of ingenious tactics to work as little as possible, I often struggled with implementing them. It was as if there were a nagging voice telling me that I really ought to work as hard as possible.

I might have known conceptually that the work was deeply exploitative and that working hard only perpetrated that exploitation, but to do it in practice was a very different matter. It was only through the support and generous sharing of methods from my colleagues that I slowly became able to make work more survivable. The same process happened at the hostel where it was a long process to learn how to become part of a precarious everyday that didn't seek to build conceptual and tangible concrete walls between me and everyone else. Coming back 'home' to an academic world was therefore a shock to me, as this 'home' was premised on self-discipline/self-exploitation and a separated existence in walled-in and self-contained units of life. I had ambitions of becoming part of this academic 'home', but as I did not dare to use the survival methods I had learned in the field, becoming part of this precarious academic world seemed harder than surviving precariously in the field ever was.

In a sense, most of this book could indeed be dismissed as academic navel gazing. It is written by someone who is still deeply embedded in academic life and practice, it still has some aspiration of being read and accepted by other academics, and it has reflective elements that are concerned with how to survive in academia. However, at the same time, it also tries to create some analytic leeway to use more precarious methods that perhaps have the potential to be less focused on individual achievements, are wary of establishing authoritarian certainty, seek to make the messy contingency of the analysis visible, are less hierarchical and determined to create separation, and more attuned to shared connections and mutual vulnerability in a precarious world.

I can't say with any certainty that seeking to experiment with precarious methods could be a small part of a process that seeks to address patterns of inequality and dynamics of separation and hierarchisation, nor do I know if it can move us towards better ways of surviving precarious worlds. However, equally, I am not convinced that the way forward is to continue to rely solely on traditional methods that delineate and separate out the 'real' issues so that they can be 'solved' in distant academic and political assemblages that are imagined to be unimpeded by the precariousness of the world. In precarious worlds, things are rarely simple. To survive and belong takes constant adjustments and manoeuvring to negotiate the ebbs and flows of vulnerability, pressures, and unfolding presents. How precarious methods play into such a world and how to make sense of it are not something I can or will seek to define.

Isn't Research Supposed to Provide Answers Rather Than a New Set of Questions?

Academic texts are normally made up like a building block set. There will be different parts and there will be a plan and clear instructions that tell you how to put together those parts in a very specific order so that in the end it looks like the ship, school, space rocket, chair, or something else that the designer specifically had in mind when creating these building blocks.

In a sense, the purpose and success of the whole process become determined by whether the reader/builder can replicate and make sense of the ship, school, space rocket, or analytic perspective in a way that fits the initial vision of the designer/author. If it is difficult to reach the same conclusions as the author intended or if the chair that the plan sets out to build ends up looking like a coffee table, it would be considered problematic. Maybe the correct building blocks were not selected or maybe the plan and instructions were not clear enough and need to be revised and redrafted so that they can more convincingly lead the reader and builder towards a fully realised vision.

As in other academic work, in this book I have provided a range of different building blocks. Where the book is perhaps slightly different is that I have tried to make the plans and instructions that tell the reader how to put together these building blocks more sketchy and incomplete. Another difference is that in more traditional academic pieces of work, the textual building blocks have been carefully selected so that each of them fits perfectly within the conclusive image the author seeks to guide the reader towards. However, I have tried to give the reader a more diverse set of building blocks that don't fit neatly together within a preconceived plan. I have done so in the hope that it perhaps makes it easier for the reader to use them in ways I could never have imagined by myself.

Any text can perhaps with enough creativity and effort be pulled apart and made into something distant from the author's intentions. The building blocks the designer carefully selects with a ship in mind can with enough ingenuity be used to make a chair, and the textual blocks that the author with great attention gathers to build up a coherent analysis that seeks to convince the reader about the importance of resistance and control can with enough effort be disassembled, reordered and used to build up worlds of allegorical giants and whatnot.

The way I keep on trying to avoid settling into definitive conclusions might seem problematic to some readers. They might say that it is all well and good to leave the conclusions open for collaboration, but when they order a flatpack set to make a chair, they expect to be told how to build a chair lest they accidentally end up with a coffee table, and when they read a text about precariousness, they expect to be told how to solve the issue of precariousness and not something that avoids this through textual contortions of several kinds.

At times, I am certainly tempted to make stronger, more definitive claims as to how this book should be read and understood. Yet it is perhaps this attempt to resist the urge for clarity and instead seek to keep the book more inconclusive, less guided towards singular meanings, and more vulnerable to become intertwined and reshaped through others that is at least one of the central 'points' of the book.

By seeking to resist robust conclusions and by gathering these diverse sets of textual blocks loosely held together by vague plans and instructions, I also hope that it becomes easier for others to make something else out of them. Perhaps this something made in collaboration with unknown others can also provide some of the answers we have been looking for.

In Terms of Social and Political Change, What Are the Potential Consequences of Experimenting with Precarious Methods?

I don't pretend that I can provide an answer to this question, but I can reflect briefly on what it might do differently from methods that seek to provide more conclusive research findings. Before starting the research, I had been working for a short spell as a social researcher in government. If at the time I had read a piece of research like this that refused to settle down on clear conclusions, I would have discarded the research as being irrelevant. Part of my job was to find research that could provide evidence for how the world 'really' was and to seek out ways to translate these findings into new impactful policies.

The methods that were appreciated and valued were therefore the ones that could provide clear-cut answers. If the issue of precarious work had come up, the research I would have been looking for would have been something that could give a clear indication of what the problem was and how policies could be designed and implemented to solve the problem.

For some readers, this might seem like a much easier and more impactful approach. You use tried-and-tested social science methods to identify a problem and then you use the same methods to try to measure and estimate the impact particular policies have – no reluctance to conclude, no fear of making defining statements based on the 'science'. If I cared for the people I lived and worked with, why not just do that? I wouldn't need to conclude something that aligned with current government policies, but if I could at least conclude something, maybe in the future it could have a real positive impact on people's lives.

The only minor problem with that approach was that the only thing that came close to being certain, was that policies without fail failed.[15] By that, I don't mean how particular policies were presented and made into political successes and failures; rather, I refer to whether they changed people's lives in the way they set out to do when they were initially conceptualised and justified. How to evaluate the exact impact of any policy is probably a next-to-impossible task, but nonetheless the impacts of policies are constantly being evaluated within government departments often using a fixed set of traditional social science methods that promise to bring out a singular reality about whether the policy succeeded or failed according to the initial intentions. What at least in my department was the result of these evaluations was that no policy, no matter how much research evidence had been used to shape it, could have been deemed to have been successful.[16]

That this was the case was common knowledge. Everyone working on these issues knew full well that the world was an incredibly complex thing, that even the best efforts to delineate it into solid analytical categories were always problematic, and that using these analytical categories to make a predicted and measurable impact was almost impossible.

Despite this, the only kind of academic research that could be considered valuable and useful was the kind of research that presented itself as being coherent, clearly defined, and based on traditional sets of methods that could bring out traditional kinds of social research conclusions. Why would that be?

Part of the reason for that is perhaps that the methods we use and the way they end up framing the world have political and social implications, as both Law (2004) and Butler (2009) would also argue. To question dominant framings and recognitions of the world and to bring together methods that bring out different realities is therefore also something that can have wider political and social consequences.

As a thought experiment, to illustrate that point, imagine that my former colleagues working on the issue of labour exploitation and precarious work started to produce research like this book. What kind of legislation could seek royal assent based on a sense of belonging in a hostel bed? What kind of policy strategy could be drafted using the evidence of conversations that effortlessly glide from discussions about the hardship of work to the ability to communicate with animals? What kind of guidelines would need to be developed for frontline workers so that they can deal with the sense that something is coming together in an unfolding but never-resting present?

Within the political-academic worlds of which I was part at the time, it would certainly have been problematic, if not impossible, to transform most of the kind of realities that are part of this book into political action of any kind (with the possible exception of Part I). This is not because the kind of realities that are brought out in this book are not full of weight and significance for people's lives; rather, it is perhaps that these realities grate against the more systematically organised, coherent, and singular kind of realities the current sociopolitical system seems to be premised on.

I do not argue for an abandonment of traditional social research methods and I do believe that there can be situations where they can be used to sway policies and social actions in particular directions. I believe that the people who are best situated to make judgements about what particular methods are best to use to bring about change are the people who are part and parcel of the issues that they face. For most people I encountered during my time in the field, there was little affinity with the kind of methods and realities that were assembled by the different government agencies, unions, and social movements that worked on labour exploitation issues. However, at times I met people active in different rank-and-file unions, and for them, it was clear that using methods that created singular realities was important for them to bring about changes that could improve their lives. What my experiments with precarious methods are trying to do is to add more possible tools that I and perhaps others can selectively use and mould in ways that help us survive these wrecked times we are facing.

Why Is There No Proper Introduction and Conclusion?

To answer this question briefly, because writing a traditional introduction and conclusion would undermine my attempt to make the text and its realities more precarious. In academic books, the author often uses tried-and-tested writing formulas and practices to convince the reader that they have always been in full control of the text, its meanings, and intentions. One trick that can be useful to convey such an image is the tactical use of an introduction and conclusion.

It is perhaps a commonly known truism in academia that the introduction and the conclusion are the last things that will be written. Yet academics are also often taught that although the introduction and the conclusion are to a large extent a retrospective rationalisation of a messy unpredictable research process, it should be portrayed to the reader as if you, the author, have always known what shape the texts would take, what arguments would be made, and what the final analytical directions and conclusions would look like. In other words, the introduction and the conclusion could be seen as narrative tactics that reconfigure the temporal dynamic of the book. So instead of portraying the text as the outcome of a continuously twisted, dismembered, and fragmented process shaped by numerous reiterations of the internal contradictions, feedback, editing, changed minds, and unsettling arguments, the introduction and the conclusion present the final text as a coherent and consistent entity that was always intended to be this way.

The argument for making this tactical temporal switch is often justified in terms of making it easier for the reader to make sense of the work. By providing the reader with an introduction that gives clear instructions on what the book will examine and why it is important, followed up by a conclusion that states that what was examined was indeed important, the reader is wrapped in a comforting narrative of certainty and linearity. Readers of academic books, so the argument goes, are in absolute need of a clear, consistent, and repetitive narrative lest they will be lost in a state of confusion and chaos. These foundational requirements of the academic reader supposedly stand in contrast with other readers, listeners, and watchers who throughout written and unwritten time have enjoyed, grappled with, and played with narratives that embrace ambiguity, contradictions, and wondrous vagueness, whether this is expressed in verbal myths and stories, visual pictures, movies, dances, and performances, or inscribed in the always unsettled and exploring texts ranging from the Daoist texts of Laozi to the interactive and interconnective poetry of Tahi Saihate. Although I recognise that there can be many good reasons to write traditional academic books with their singular portrayals of reality, I also believe that it is possible for academic readers to engage with the textual enactment of more messy, entangled, and precarious realities.

Furthermore, I believe that using introductions and conclusions to reconfigure the temporal dynamics also has consequences for how the academic as a narrative entity is being portrayed. when the text is wrapped in the comforting certainty of the introduction and conclusion the academic becomes almost a caricature of the great man theories (Mouton, 2019; Spector, 2016) where great leaders, geniuses, and change makers through their sheer excellence and brilliance overcome the complexities of the world to make an intended, lasting, and marked difference in the world. Although the great man theories have long since been put on the academic dustheap of inadequate theories, much of academic everyday practice, such as how introductions and conclusions are written, is perhaps still premised on enacting these theories in order to portray a convincing, competent and authoritative 'great academic' whose truths sayings matter. In this book, I have decided to attempt, perhaps not quite wholeheartedly, to try to forgo any such pretence. By trying to avoid some of the tactical trickeries embedded in introductions and conclusions, I hope to give some sense of an author who might be heavily involved in the process, but who just like everyone else is trying to make sense of a messy, confusing process and haphazardly assembled texts.

Why Do You Call It Methods and Not Methodologies or Method Assemblages?

I have no particular strong affinity with any particular one of these terms. My understanding of methods might be seen to align well with much work on method assemblage – e.g., Law's work – in that I consider methods to be entangled in social relations, practices, and materialities, and that the unfolding of these entanglements can shape realities. However, I also realise that this perspective and the particular vocabularies they use, just like any other academic terminology, are deeply embedded in specific disciplinary customs and border-building processes that seek to delineate who belongs within the discipline. The word 'method' standing alone also has these issues. What constitutes 'methods' varies widely across disciplines and theoretical tribes, and there are daily ongoing struggles to create boundaries around what is considered proper methods and who is deemed capable of utilising them. However, on the flipside, 'methods' as a word by itself is perhaps less wedded to one particular approach and therefore has greater potential to be reconstituted and shaped in diverse forms across disciplinary and theoretical divides.

In social science, methods and methodologies are often understood as relating to different spheres of the research process. Methods are sometimes understood as referring to a number of techniques that are used to collect data (e.g., interview questionnaires), whereas methodology is seen to refer to the practices and underlying assumptions that inform the data generation. However, these distinctions are also often discussed, and how these distinctions are conceptualised doesn't overlap neatly with how they are enacted in practice (Bryman, 2008; Mair et al., 2016). Some might think that methodology would be a much more appropriate term to use in the context of this book, and they would not be wrong, but equally they would not be entirely correct. The same could be said for using 'method assemblages' or 'method'. If the technology allowed for it, I would probably prefer to leave it open for the reader to choose in a drop-down menu whatever term they feel puts them most at ease. As an interim choice, I have settled for 'methods', but feel free to ignore it, tear it out, or replace it in whatever way that works for you.

Are You Not Privileged Since You Have Been a Civil Servant and Are Highly Educated?

Yes, that is absolutely a privileged position and when it comes to race, nationality, gender, sexuality, and embodied compositions, I am also benefiting from historical, cultural, political, and economic entrenched and enforced privileges. I most likely would never have been in a position to write this book if I had not benefited from these privileged social positions. Throughout all stages of my education as well as my working history, I have experienced how people who did not align with these dominant positions were institutionally cleansed and discarded as if they were nothing.

When it comes to class and financial circumstances, things are perhaps less clear. I am in my mid-forties and for a combined three years I have earned more than £30,000 per annum. All other years I have earned less than £17,000 per annum. The capability of my family and friend networks to support me is limited as they are mostly working in low-paid sectors like care or construction and some are on benefits.

These self-selected 'facts' about my life are not without importance, as they give some indications of my situated social positions, but they do not in themselves encompass the complex ways in which privileges, precariousness, and patterns of oppression and inequality play out in immediate moments and over time. Whilst these experiments with precarious methods are shaped by the particular lived circumstances in which I found myself, I don't think it is necessary to have particular precarious social positions in order to experiment with the methods. As was discussed in the question on academic naval gazing, I am sceptical about the political implications of maintaining hierarchies of silenced misery and exclusionary stakeholder privileges and seeking to erect boundaries around who is precarious enough to experiment with precarious methods would play into a similar kind of dynamic.

Why Do You Use 'You' (i.e., Second-Person Narrative) So Much?

When I first used 'you', I didn't even notice, and my grammatical comprehension was not extensive enough to put a label on it, but I later found out that the use of the second-person point of view in social science texts could be problematic. This is because it can be seen to be too informal and as it can 'alienate' the reader, who might not feel included in the 'you' of the text (Aims Writing Center, 2020; College Writing Center, 2013). Nonetheless, the second-person point of view can be found in academic texts, including in Stewart's work (2007), where it is utilised at different points throughout her texts. However, she does not give any justification for why it might be appropriate to do so.

What kind of perspective comes to be used in ethnographic narratives is not just a matter of style, but has several implications related to linguistic,[17] political, cultural, and social notions about knowledge and authority (Clifford and Marcus, 1986; Malcomson, 2019; Venkatesh, 2013). However, whilst the implications of using the first and third person have been explored,[18] the use of the second person is less commonly used in ethnographies (Malcomson, 2019) and therefore less examined.

Sacks did examine the use of 'you' in one lecture where he points out the ambiguous nature of it as it does not differentiate between singular and plural forms. This means that 'you' has a 'this and that format' (Sacks, 2006: 166) where it can mean 'you alone' or 'you and others' (Sacks, 2006: 166). There are more nuances to the use of 'you': it can be used to refer to the speaker/writer, but in a way that refers to the speaker 'as a member of 'anybody'' (Sacks, 2006: 166) and in its plural form can have a 'sense of it which is much larger but at least includes yourself' (Sacks, 2006: 166). The use of 'you' therefore has some tenuous affinity with precariousness in its ambiguity, and in that it seeks to refer to experiences that are interconnected and potentially, but not necessarily, could refer to 'anybody'.

The use of a second-person point of view might be seen as potentially alienating, as it frames and implicates the reader in what is going on, which could cause offence (the reader might think 'I had nothing to do with this, don't drag me into your mess'). On the other hand, perhaps the use of the second-person form could also be seen as a gentle invitation to care, become involved, and recognise our mutual interdependence on others, no matter how far and distant they may seem. By relying solely on the use of first and third-person perspectives, there is perhaps a sense of implicit understanding that the vague and uncertain links that the text has to lived realities are only of immediate concern to someone other than the reader. If, however, precariousness relates to being interdependent and vulnerable to each other, is the use of second-person narrative perhaps in some circumstances a better linguistic tool to use that can bring that sense out?

How I have used the second-person narrative is sporadic and intermittent, which aligns with literary writings where this more fluctuating use seems to be the norm (Parker, 2012). As mentioned earlier, my use of the second-person voice wasn't planned and my motivations weren't explicitly thought out. So whether I like other authors use it as an act of self-preservation to create distance between myself and particularly troubling experiences, whether I use it as a middle ground between first-person narrative's claims to total ownership and the distant alterity of third-person narrative, or whether I use it to put the reader and 'the narrated self in a position of a seemingly shared subjectivity' (Parker, 2012: 173) is not something I seek to determine. What I do know is that when I tried to eliminate the use of second-person narratives, the texts to me came across as more definitive and distant. How the reader will approach it and make sense of it I cannot say, but as an experiment, I have kept the use of 'you' to see if 'something' might happen.

What's with the Blank Conclusive Page?

It somehow felt right to end the book with a blank page, but for a long time, I didn't have any articulated reason or allegory that I could draw on to justify that. However, at the very end of the writing phase, pictures of protestors from around the world that were being arrested for holding up blank pieces of paper started to crop up on the social media platforms I used for distraction and these pictures helped me make some sense of what it is a blank page can do.

The protestors might have been arrested because the police suspected that the blank piece of paper implied slogans that were banned, though presenting blank pieces of paper could also signify something else. Perhaps it ties in with other more diversely structured forms of protest that refused to settle on explicit and clearly defined demands in the hope that this would prevent easy incorporation into the existing order (Scott, 2012).

There is always a complex context behind the blank page filled with fragmented interdependencies to a precarious world. Presenting the blank page is therefore not a claim that it is possible to stand outside of a precarious weighted present with all its powerful sets of intensities, pressures, and disruption. Instead, by keeping the conclusive page blank, there is perhaps an implied invitation to unknown others to become part of something that can fill out the blanks and there is perhaps also an insistence that in order to move towards something else and better, it is necessary to rely on and be vulnerable to the sway of others.

The indefinable blank page, the inconclusive and vague realities it presents, and the precarious methods that underpin it can perhaps both be seen as a threat to an existing order and as a possibility of something else. That something else does not have to be concluded into predetermined future realities. A blank page with its unsettled conclusions and invitations for collaboration can perhaps sometimes be the best way to start experimenting with new vulnerable ways to survive these wrecked worlds in which we find ourselves. The stakes of this book are nowhere near as high as the protesters risking their lives by holding up a blank piece of paper, yet despite that, I do not have the full courage to submit 200 blank pages full of collaborative possibilities of something else. Instead, after much delay, let us return to the conclusive blank page.

What do you want us to write?

Notes

1. For example, the November 2014 Modern Slavery Strategy, the 2015 Modern Slavery Act, the establishment of a Director of Labour Market Enforcement (Home Office, 2017), and a Select Committee focusing on the future of work and the status and rights of workers in the more precarious segments of the labour market (Business, Energy, and Industrial Strategy Committee, 2016).
2. I found it difficult to settle on a single term that could cover this aspect and at various points I considered other terms such as 'personal', 'practice', 'experiential', and 'embodied'. With 'practical', I understand it in a similar way to Smith's 'world of concrete practical activities' (Smith, 1974b: 10) that stands in contrast to a conceptual disentangled world of theory making, although here the focus will be on how precarious social positionings of researchers influence these dynamics rather than Smith's focus on how this dynamic plays out within unequal and oppressive gender dynamics. The term 'practical' also aligns with Law's call for methods that can notice the practicalities of knowing and making realities (Law, 2004: 152).
3. I have chosen not to stick with Butler's sharp differentiation between precarity and precariousness. This is partly because other authors write about precarity in a way that aligns more with Butler's version of precariousness. Keeping the categorical delineations unsettled is perhaps also in the spirit of my approach.
4. Tsing, however, does not make the same distinction between precarity and precariousness that Butler does.
5. Inspired by the poem 'The Second Coming' by William Butler Yeats first published in 1920.
6. This social positioning is not singular or static and can relate to a number of intersecting factors related to gender, race, class, age, migration status, disability, sexuality, nationality, language, etc.
7. That is, regardless of whether that mess is the academic embedded practicalities of teaching, dealing with administration, or filling out research funding applications, or whether it is dealing with the time-consuming task of everyday surviving in precarious lifeworlds shaped by gendered, racial, and classed patterns of inequality.
8. While Law argues that representation in the social sciences is 'allegory that denies its character as allegory' (Law, 2004: 89), I believe that some of the fragments I present here will be close to screaming out loud their allegorical character.
9. Although I did stay in a York hostel after returning from the field, the fragments in this part relate to my fieldwork experiences in London.
10. I shamelessly blamed these types of questions on non-existent readers, but really they are questions raised by me in particular moments of doubt and insecurity.

11. It could have been the case that he was classified as 'self-employed' by the multinational company he was working for. Due to the vague formulation of the regulation, a self-employed person can in all practical respects be an employee, but in technical legal terms be defined as a contractor, which means that they are not bound by most labour law regulations such as minimum wage regulations. How the scam then works is that the self-employed might be paid a contract fee of £200 to complete a task, which is fine if the task takes a few hours to complete, but if it takes 100 hours to finish, you are looking at an hourly pay of £2 or less than a quarter of the UK minimum wage.
12. Spivak's work 'Can the Subaltern Speak?', exploring from a postcolonial view how the voice of subaltern groups are systematically silenced even when they are the supposed focus of 'charitable' interventions (Spivak, 2010), comes to mind as one analytical direction that links directly to this dynamic.
13. After all, being seen as a member of a strange cult was not really the kind of position in which I wanted to find myself.
14. Most of them were rank-and-file workers in precarious jobs.
15. This is based on a rough and unsubstantiated sense of how policies worked. I won't be able to support nor talk about it in any legally viable way. Also, this only applies to the ministry I was working with at the time.
16. This is not quite correct; there was a brief period where one, and only one, policy was deemed to have been successful. Any talk of it was like talking about the holy grail and all newcomers would quickly learn about its mythological status. Unfortunately, later on, it turned out not to have had the impact it had set out to have, so it was put in the pile of other decent but failed policies.
17. My own situatedness between three different languages, each of which has its own fluid grammatical nets that it throws out into the world to capture something, does perhaps also play a particular role in how the text has been shaped.
18. See, for example, Malcomson (2019), who draws out the argument that the use of the third person is problematic as it portrays the researcher as an all-knowing objective observer disentangled from the world they study. Furthermore, the use of the first-person perspective can also play into processes of othering and it can centre the attention and authority on the author rather than the lives of the research participants. She goes on to argue for the use of more experimental techniques in relation to how perspectives are drawn out in the text.

References

Abu-Lughod L (1996) Writing against culture. In: Fox RG (ed.), *Recapturing Anthropology: Working in the Present*. Santa Fe, NM: School of American Research Press, pp. 62–71.

———. (2000) *Writing Women's Worlds: Bedouin Stories*. Berkeley: University of California Press.

Advani A, Bangham G and Leslie J (2021) The UK's wealth distribution and characteristics of high-wealth households. *Fiscal Studies* 42(3–4): 397–430.

Agustín LM (2007) *Sex at the Margins: Migration, Labour Markets and the Rescue Industry*. London: Zed Books.

Ahmed S (2013) Making feminist points. Available at: https://feministkilljoys.com/2013/09/11/making-feminist-points (accessed 13 April 2024).

———. (2017) *Living a Feminist Life*. Durham, NC: Duke University Press.

Aims Writing Center (2020) Tools for writing: points of view in writing. Available at: https://www.aims.edu/student/online-writing-lab/tools/point-of-view.php (accessed 15 August 2020).

Alberti G (2014) Mobility strategies, 'mobility differentials' and 'transnational exit': the experiences of precarious migrants in London's hospitality jobs. *Work, Employment & Society* 28(6): 865–81.

Alberti G, Bessa I, Hardy K, et al. (2018) In, against and beyond precarity: work in insecure times. *Work, Employment and Society* 32(3): 447–57.

Anderson B (2007) Battles in time: the relation between global and labour mobilities. Centre on Migration. Policy and Society. Working Paper 55.

Andrees B (2014) Why definitions matter. Available at: https://www.ilo.org/resource/article/why-definitions-matter (accessed 22 September 2024).

Andreß H-J and Lohmann H (2008) *The Working Poor in Europe: Employment, Poverty and Globalisation*. Cheltenham: Edward Elgar.

Aradau C (2016) Governing mobile bodies: human trafficking and (in)security states. In: Dickinson J, Cameron A, and Smith N (eds) *Body/State*. Abingdon: Routledge, pp. 185-198.

Armano E and Murgia A (2013) The precariousnesses of young knowledge workers: a subject-oriented approach. *Global Discourse* 3(3–4): 486–501.

Armano E, Bove A and Murgia A (2017) Mapping precariousness: subjectivities and resistance – an introduction. In: Armano E, Bove A, and Murgia A (eds), *Mapping Precariousness, Labour Insecurity and Uncertain Livelihoods: Subjectivities and Resistance*. New York: Routledge, pp. 1-12.

Asad T (1986) The concept of cultural translation in British social anthropology. In: Clifford J and Marcus GE (eds), *Writing Culture: The Poetics and Politics of Ethnography*. Berkeley: University of California Press, pp. 141–64.

Association of Social Anthropologists of the UK (ASA) (2021) Ethical guidelines 2021 for good research practice. Available at: https://www.theasa.org/ethics (accessed 21 January 2022).

Atkinson R and Bridge G (2004) *Gentrification in a Global Context*. Abingdon: Routledge.

Back L (2012) Live sociology: social research and its futures. *Sociological Review* 60(1_suppl): 18–39.

Back L and Puwar N (2012) A manifesto for live methods: provocations and capacities. *Sociological Review* 60(1_suppl): 6–17.

Badenhorst C, Arif A and Quintyne K (2022) Doctoral writing and the politics of citation use. *Discourse and Writing/Rédactologie* 32: 262–80.

Bailey C and Madden A (2017) Time reclaimed: temporality and the experience of meaningful work. *Work, Employment and Society* 31(1): 3–18.

Balch DA, Craig PG, Roberts K, et al. (2017) *The Co-op's Bright Future Programme: An Independent Interim Review*. Manchester: Co-op.

Bales K, Trodd Z and Williamson AK (2009) *Modern Slavery: The Secret World of 27 Million People*. Oxford: Oneworld Publications.

Beck U (2015) Emancipatory catastrophism: what does it mean to climate change and risk society? *Current Sociology* 63(1): 75–88.

Beels M (2017) *Preventing Labour Exploitation*. Warwick Papers in Industrial Relations 107. Coventry: Industrial Relations Research Unit. Available at: https://www.gla.gov.uk/media/2996/wpir_107-margaret-beels-lecture-2017.pdf (accessed 15 June 2020).

Bekar M and Fay R (2020) Developing Anglo-centred academic literacy: problematizing understandings of criticality. In: Simpson A and Dervin F (eds), *The Meaning of Criticality in Education Research: Reflecting on Critical Pedagogy*. Cham: Springer International Publishing, pp. 23–45.

Berardi F (2009) *The Soul at Work: From Alienation to Autonomy*. Semiotext(e) foreign agents series. Los Angeles, CA: Semiotext(e).

Berlant LG (2011) *Cruel Optimism*. Durham, NC: Duke University Press.

Berry C and McDaniel S (2020) Post-crisis precarity: understanding attitudes to work and industrial relations among young people in the UK. *Economic and Industrial Democracy*: 1–22.

Bhatt C (2016) White sociology. *Ethnic and Racial Studies* 39(3): 397–404.

Bone J (2014) Neoliberal nomads: housing insecurity and the revival of private renting in the UK. *Sociological Research Online* 19(4): 1–14.

Bone KD (2019) 'I don't want to be a vagrant for the rest of my life': young peoples' experiences of precarious work as a 'continuous present'. *Journal of Youth Studies* 22(9): 1218–37.

Bosch G (2004) Towards a new standard employment relationship in Western Europe. *British Journal of Industrial Relations* 42(4): 617–36.

Bradley K (2014) Modern slavery a hidden crime, says minister. *BBC News*, 29 November. Available at: http://www.bbc.co.uk/news/uk-30257981 (accessed 16 April 2017).

Breeze M (2018) Imposter syndrome as a public feeling. In: Taylor Y and Lahad K (eds), *Feeling Academic in the Neoliberal University: Feminist Flights, Fights and Failures*. Cham: Palgrave Macmillan, pp. 191–219.

Breman J (2013) A bogus concept? [Review of: G. Standing (2011) The precariat: the new dangerous class]. *New Left Review*, 84.

Brenner N (1999) Beyond state-centrism? Space, territoriality, and geographical scale in globalization studies. *Theory and Society* 28(1): 39–78.

Breuil BCO et al. (2011) Human trafficking revisited: legal, enforcement and ethnographic narratives on sex trafficking to Western Europe. *Trends in Organized Crime* 14(1): 30–46.

British Sociological Association (2017) *BSA Statement of Ethical Practice*. Durham: BSA Publications. Available at: https://www.britsoc.co.uk/media/24310/bsa_statement_of_ethical_practice.pdf (accessed 26 January 2022).

Broadbent P and Green K (2017) *REC webinar – reform of the GLA*. [Online] 21 March, the Recruitment and Employment Confederation, Nottingham. Available at: https://www.gla.gov.uk/whats-new/transition-to-the-glaa/rec-webinar-gla-reform (accessed 22 September 2024).

Bryman A (2008) Of methods and methodology. *Qualitative Research in Organizations and Management: An International Journal* 3(2): 159–68.

Bryson A and Gomez R (2005) Why have workers stopped joining unions? The rise in never-membership in Britain. *British Journal of Industrial Relations* 43(1): 67–92.

Burawoy M (2015) Facing an unequal world. *Current Sociology* 63(1): 5–34.

Burton S and Bowman B (2022) The academic precariat: understanding life and labour in the neoliberal academy. *British Journal of Sociology of Education* 43(4): 497–512.

Business, Energy, and Industrial Strategy Committee (2016) Future world of work and rights of workers inquiry launched – news from Parliament. Available at: https://www.parliament.uk/business/committees/committees-a-z/commons-select/business-energy-industrial-strategy/news-parliament-2015/the-future-world-of-work-and-rights-of-workers-launch-16-17 (accessed 22 April 2017).

Butler J (1999) *Gender Trouble: Feminism and the Subversion of Identity*. New York: Routledge.

———. (2004) *Precarious Life: The Powers of Mourning and Violence*. New York: Verso.

———. (2009) *Frames of War: When Is Life Grievable?* New York: Verso.

Byrne M (2020) Generation rent and the financialization of housing: a comparative exploration of the growth of the private rental sector in Ireland, the UK and Spain. *Housing Studies* 35(4): 743–65.

Canagarajah AS (2002) *A Geopolitics of Academic Writing*. Pittsburgh: University of Pittsburgh Press.

Cant C (2019) *Riding for Deliveroo: Resistance in the New Economy*. Cambridge: John Wiley & Sons.

Castel R (2003) *From Manual Workers to Wage Laborers: Transformation of the Social Question*. New Brunswick, NJ: Transaction Publishers.

Cederström C and Fleming P (2012) *Dead Man Working*. Winchester: Zero Books.

Celikates R (2012) Karl Marx: Critique as emancipatory practice. In: de Boer K and Sonderegger R (eds), *Conceptions of Critique in Modern and Contemporary Philosophy*. Basingstoke: Palgrave Macmillan, pp. 101–18.

Chakravartty P, Kuo R, Grubbs V, et al. (2018) #CommunicationSoWhite. *Journal of Communication* 68(2): 254–66.

Chan S (2013) 'I am king': financialisation and the paradox of precarious work. *Economic and Labour Relations Review* 24(3): 362–79.

Chari A (2010) Toward a political critique of reification: Lukács, Honneth and the aims of critical theory. *Philosophy & Social Criticism* 36(5): 587–606.

CLEAR (2021) Citational politics. Available at: https://civiclaboratory.nl/citational-politics (accessed 16 April 2024).

Clifford J and Marcus GE (1986) *Writing Culture: The Poetics & Politics of Ethnography*. Berkeley: University of California Press.

College Writing Center (2013) *Point of View in Academic Writing*. St Louis: St Louis Community College.

Conrad P (1997) It's boring: Notes on the meanings of boredom in everyday life. *Qualitative Sociology* 20(4): 465–75.

Conservative Party (2019) *The Conservative and Unionist Party Manifesto 2019*. Available at: https://assets-global.website-files.com/5da42e2cae7ebd3f8bde353c/5dda924905da587992a064ba_Conservative%20 2019%20Manifesto.pdf (accessed 8 June 2020).

Costas J and Fleming P (2009) Beyond dis-identification: a discursive approach to self-alienation in contemporary organizations. *Human Relations* 62(3): 353–78.

Davidson JO (2010) New slavery, old binaries: human trafficking and the borders of 'freedom'. *Global Networks* 10(2): 244–61.

———. (2013) Troubling freedom: migration, debt, and modern slavery. *Migration Studies* 1(2): 176–95.

Davies J (2019) From severe to routine labour exploitation: the case of migrant workers in the UK food industry. *Criminology & Criminal Justice* 19(3): 294–310.

Department for Business Innovation & Skills (2016) *Tackling Exploitation in the Labour Market: Government Response*. London: BIS. Available at: https://assets.publishing.service.gov.uk/media/5f2982868fa8f57acba2bd55/BIS-16-11-government-response-to-tackling-exploitation-in-the-labour-market.pdf (accessed 25 August 2024).

Derrida J (1988) *Limited Inc*. Evanston, IL: Northwestern University Press.

Desyllas MC (2007) Critique of the global trafficking discourse and US policy. *Journal of Sociology & Social Welfare* 34(4): 57-79.

Di Nicola A (2007) Researching into human trafficking: issues and problems. In: Lee M (ed.), *Human Trafficking*. Cullompton: Willan, pp. 49-72.

Ellis C, Adams TE and Bochner AP (2011) Autoethnography: an overview. *Historical Social Research* 36(4): 19.

Eyles A (2019) Real wage changes on the JNCHES pay spine (updated for August 2019 inflation release). *Universities and Colleges Employers Association (UCEA)*, 10 October. Available at: https://www.bera.ac.uk/blog/pay-and-conditions-in-universities-beras-solidarity-with-academics (accessed 25 August 2024).

Ferreri M, Dawson G and Vasudevan A (2017) Living precariously: property guardianship and the flexible city. *Transactions of the Institute of British Geographers* 42(2): 246–59.

Fields DJ and Hodkinson SN (2018) Housing policy in crisis: an international perspective. *Housing Policy Debate* 28(1): 1–5.

Foucault M (1979) Authorship: what is an author? *Screen* 20(1): 13–34.

Frayne D (2015) *The Refusal of Work: The Theory and Practice of Resistance to Work*. London: Zed Books.

Furlong A, Goodwin J, O'Connor H, et al. (2017) *Young People in the Labour Market : Past, Present, Future*. Abingdon: Routledge.

Gambino F (2007) A critique of the Fordism of the Regulation School. *The Commoner* 12: 39–62.

Gangmasters and Labour Abuse Authority (2017) *Problem Profile: The Nature and Scale of Labour Exploitation across all sectors within the United Kingdom*. London: Gangmasters and Labour Abuse Authority.

Garfinkel H (1996) Ethnomethodology's program. *Social Psychology Quarterly* 59(1): 5–21.

Garfinkel H and Rawls AW (2002) *Ethnomethodology's Program: Working out Durkeim's Aphorism*. Lanham, MD: Rowman & Littlefield.

Goodley S (2016) Undercover at Sports Direct: rewarding, exhilarating and sometimes petrifying. *The Guardian*, 27 June. Available at: https://www.theguardian.com/membership/2016/jun/27/undercover-sports-direct-rewarding-mike-ashley (accessed 15 October 2018).

Gorczynski PF, Hill D and Rathod S (2017) Examining the construct validity of the transtheoretical model to structure workplace physical activity interventions to improve mental health in academic staff. *EMS Community Medicine Journal* 1(1): 1–4.

Graeber D (2004) *Fragments of an Anarchist Anthropology*. Chicago: Prickly Paradigm Press.

———.(2018) *Bullshit Jobs: A Theory*. London: Simon & Schuster.

Green K (2016) Gig economy: the business benefits. *Director Magazine*. Available at: https://www.director.co.uk/blog-gig-economy-20104-2 (accessed 8 December 2018).

Gunaratnam Y (2012) Learning to be affected: social suffering and total pain at life's borders. *Sociological Review* 60(1_suppl): 108–23.

Haraway DJ (1989) *Primate Visions: Gender, Race, and Nature in the World of Modern Science*. New York: Routledge.

———. (1991) *Simians, Cyborgs, and Women: The Reinvention of Nature*. New York: Routledge.

Harris D, Sheehan DJ and Toft DA (2014) Supporting victims of severe forms of labour exploitation in having access to justice in EU Member States: United Kingdom. Available at: https://fra.europa.eu/sites/default/files/fra_uploads/severe-labour-exploitation-country_uk.pdf (accessed 25 August 2024).

Harris J (2018) Are dark kitchens the satanic mills of our era? *The Guardian*, 9 October. Available at: https://www.theguardian.com/commentisfree/2018/oct/09/dark-kitchens-satanic-mills-deliveroo (accessed 8 December 2018).

Hasegawa K (2014) The Fukushima nuclear accident and Japan's civil society: context, reactions, and policy impacts. *International Sociology* 29(4): 283–301.

Holman Jones SL, Adams TE and Ellis C (2013) *Handbook of Autoethnography*. Walnut Creek, CA: Left Coast Press.

Home Office (2014) *Modern Slavery Strategy*. London: Home Office.

———. (2017) Sir David Metcalf named as the first Director of Labour Market Enforcement. Available at: https://www.gov.uk/government/news/sir-david-metcalf-named-as-the-first-director-of-labour-market-enforcement (accessed 22 April 2017).

———. (2019) *2019 UK Annual Report on Modern Slavery*. London: Home Office. Available at: https://assets.publishing.service.gov.uk/government/uploads/system/uploads/attachment_data/file/840059/Modern_Slavery_Report_2019.pdf (accessed 8 June 2020).

Human Rights Council (2019) *Visit to the United Kingdom of Great Britain and Northern Ireland: Report of the Special Rapporteur on extreme poverty and human rights*. 2 April. Available at: https://digitallibrary.un.org/record/3806308?ln=en&v=pdf (accessed 22 September 2024).

Hussein RA (2015) The existing tensions in the defining of human trafficking at a UK and international level: a critical overview. *International Journal of Comparative and Applied Criminal Justice* 39(2): 129–38.

Idris I (2017) *Interventions to Support Victims of Modern Slavery*. Birmingham: GSDRC.

Jenkins RH et al. (2021) The relationship between austerity and food insecurity in the UK: a systematic review. *EClinicalMedicine* 33(100781): 1-10.

Johnson M (2013) The precariat. *Global Discourse* 3(3–4): 385–87.

Kalleberg AL (2009) Precarious work, insecure workers: employment relations in transition. *American Sociological Review* 74(1): 1–22.

Kallis A (2018) Populism, sovereigntism, and the unlikely re-emergence of the territorial nation-state. *Fudan Journal of the Humanities and Social Sciences* 11(3): 285–302.

Kondo DK (1990) *Crafting Selves: Power, Gender, and Discourses of Identity in a Japanese Workplace*. Chicago: University of Chicago Press.

Kubota R (2022) Decolonizing second language writing: possibilities and challenges. *Journal of Second Language Writing* 58(100946): 1-11.
Labour Party (2019) *Workers' Rights Manifesto*. London. Available at: https://web.archive.org/web/20240309153743/https://labour.org.uk/wp-content/uploads/2019/12/13238_19-Work-manifesto.pdf (accessed 22 September 2024).
Lambert R and Herod A (2016) Neoliberalism, precarious work and remaking the geography of global capitalism. In: Lambert R and Herod A (eds), *Neoliberal Capitalism and Precarious Work: Ethnographies of Accommodation and Resistance*. Cheltenham: Edward Elgar, pp. 1-35.
Latour B and Woolgar S (1986) *Laboratory Life: The Construction of Scientific Facts*. Princeton: Princeton University Press.
Law J (2004) *After Method: Mess in Social Science Research*. London: Routledge.
Lean G (2015) *Transformative Travel in a Mobile World*. Boston, MA: CABI.
Lees L, Slater T and Wyly E (2013) *Gentrification*. New York: Routledge.
Lemert C (2002) The pleasure of Garfinkel's indexical ways. In: Rawls AW (ed.), *Ethnomethodology's Program: Working out Durkeim's Aphorism*. Lanham, MD: Rowman & Littlefield, pp. xi-xiii.
Lewis H, Dwyer P, Hodkinson S, et al. (2015) Hyper-precarious lives: migrants, work and forced labour in the Global North. *Progress in Human Geography* 39(5): 580–600.
Lorey I (2015) *State of Insecurity: Government of the Precarious*. New York: Verso.
Lori NA (2017) Statelessness, 'in-between' statuses, and precarious citizenship. In: Shachar A et al. (eds), *The Oxford Handbook of Citizenship*. Oxford University Press, pp. 742–66.
Machin S (2000) Union decline in Britain. *British Journal of Industrial Relations* 38(4): 631–45.
Mair M, Greiffenhagen C and Sharrock WW (2016) Statistical practice: putting society on display. *Theory, Culture & Society* 33(3): 51–77.
Malcomson H (2019) Point of view, narrative violence, and ethnographic representation: writing everyday violence in 2010s Mexico. *Irish Journal of Anthropology* 22(1): 99–103.
Maley W (2007) Ten ways of thinking about deconstruction. *Affirmez la survie*. Available at: http://derridaworks.blogspot.com/2007/08/ten-ways-of-thinking-about.html (accessed 30 July 2020).
Malinowski B (1922) *Argonauts of the Western Pacific: Account of Native Enterprise and Adventure in the Archipelagoes of Melanesian New Guinea*. London: Routledge.
Marcus GE (2007) Ethnography two decades after writing culture: from the experimental to the baroque. *Anthropological Quarterly* 80(4): 1127–45.
Marcus GE (2012) The legacies of writing culture and the near future of the ethnographic form: a sketch. *Cultural Anthropology* 27(3): 427–45.
Margalioth SR (1998) The significance of worker attitudes: individualism as a cause for labor's decline. *Hofstra Labor and Employment Law Journal* 16(1): 133–66.

Marx K (1844) *Economic and Philosophic Manuscripts of 1844*. Amherst, NY: Prometheus Books.
Mauss M (2002) *The Gift: Forms and Functions of Exchange in Archaic Societies*. London: Routledge.
McCarthy LA (2014) Human trafficking and the new slavery. *Annual Review of Law and Social Science* 10(1): 221–42.
McCartin JA (2014) *Bargaining for the Future: Rethinking Labor's Recent Past and Planning Strategically for Its Future*. Washington, DC: Georgetown University.
Milkman R and Ott E (2014) *New Labor in New York: Precarious Workers and the Future of the Labor Movement*. Ithaca, NY: Cornell University Press.
Millar KM (2017) Toward a critical politics of precarity. *Sociology Compass* 11(6): 1–11.
Mills CW (1953) *White Collar: The American Middle Classes*. New York: Oxford University Press.
Mishel L et al. (2012) *The State of Working America*. Ithaca, NY: Cornell University Press.
Miyazaki H (2006) Economy of dreams: hope in global capitalism and its critiques. *Cultural Anthropology* 21(2): 147–72.
Mol A (2002) *The Body Multiple: Ontology in Medical Practice*. Durham, NC: Duke University Press.
Mollona M (2009) *Made in Sheffield: An Ethnography of Industrial Work and Politics*. New York: Berghahn Books.
Molstad C (1986) Choosing and coping with boring work. *Urban Life* 15(2): 215–36.
Monaghan A (2017) Number of zero-hours contracts stalls at 'staggering' 1.7m. *The Guardian*, 11 May. Available at: https://www.theguardian.com/uk-news/2017/may/11/number-of-zero-hours-contracts-stalls-at-staggering-1-7-million (accessed 8 December 2018).
Morris J (2018) Hauntology and the trauma of social change: deindustrializing communities in Mumbai and provincial Russia. *City & Society* 30(1).
Morrow RA and Brown DD (1994) *Critical Theory and Methodology*. Thousand Oaks, CA: Sage Publications.
Mouton N (2019) A literary perspective on the limits of leadership: Tolstoy's critique of the great man theory. *Leadership* 15(1): 81–102.
Mulholland K (2004) Workplace resistance in an Irish call centre: slammin', scammin' smokin' an' leavin'. *Work, Employment and Society* 18(4): 709–24.
Mumby DK (2005) Theorizing resistance in organization studies: a dialectical approach. *Management Communication Quarterly* 19(1): 19–44.
Mumby DK, Thomas R, Martí I, et al. (2017) Resistance redux. *Organization Studies* 38(9): 1157–83.
Nakane C (1970) *Japanese Society*. Berkeley: University of California Press.
Neilson B and Rossiter N (2008) Precarity as a political concept, or, Fordism as exception. *Theory, Culture & Society* 25(7–8): 51–72.

Ng ESW, Schweitzer L and Lyons ST (2010) New generation, great expectations: a field study of the millennial generation. *Journal of Business and Psychology* 25(2): 281–92.

Nolas S-M and Varvantakis C (2018) Entanglements that matter. *Entanglements* 1(1): 1–4.

Oliver D (2006) An expectation of continued success: the work attitudes of Generation Y. *Labour & Industry* 17(1): 61–84.

ONS (2023) *Trade Union Membership, UK 1995–2022: Statistical Bulletin*. London: Office for National Statistics.

Otherwise (2023) About *Otherwise*. Available at: https://www.otherwisemag.com/magazine (accessed 30 November 2023).

Paret M and Gleeson S (2016) Precarity and agency through a migration lens. *Citizenship Studies* 20(3–4): 277–94.

Parker J (2012) In their own words: on writing in second person. *Connotations* 21(2–3): 165–76.

Pearce JJ (2011) Working with trafficked children and young people: complexities in practice. *British Journal of Social Work* 41(8): 1424–41.

Perlow LA (1999) The time famine: toward a sociology of work time. *Administrative Science Quarterly* 44(1): 57–81.

Piketty T (2014) *Capital in the Twenty-First Century* (A Goldhammer, trans.). Cambridge, MA: Belknap Press of Harvard University Press.

Potter M and Hamilton J (2014) Picking on vulnerable migrants: precarity and the mushroom industry in Northern Ireland. *Work, Employment & Society* 28(3): 390-406.

Quirk J (2011) *The Anti-Slavery Project: From the Slave Trade to Human Trafficking*. Pennsylvania studies in human rights. Philadelphia: University of Pennsylvania Press.

Ray VE (2019) Reproducing inequality in sociology. *Sociological Forum* 34(1): 236–44.

Rosaldo R (1993) *Culture & Truth: The Remaking of Social Analysis*. Boston: Beacon Press.

Rubenstein SL (2007) Circulation, accumulation, and the power of Shuar shrunken heads. *Cultural Anthropology* 22(3): 357–99.

Rubery J et al. (2018) Challenges and contradictions in the 'normalising' of precarious work. *Work, Employment and Society* 32(3): 509–27.

Ryang S (2004) *Japan and National Anthropology: A Critique*. New York: RoutledgeCurzon.

Sacks H (2006) *Lectures on Conversation: Volumes I & II*. Oxford: Blackwell.

Said EW (1979) *Orientalism*. New York: Vintage Books.

Sandoval M (2018) From passionate labour to compassionate work: cultural co-ops, do what you love and social change. *European Journal of Cultural Studies* 21(2): 113–29.

Savage M (2010) *Identities and Social Change in Britain since 1940: The Politics of Method*. Oxford: Oxford University Press.

Scott JC (1985) *Weapons of the Weak*. New Haven: Yale University Press.

———. (2012) *Two Cheers for Anarchism: Six Easy Pieces on Autonomy, Dignity, and Meaningful Work and Play*. Princeton: Princeton University Press.

Seeman M (1959) On the meaning of alienation. *American Sociological Review* 24(6): 783–91.

Selby A (2017) Timed toilet breaks, impossible targets and workers falling asleep on feet: brutal life working in Amazon warehouse. *Mirror Online*, 9 December. Available at: https://www.mirror.co.uk/news/uk-news/timed-toilet-breaks-impossible-targets-11587888 (accessed 25 August 2024).

Silverman B (2014) Modern slavery an application of multiple systems estimation. Available at: https://assets.publishing.service.gov.uk/media/5a7509c640f0b6397f35d2e9/Modern_Slavery_an_application_of_MSE_revised.pdf (accessed 25 August 2024).

Skrivankova K (2010) *Between decent work and forced labour: examining the continuum of exploitation*. York: Joseph Rowntree Foundation. Available at: https://humantraffickingsearch.org/wp-content/uploads/2017/06/jrf-between-decent-work-and-forced-labour.pdf (accessed 22 September 2024).

Smith DE (1974a) Smith: theorizing as ideology. In: Turner R (ed.), *Ethnomethodology*. London: Penguin, pp. 41–44.

———. (1974b) Women's perspective as a radical critique of sociology. *Sociological Inquiry* 44(1): 7–13.

Spector BA (2016) Carlyle, Freud, and the great man theory more fully considered. *Leadership* 12(2): 250–60.

Spivak GC (2010) Can the subaltern speak? In: Morris R (ed.), *Can the Subaltern Speak? Reflections on the History of an Idea*. New York: Columbia University Press, pp. 21-80.

Standing G (2011) *The Precariat: The New Dangerous Class*. London & New York: Bloomsbury.

Steinhoff PG (1999) Student Protest in the 1960s. *Social Science Japan* 15(3): 3–7.

Stewart K (2007) *Ordinary Affects*. Durham, NC: Duke University Press.

———. (2012) Precarity's forms. *Cultural Anthropology* 27(3): 518–25.

Stop the Traffik (2017) Resilience building. Available at: https://www.stopthetraffik.org/resilience-building (accessed 8 December 2018).

Strangleman T (2017) Deindustrialisation and the historical sociological imagination: making sense of work and industrial change. *Sociology* 51(2): 466–82.

Tailby S and Pollert A (2011) Non-unionized young workers and organizing the unorganized. *Economic and Industrial Democracy* 32(3): 499–522.

Taylor M (2017) *Good Work: The Taylor Review of Modern Working Practices*. Available at: https://assets.publishing.service.gov.uk/government/uploads/system/uploads/attachment_data/file/627671/good-work-taylor-review-modern-working-practices-rg.pdf (accessed 25 August 2024).

Thomas N (1994) *Colonialism's Culture: Anthropology, Travel, and Government*. Princeton: Princeton University Press.

Todd Z (2016) An Indigenous feminist's take on the ontological turn: 'ontology' is just another word for colonialism. *Journal of Historical Sociology* 29(1): 4–22.

Tsianos V and Papadopoulos D (2006) Precarity: a savage journey to the heart of embodied capitalism. *Machines and Subjectivation* 10: 1–12.

Tsing AL (2015) *The Mushroom at the End of the World: On the Possibility of Life in Capitalist Ruins*. Princeton: Princeton University Press.

Tsurumi EP (1984) Female textile workers and the failure of early trade unionism in Japan. *History Workshop Journal* 18(1): 3–27.

TUC and Hudson M (2015) *The Decent Jobs Deficit: The human cost of zero-hours working in the UK*. London: Trade Union Congress. Available at: https://www.tuc.org.uk/sites/default/files/DecentJobsDeficitReport_0.pdf (accessed 14 June 2020).

Tyler DI (2013) *Revolting Subjects: Social Abjection and Resistance in Neoliberal Britain*. London: Zed Books.

UCU (2016a) *Precarious Work in Higher Education*. London: University and College Union. Available at: https://www.ucu.org.uk/media/8384/Precarious-work-in-higher-education-November-2016-update/pdf/ucu_precariouscontracts_hereport_nov16_.pdf (accessed 9 May 2020).

———. (2016b) *Workload Is an Education Issue: UCU Workload Survey 2016*. University and College Union. Available at: https://www.ucu.org.uk/media/8195/Workload-is-an-education-issue-UCU-workload-survey-report-2016/pdf/ucu_workloadsurvey_fullreport_jun16.pdf (accessed 9 May 2020).

———. (2018) *Data from NTU Branch UCU Workload Survey*. University and College Union. Available at: https://www.ucu.org.uk/media/10195/NTU-branch-workload-survey-2018/pdf/NTU-UCU-workload-survey_mar19.pdf (accessed 9 May 2020).

University of Liverpool (2020) Library guides: referencing – about referencing. Available at: https://libguides.liverpool.ac.uk/referencing/home (accessed 24 July 2020).

Venkatesh SA (2013) The reflexive turn: the rise of first-person ethnography. *Sociological Quarterly* 54(1): 3–8.

Volti R (2012) *An Introduction to the Sociology of Work and Occupations*. Thousand Oaks, CA: Sage Publications.

Wajcman J and Dodd N (eds) (2017) *The Sociology of Speed: Digital, Organizational, and Social Temporalities*. Oxford: Oxford University Press.

Weeks K (2011) *The Problem with Work: Feminism, Marxism, Antiwork Politics, and Postwork Imaginaries*. Durham, NC: Duke University Press.

Weitzer R (2014) New directions in research on human trafficking. *Annals of the American Academy of Political and Social Science* 653(1): 6–24.

———. (2015) Human trafficking and contemporary slavery. *Annual Review of Sociology* 41(1): 223–42.

WES (2024) *Work, Employment and Society Notes to Contributors*. Available at: https://journals.sagepub.com/author-instructions/wes (accessed 22 September 2024).

Wikipedia (2020) Criticism of Wikipedia. *Wikipedia*. Available at: https://en.wikipedia.org/w/index.php?title=Criticism_of_Wikipedia&oldid=954695465 (accessed 8 May 2020).

Wills J, Datta K, Evans Y, et al. (2010) *Global Cities at Work: New Migrant Divisions of Labour*. London: Pluto Press.

Woodcock J (2017) *Working the Phones: Control and Resistance in Call Centres*. London: Pluto Press.

Xu X, Waters T, Cribb J, et al. (2019) *Why Has In-Work Poverty Risen in Britain?* London: IFS. Available at: https://www.ifs.org.uk/publications/14154 (accessed 8 June 2020).

Youkhana E (2015) A conceptual shift in studies of belonging and the politics of belonging. *Social Inclusion* 3(4): 10–24.

Yuval-Davis N (2010) Theorizing identity: beyond the 'us' and 'them' dichotomy. *Patterns of Prejudice* 44(3): 261–80.

Yuval-Davis N, Wemyss G and Cassidy K (2018) Everyday bordering, belonging and the reorientation of British immigration legislation. *Sociology* 52(2): 228–44.

Index

www.ingramcontent.com/pod-product-compliance
Ingram Content Group UK Ltd.
Pitfield, Milton Keynes, MK11 3LW, UK
UKHW021836150926
8656IPUK00004B/20

9 781805 3989